EUSTRATIOS ARGENTI

A Study of the Greek Church
under Turkish Rule

EUSTRATIOS ARGENTI

A Study of the Greek Church under Turkish Rule

BY

KALLISTOS WARE

WIPF & STOCK · Eugene, Oregon

Wipf and Stock Publishers
199 W 8th Ave, Suite 3
Eugene, OR 97401

Eustratios Argenti
A Study of the Greek Church under Turkish Rule
By Ware, Kallistos

ISBN 13: 978-1-62564-082-6
Publication date 5/15/2013
Previously published by Oxford University Press, 1964

ACKNOWLEDGEMENTS

I AM deeply grateful for the invaluable assistance which I have received from Dr. P. P. Argenti. Learning of my interest in Orthodox theology, he generously placed at my disposal all the material relating to Eustratios Argenti which he had collected, in particular microfilms and transcripts of manuscripts in Hungary, Athens, Alexandria, and elsewhere. He has offered me advice on many points of detail, and saved me from numerous mistakes.

My thanks are due to Dr. Henry Chadwick and Mr. W. Jardine Grisbrooke for their kind advice and encouragement.

The greater part of Chapter III, section (ii), originally appeared as an article in *Chrysostom*. I am grateful to the Editor for permission to reproduce it here.

The first draft of this book was written in the spring of 1960, when I was Jane Eliza Procter Visiting Fellow at Princeton Graduate College. I must express my gratitude to Princeton University for hospitality, and to the Librarian of Princeton Theological Seminary for permission to use his admirable library.

CONTENTS

NOTE

WHEN books appear in the bibliography, they are cited in the notes by author and title (or short title) alone; for full details of the edition consulted, see the bibliography.

In the transcription of Greek names I have tried, so far as possible, to reproduce the original spelling; but where there is an accepted English form (e.g. Cyril, Peter, Athanasius, Cerularius), it has been adopted. This involves, as I am painfully aware, a certain lack of uniformity, but it seemed on consideration the least inconvenient method.

Introduction to the 2014 Reprint Edition

I AM BOTH GRATIFIED and surprised that, fifty years after its first appearance, a proposal has been made to reissue my monograph *Eustratios Argenti: A Study of the Greek Church under Turkish Rule*. It is encouraging to find that there is a continuing interest in Orthodox theology during the Ottoman period, and more particularly in the contribution made by the Chiot writer Argenti. *Eustratios Argenti* was originally published in 1964 by the Clarendon Press, the academic branch of the Oxford University Press. It was then reprinted photographically in 1977 by Eastern Orthodox Books (Willits, CA), but most of this re-edition was later destroyed in a warehouse fire. In the present reprint by Wipf and Stock (Eugene, OR), the text of the 1964 publication has been left unchanged, but I have taken advantage of the opportunity to add a new introduction.

Without attempting a comprehensive overview, let me mention some of the leading studies on Greek Orthodoxy during the Turcocratia that have appeared during the past half century. To the best of my knowledge no major work relating to Argenti himself has been published since 1964. One new piece of evidence, however, has been kindly brought to my attention by Metropolitan Athenagoras (Peckstadt) of Belgium. On 16 September 1720 Argenti was admitted as a student in the University of Leiden, Holland, which was under Protestant and more particularly Calvinist auspices. His enrolment is recorded in *Album Studiosorum Academiae Lugduno Batavae MDLXXV - MDCCCLXXV* (The Hague: Martin Nijhoff, 1875), col. 869.

This fills a significant gap in our information about Argenti's studies in the West. It fits with the fact, already known to us, that in

1719 he was journeying from Venice to Innsbruck (Ware, *Eustratios Argenti*, p. 45). Hitherto it was not definitely established to what university or universities he was attached. It has been speculated that he went to Halle in Saxony (*Eustratios Argenti*, p. 45), and this may well be the case, although it is not supported by any specific evidence. The *Album Studiosorum* provides us with a firm date and place, although it does not indicate how long he remained at Leiden. It is of course possible that he also pursued studies elsewhere in Western Europe.

The best general account of Greek Christianity during the Ottoman era to be published in English since the appearance of my book on Argenti is Steven Runciman, *The Great Church in Captivity: A Study of the Patriarchate of Constantinople from the Eve of the Turkish Conquest to the Greek War of Independence* (Cambridge: University Press, 1968): see Book II, pp. 165-412. This is still of great value. It relies, however, mainly on Western rather than Greek sources and, as its title indicates, it deals primarily with the Ecumenical Patriarchate. It is for the most part a 'diplomatic' history of the Patriarchate's relations with the West, and it says relatively little about the daily life and personal spirituality of Orthodox Christians during the Turcocratia.

On the wider history of the Greek people during the fifteenth to the nineteenth centuries, a basic work of reference is A. E. Vacalopoulos, *'Ιστορία τοῦ Νεοῦ 'Ελληνισμοῦ*, 8 volumes (Thessaloniki, 1961-88). This has been partly translated into English: see in particular the second volume of the English version, *The Greek Nation, 1453- 1669. The cultural and economic background of Modern Greek Society* (New Brunswick: Rutgers University Press, 1976). Regrettably the author, while undoubtedly learned, shows a lack of sympathy for the Church.

Much information on the cultural background of the eighteenth-century Greek world is shed by the writings of Paschalis M. Kitromilides: see *Enlightenment, Nationalism, Orthodoxy: Studies in the culture and political thought of south-eastern Europe*, Variorum Collected Studies Series CS 453 (Aldershot/ Burlington: Ashgate, 1994); *An Orthodox Commonwealth: Symbolic Legacies and Cultural Encounters in Southeastern Europe*, Variorum Collected Studies Series CS 891 (Aldershot/ Burlington: Ashgate, 2007); *Enlightenment and Revolution. The Making of Modern Greece* (Cambridge, MA/ London: Harvard University Press, 2013). Although referring mainly to the period after Argenti's death, these works also shed light on the *milieu* in which Argenti himself lived and worked.

Bibliographical details about Greek theological writers in the post-Byzantine era are provided by Gerhard Podskalsky, *Griechische Theologie in der Zeit der Türkenherrschaft (1453-1821). Die Orthodoxie im Spannungsfeld der nachreformatorischen Konfessionen des Westens* (Munich: Beck, 1988). There is an updated Greek translation by Georgios D. Metallinos, *'Η 'Ελληνικὴ Θεολογία ἐπὶ Τουρκοκρατίας 1453-1821. 'Η* Ὀρθοδοξία στὴ σφαῖρα ἐπιρροῆς τῶν *Δυτικῶν δογμάτων μετὰ τὴ Μεταρρύθμιση* (Athens: Morphotiko Idryma Ethnikis Trapezis, 2005). On Eustratios Argenti, see in the German edition, pp. 331-5; in the Greek translation, pp. 413-18. Podskalsky's encyclopedic survey supersedes the work of Martin Jugie, of which I made use when writing my book on Argenti in the early 1960s. I wish that his *Griechische Theologie* had been available to me at that time!

Less thorough than the work of Podskalsky, yet nevertheless useful, is George A. Maloney, *A History of Orthodox Theology since 1453* (Belmont: Nordland, 1976). Also helpful are the two opening chapters of Yannis Spiteris, *La teologia ortodossa neo-greca* (Bologna: Edizioni Dehoniane, 1992). There are many references to theological authors in G. P. Henderson, *The Revival of Greek Thought 1620-1830* (Albany: State University of New York Press, 1970). The Orthodox Confessions of Faith from the post-Byzantine epoch – often described as the Orthodox 'symbolical books' – are conveniently collected in Jaroslav Pelikan and Valerie Hotchkiss (ed.), *Creeds and Confessions of Faith in the Christian Tradition*, vol. 1 (New Haven/London: Yale University Press, 2003), pp. 385-635.

The discussion of Orthodox- Catholic relations in *Eustratios Argenti*, pp. 16-33, is supplemented by my article 'Orthodox and Catholics in the seventeenth century: schism or intercommunion?', in Derek Baker (ed.), *Schism, Heresy and Religious Protest*, Papers read at the Tenth Summer Meeting and the Eleventh Winter Meeting of the Ecclesiastical History Society (Cambridge: University Press, 1972), pp. 259-76. For Catholics and Orthodox in Argenti's homeland, see Philip P. Argenti, *The Religious Minorities of Chios: Jews and Roman Catholics* (Cambridge: University Press, 1970), especially pp. 287-94, 359-66.

The aspect of Argenti's career that continues to attract the greatest attention is his involvement in the rebaptism controversy at Constantinople during the 1750s. On this, see Evangelos A. Skouvaras, Στηλητευτικὰ Κείμενα τοῦ *ΙΗ'* Αἰῶνος (Κατὰ τῶν Ἀναβαπτιστῶν), *Byzantinisch- Neugriechische Jahrbücher* 20 (Athens, 1967). On the activities of Auxentios of Katirli (*Eustratios Argenti*, pp. 71-72), there is an important study by Joseph Vivilakis, Αὐξεντιανὸς Μετανοημένος *[1752]* (Athens: Academy of Athens, 2010), which discusses in detail the whole dispute. For the *apologia* of Patriarch Kallinikos IV (*Eustratios Argenti*, pp. 77-78), see his lengthy (not to say interminable) poem Τὰ κατὰ καὶ μετὰ τὴν ἐξορίαν ἐπισύμβαντα, ed. Agamemnon Tselikas (Athens: Morphotiko Idryma Ethnikis Trapezis, 2004).

The concept of economy (*Eustratios Argenti*, pp. 83-86) is analysed at length by F. J. Thomson, 'Economy: An Examination of the Various Theories of Economy Held within the Orthodox Church, with Special Reference to the Ecumenical Recognition of the Validity of non-Orthodox Sacraments', *Journal of Theological Studies*, n. s. 16 (1965), pp. 368-420. Briefer but more illuminating is the discussion by John H. Erickson, *The Challenge of Our Past: Studies in Orthodox Canon Law and Church History* (Crestwood: St. Vladimir's Seminary Press, 1991), pp. 115-32. See also his essay, 'On the Cusp of Modernity: The Canonical Hermeneutic of St. Nikodemos the Hagiorite (1748-1809)', *St. Vladimir's Theological Quarterly* 42:1 (1998), pp. 45-66, where he calls in question the use made by Nicodemus of the distinction between 'strictness' and 'economy', which I myself follow (*Eustratios Argenti*, p. 83).

Valuable insights on the rebaptism issue can be found in Georgios D. Metallinos, *I confess One Baptism... Interpretation of Canon VII of the Second Ecumenical Council by the Kollyvades and Constantine Oikonomos*, translated by Priestmonk Seraphim (Athos: St Paul's Monastery, 1994). I have updated my own treatment of this question in my contribution to the 2009 International Medieval Congress at Leeds, 'The Rebaptism of Heretics in the Orthodox Canonical Tradition', in Andrew P. Roach and James R. Simpson (ed.), *Heresy and the Making of European Culture: Medieval and Modern Perspectives* (Farnham/ Burlington: Ashgate, 2013), pp. 31-50. See also my remarks in 'The Fifth Earl of Guilford and his Secret Conversion to the Orthodox Church', in Peter M. Doll (ed.), *Anglicanism and Orthodoxy: 300 Years After the 'Greek College' in Oxford* (Oxford/ Bern: Peter Lang, 2006), pp. 289-326, especially pp. 302-9. Compare George Dion Dragas, 'The Manner of Reception of Roman Catholic Converts into the Orthodox Church with Special Reference to the Decisions of the Synods of 1484 (Constantinople), 1755 (Constantinople) and 1667 (Moscow)', *The Greek Orthodox Theological Review* 44 (1999), pp. 235-71.

Finally, following the example of Saint Augustine, I wish to conclude with a *retractatio*. In my epilogue (*Eustratios Argenti*, pp. 170-5) I fear that I was overenthusiastic in the defence of my protagonist. Comparing Argenti with two other figures from eighteenth-century Greek Orthodoxy, Saint Nicodemus of the Holy Mountain and Eugenios Bulgaris (or Vulgaris), I acknowledged the greater significance of Nicodemus *vis-à-vis* Argenti; and there certainly my views have not changed. But I was less than just in what I said about Bulgaris, whom I compared unfavourably with the Chiot theologian. Nicodemus and Bulgaris have both contributed positively, in their different ways, to the renewal of Orthodox thought in the eighteenth and nineteenth centuries. This cannot be claimed to the same degree for Argenti. He was a loyal defender of Orthodoxy during a period of oppression and suffering for the Greek Church, and he has true value as a typical and at the same time articulate spokesman of his era. I do not regret having written about him. But, while he displays the better qualities of Greek polemical theology during the Turcocratia, he also illustrates its limitations. He was not able to transmit in its fullness the creative vision of traditional Orthodoxy.

Kallistos [Timothy] Ware
Metropolitan of Diokleia

INTRODUCTION

Four centuries of Turkish rule have left—for good or evil—a permanent mark upon the Greek Orthodox world. It is unfortunate that contemporary writers, Orthodox and non-Orthodox alike, usually pass over the Ottoman period of Orthodox history and seriously underestimate its importance. For without taking into account the way Greeks thought and felt under Turkish domination, and the way their theology developed between 1453 and 1821, it is all but impossible to understand the present condition of Greek Orthodoxy.

The subject of this book, Eustratios Argenti of Chios (*c.* 1687–*c.* 1757), is in many ways typical of the Turkish period. The most eminent Greek theologian of the eighteenth century, he displays both the limitations and (more notably) the good qualities of Orthodox religious thought at that time. His writings, like those of most Greek theologians between the fifteenth and the nineteenth centuries, are devoted almost entirely to polemics. Today discussion between east and west is normally carried out in a different spirit and with a different emphasis, and there must be few if any who wish to revive the bitter and aggressive style of an earlier era. Yet past controversy has still its relevance, for Orthodox of the present time have by no means abandoned all that Argenti and other such authors had to say.

Argenti is chiefly remembered as the author of a long dissertation concerning the Eucharist—probably the most elaborate polemical work on this subject ever composed by an Orthodox writer. He also made a decisive contribution to the Baptism Controversy at Constantinople in the 1750s. The issue at stake in this dispute—is it necessary to baptize Latin converts anew when receiving them into the Orthodox Church?—today seems at first sight remote and academic. But it is an issue which involves fundamental questions regarding the validity of non-Orthodox sacraments and the status of other Christian Churches in Orthodox eyes; and these are questions which inevitably arise in the 'ecumenical' situation of the present day, whenever Orthodox and non-Orthodox encounter one another.

The one existing study of Argenti, *Βίος Εὐστρατίου 'Αργέντη τοῦ Χίου Θεολόγου*, by A. K. Sarou (Athens, 1938), is written with care and is full of detailed information; but Mrs. Sarou limits herself to biographical and bibliographical matters. The present book is somewhat wider in scope. First, an attempt is here made not only to describe Argenti's life, but to assess his achievement as a theologian and to compare his views with those of other Greek writers at this time. In the second place, I have used several of Argenti's works to which Mrs. Sarou did not have access, most notably his essay on purgatory and his three treatises on the Papacy.

I have found Martin Jugie's great work, *Theologia Dogmatica Christianorum Orientalium ab Ecclesia Catholica Dissidentium* (Paris, 1926–35), most valuable as a general guide to Greek theological writing since the fall of the Byzantine Empire; there are times, however, when it must be used with some caution. The only full-scale study of the Orthodox Church under the Turks which has so far appeared in English is T. H. Papadopoullos, *The History of the Greek Church and People under Turkish Domination* (Brussels, 1952). The author has collected much curious and interesting material, but his conclusions, particularly on ecclesiastical issues, are often open to question. Because so little has been published about Orthodoxy in the Ottoman period, I have felt it desirable to begin this book with a fairly long chapter on the general religious situation in which Argenti was brought up; and I have described in detail the relations which prevailed between Orthodox and Roman Catholics in the Turkish Empire, in order that the anti-Latin polemics of Argenti and his contemporaries may be placed in their proper historical context. In this way I hope that the present book will provide a picture not only of Eustratios Argenti himself, but also of the Greek Orthodox world as a whole during the seventeenth and eighteenth centuries.

I

THE BACKGROUND

How doth the city sit solitary, that was full of people! How is she become as a widow, she that was great among the nations! LAMENTATIONS i. 1.

(i) *Orthodoxy under Islam*

The long centuries of Ottoman rule were a disheartening era for the Greek nation and the Orthodox Church. Friends and visitors from the west, recalling the position once enjoyed by the Church in the Byzantine Empire, sadly compared its former greatness with its subsequent degradation. 'It doth go hugely against the grain', wrote Edward Browne on his arrival in 1677 as chaplain to the English Embassy at Constantinople, 'to see the crescent exalted everywhere, where the Cross stood so long triumphant: and I could wish this mighty tyrant turned upside down, but that 'tis only a silly wish and hath nothing in it: but really it would grieve any Christian in the world to see this grand empire in such hands as it is, and the Stately Church of Santa Sophia so abused, and a most pleasant fruitful country possessed by infidells.'[1] A century before, Martin Crusius complained: 'Alas! unhappy Greece . . . no more is any free breath drawn there; there are no schools, no learning; the ancient glories remain no longer; with difficulty they scrape together the tribute which they have to pay; in place of the saving Gospel of Christ they have the accursed Koran; where once the voice of Basils, Nazianzens, and Chrysostoms made God's oracles resound, there the prophets of Mohammed, hateful to God, now cry aloud.'[2]

But Crusius in his indignation exaggerates: the situation, although depressing, was never as desperate as his words suggest. Greek writers of today usually speak as if Turkish domination meant utter slavery both of soul and body; yet in fact the Turks displayed on the whole a remarkable tolerance,

[1] Letter quoted in G. Williams, *The Orthodox Church of the East in the Eighteenth Century*, p. xv.

[2] *Germanograecia*, p. 18.

not least in religious matters. Islam in 1453 was far more generous to its Christian subjects than Christians of western Europe were towards one another in the sixteenth and seventeenth centuries. Since Mohammedans regard the Bible as a holy book and Jesus Christ as a prophet, the Christian religion from their point of view, although incomplete, is not entirely false, and Christians, being a 'People of the Book', are not to be treated on a level with mere pagans. They are not to be converted at the point of the sword nor persecuted, but can continue undisturbed in the exercise of their faith, so long as they remain submissive and acknowledge their subjection to the power of Islam. Such were the principles which Mohammed II, the conqueror of Constantinople, put into effect in 1453. The Orthodox Church, in other words, was allowed to survive, but its members were kept in a position of permanent inferiority, maintained like sheep or cows for the support of their Moslem masters. Turkish tolerance had thus its disadvantages: it deprived the Greeks of the more heroic ways of witnessing to their faith, while exposing them to the demoralizing effects of a steady social pressure.

The Turkish state was a theocracy, and as such admitted no distinction between religion and politics, so that if Christians were to be recognized as an independent religious faith, it was also necessary for them to be organized as an independent nation, an *imperium in imperio*. The Orthodox Church under the Turks became in this way a civil as well as a religious institution —the *Rum Millet*, the 'Roman Nation', with the Patriarch of Constantinople as both civil and religious head. On other occasions when one people has conquered another, the two have in course of time become so fused that all distinction between them is eventually lost; but on Turkish principles a difference of religion set up an absolute barrier between the conqueror and the conquered. The *Millet* system made it possible for the Greek people to endure as a distinctive unit through four centuries of alien rule; but by preserving Greek national consciousness, and yet keeping the Greeks for ever in a position of subjection, it made revolts inevitable. Hence it is that, in spite of Turkish tolerance, the story of Turkish rule is in its later stages one long chronicle of bloodshed, of patriotic uprisings followed by savage reprisals.

But if Greek Orthodoxy was enabled to survive under the Ottomans it paid a heavy price. The outward restrictions which the Turks imposed were, it is true, depressing rather than intolerable. The taxes of which Crusius complains were certainly severe, but the most objectionable item—the levy of Greek children for the Sultan's Janissary guard—fell into disuse in the early part of the seventeenth century. Christians had to wear a distinctive dress and were not allowed to serve in the army. They must not attempt to convert a Moslem to their faith, must not seduce or marry a Moslem woman, revile or show disrespect for the Prophet or the Koran, make an alliance or treaty with a nation outside Moslem territory. They were permitted to display little or no outward sign of their religion; Sir Paul Rycaut, an English resident in the Levant during the seventeenth century, speaks of:

> . . . the Mysteries of the Altar conceal'd in secret and dark places; for such I have seen in Cities and Villages where I have travelled, rather like Vaults or Sepulchres than Churches, having their Roofs almost levelled with the Superficies of the Earth, lest the most ordinary exsurgency of structure should be accused for triumph of Religion, and to stand in competition with the lofty Spires of the *Mahometan* Moschs.[1]

Such were the outward restrictions. But far more serious than this was the inner decay which the Orthodox Church suffered as a result of its relations with the Turkish government. Intrigue, simony, and corruption dominated the higher administration of the Church. Each Patriarch of Constantinople on his election required a *berat* from the Sultan, as a confirmation of his spiritual and secular authority. It quickly became the regular practice for him to pay a large fee in order to obtain this official recognition, and it was therefore in the financial interests of the

[1] *The Present State of the Greek and Armenian Churches*, pp. 11–12. See also Thomas Smith, *An Account of the Greek Church*, p. 51: 'Christianity here, as to the exteriour part of it, being reduced to the same state and condition, as it was before the times of *Constantine* the Great.' Joseph Georgirenes, Archbishop of Samos, writes in the same way: 'Nor is it expedient in that Country, that any thing which concerns the Christian Religion should make any outward appearance of Magnificence, or costliness, least it should provoke the envy and avarice of their proud Masters to Sacrilegious rapine' (*A Description of the Present State of Samos*, p. 12). Compare Peter Hammond, *The Waters of Marah*, London, 1956, pp. 21–22, on the 'secret' churches of Kastoria.

government to change the occupier of the see as frequently as possible. The Sultan had no difficulty in finding excuses for the deposition of the Patriarch. Among the Metropolitans who composed the Holy Synod, there was normally a number of parties, each anxious to secure the throne for its own candidate and willing to reward the civil authorities generously for their co-operation. The Sultan had only to encourage one of these groups in its agitation and then yield to its demands.

Patriarchs were removed and reinstated with bewildering rapidity. 'Out of 159 Patriarchs who held office between the fifteenth and the twentieth century, the Turks have on 105 occasions driven Patriarchs from their throne; there have been 27 abdications, often involuntary; 6 Patriarchs have suffered violent deaths by hanging, poisoning or drowning; and only 21 have died natural deaths while in office.'[1] In the seventy-five years between 1625 and 1700 there were fifty Patriarchs: an average of eighteen months each.[2] At any given moment there was usually a number of ex-Patriarchs living in exile, who were often recalled to resume office once more; some even occupied the Patriarchate on four or five distinct occasions. Many Patriarchs were men of ability and deep sincerity, but they were the victims of a system which they could do little to improve.

Western visitors were not slow to comment on the pernicious effects of the bribery and intrigue which prevailed in the Church. Sir George Wheler says of the Patriarchs:

> The Authority which they thus obtain by Simony, they maintain by Tyranny: For as soon as they are promoted, they send to all their Bishops, to contribute to the Sum they have disbursed for their Preferment, and such as deny, they depose and send others to their Charge. Again, the Bishops send to their inferiour Clergy; who are forced to do the same to the poor People, or to spare it out of their Wives and Childrens Mouths. But many times they engage for more, than they can perform; and bring the Church so much in debt to the *Turk*, that its Ruin is daily threatened thereby; which, without *God's* great Mercy uphold it, cannot long subsist.[3]

[1] B. J. Kidd, *The Churches of Eastern Christendom*, p. 304.

[2] See A. K. Fortescue, *The Orthodox Eastern Church*, p. 242.

[3] *A Journey into Greece*, p. 195 (quoted in part by P. Sherrard, *The Greek East and the Latin West*, pp. 102–3).

This debt, a permanent feature in the ecclesiastical finances, had attained alarming dimensions by the middle of the eighteenth century, when efforts were made to restrict it; but on the eve of the Greek War of Independence it still amounted to more than 3,000 purses, or one and a half million Turkish piastres.[1]

The Patriarch saw in the members of the Synod nothing but rival claimants for the throne which he held, and only too often the prevailing relation between Patriarch and Synod was one of mutual suspicion. So great was their distrust of one another that during his third period of office (1744–8) Patriarch Païsios II resorted to the extraordinary expedient of summoning his Metropolitans into the Patriarchal church on the Sunday of Pentecost, and forcing them to swear over the Book of the Gospels that they would not attempt to overthrow him; he in turn undertook not to persecute any of them.[2] 'Every good Christian', Rycaut justly remarked, 'ought with sadness to consider, and with compassion to behold this once glorious Church to tear and rent out her own bowels, and give them for food to Vultures and Ravens, and to the wild and fierce Creatures of the World.'[3]

(*ii*) *The State of Learning and Theology*

But western visitors to the Levant during the Turkish period found occasion to deplore not only the corruption and the internal dissensions of the Orthodox Church, but also its want of scholarship and the ignorance of its priests. 'Most Mechanicks amongst us [are] more learned and knowing than the Doctors and Clergy of *Greece*,' wrote Rycaut.[4] 'The ancient Structures and Colleges of *Athens* are become ruinous, and only a fit habitation for its own Owle, and all *Greece* poor and illiterate.'[5] M. Pitton de Tournefort claimed that the Greek clergy were scarcely capable of reading the service books; as for under-

[1] T. H. Papadopoullos, *The History of the Greek Church and People under Turkish Domination*, p. 132.

[2] A. K. Hypsilantis (Ypsilanti), *Τὰ μετὰ τὴν ἅλωσιν*, p. 362; G. Vendotis, *Προσθήκη τῆς Ἐκκλησιαστικῆς Ἱστορίας Μελετίου*, p. 87. Vendotis adds that the Metropolitans, as soon as they left the church, 'gobbled up their oath like donkeys gobbling up cabbages'.

[3] *The Present State of the Greek and Armenian Churches*, p. 107.

[4] Ibid., Preface.

[5] Ibid., pp. 28–29.

standing what they read, this was completely beyond them.[1] But such sweeping changes as this are without doubt grossly exaggerated. The proportion of Greeks in the Turkish period who could read and write was probably as great as in any European nation at the same time;[2] and in every century there were at least one or two Greek theological writers little inferior to their Latin counterparts, or to most of their Byzantine predecessors.

But if learning never wholly disappeared among the Greeks under Ottoman rule, the general position in the seventeenth and eighteenth centuries was not encouraging. They possessed a few educated theologians, but only a few. They had a number of local 'colleges' or *gymnasia*, the most notable being those at Jannina, Patmos, and Chios, while at Constantinople itself there was the celebrated Patriarchal Academy, attended by Greeks from all parts of the Near East, 'the School of the Nation' (*ἡ Σχολὴ τοῦ Γένους*), as it was called. Outside the Turkish Empire there was an Orthodox College at Venice. These places were often thorough and efficient as far as they went, but in higher academic studies they obviously could not compare with the great universities of western Europe. In hopes of improving the situation, Patriarch Cyril V in 1753 founded a college on Mount Athos, with the aim of introducing into the Greek world the methods and standards of western scholarship; but the venture did not meet with success. The Principal, Eugenios Bulgaris, was at this time the leading Greek protagonist of European 'enlightenment' and scientific rationalism, and in his lectures on philosophy he used the works not of Aristotle but of Descartes, Leibniz, and Locke. The school was welcomed by many—in the words of one contemporary, 'here was something greater than the Academy or the Lyceum, . . . a place of learning such as the Greeks in their misfortune had not seen before'[3]—but there were others who viewed the new school with less enthusiasm, feeling that the secular outlook of the Principal was scarcely in harmony with the traditions of Mount Athos. So great indeed was the opposition, particularly among the monks of the Holy Mountain, that within a few years the

[1] J. Pitton de Tournefort, *Relation d'un Voyage du Levant*, vol. i, p. 98.

[2] See G. Finlay, *A History of Greece*, vol. v, p. 283.

[3] S. Makraios, '*Ὑπομνήματα*, in K. N. Sathas, *Μεσαιωνικὴ Βιβλιοθήκη*, vol. iii, p. 219.

Athonian Academy was forced to close. The ambitious scheme of Cyril and Eugenios came to nothing.[1]

Promising Greek students, then, who wished to continue their early studies, had no choice but to go to the universities of western Europe. Among the leading theologians of the Turkish period, a few were self-taught (for example, Dositheos, the great seventeenth century Patriarch of Jerusalem), but the overwhelming majority had been trained in the west, under Protestant or Roman Catholic masters. Greeks went to Padua,[2] to Pisa or Florence, to Halle, Paris, or even as far afield as Oxford;[3] they went also to Rome, where in 1576 Pope Gregory XIII had founded the College of Saint Athanasius, specially intended for Greek students.

This western training, given under non-Orthodox auspices, inevitably influenced the way in which Greek theologians of the seventeenth and eighteenth centuries approached and interpreted their faith.[4] However great their desire to remain loyal Orthodox, most of them looked at theology to a greater or lesser extent through western spectacles. Naturally this tendency towards westernization was not limited to those who had actually studied in the west, but also affected many who themselves had never left the Orthodox world. Consciously or unconsciously, most Greek writers of the time adopted theological categories, terminology, and forms of argument foreign to the tradition of their own Church; Orthodox religious thinking underwent what a contemporary Russian theologian, Father George Florovsky, has appropriately termed a *pseudomorphosis*. Writers for the most part fall into two broad classes, the 'Latinizers' and the 'Protestantizers', although there is also a number

[1] For a somewhat idealized picture of Greek schools in the Turkish Empire at the start of the eighteenth century, see A. Helladius, *Status Praesens Ecclesiae Graecae*, pp. 21–61. Compare the description by Richard Pococke of the school or 'university', as he terms it, of Patmos (*A Description of the East*, vol. ii, Part 2, p. 31). See also G. Chassiotis, *L'instruction publique chez les Grecs*, pp. 13–128.

[2] With good reason the university of Padua has been called 'véritable *Alma Mater* de la Grèce moderne' (M.-J. le Guillou, 'La renaissance spirituelle du XVIIIe siècle', *Istina*, 1960, No. 1, p. 99).

[3] The most notable among the Greek students at Oxford was Mitrophanis Kritopoulos, who studied there from 1617 to 1624, and later became Patriarch of Alexandria. At the end of the seventeenth century there was actually a scheme to establish a special 'Greek College', but after a few years this came to nothing. (See G. Williams, *The Orthodox Church of the East in the Eighteenth Century*, p. xviii–xxv.)

[4] On this question of western influences, see J. N. Karmiris, '*Ετερόδοξοι ἐπιδράσεις ἐπὶ τὰς ὁμολογίας τοῦ ιζ' αἰῶνος*.

—including Eustratios Argenti himself—whom neither label fits. But while the pseudomorphosis is unmistakable, its extent must not be unduly exaggerated: the great majority of those who used outward forms borrowed from the west none the less remained basically Orthodox in the inward substance of their thought.

As examples of the Protestantizing tendency in Orthodox theology, we may take two Patriarchs of the early seventeenth century: Cyril Lukaris, Patriarch of Alexandria from 1601 to 1621 (Patriarch of Constantinople for three weeks in 1612, and also subsequently on six different occasions between 1621 and 1638);[1] and Mitrophanis Kritopoulos, Patriarch of Alexandria from 1636 to 1639. But while the writings of Kritopoulos are marked at the most by a faint Protestant tinge—indeed, his *Confession*[2] is reckoned among the so-called 'symbolical books' of the Orthodox Church—in the case of Lukaris the position is altogether different. He formed close friendships with a number of Protestants, above all with Cornelius Van Haga, the Dutch envoy at Constantinople, and fell so much under their influence that by the end of his life there is little in his religious thought which can be considered distinctively Orthodox.

Cyril's views are concisely set forth in his *Confession*, first published in Latin at Geneva in 1629; a Greek edition was issued at Geneva in 1633. Dr. Karmiris, Professor of Theology at the University of Athens, justly terms the *Confession* 'a Calvinist symbolical book written under Orthodox influence, rather than an Orthodox book written under Protestant influence'.[3] Were it not (Karmiris continues) for a few Orthodox

[1] On Lukaris, see the very partisan and often unreliable biography by G. A. Hadjiantoniou, *Protestant Patriarch. The Life of Cyril Lucaris (1572–1638), Patriarch of Constantinople*; also J. M. Hornus, 'Cyrille Lucaris—A propos d' un livre récent', in *Proche-Orient Chrétien*, vol. xiii, Jerusalem, 1963, pp. 21–36. Lukaris was finally strangled by the Sultan's Janissary Guards and his body thrown into the Bosphorus. The story of his life is a striking illustration of the way in which religion and politics were intertwined in the Greek world at this time.

[2] By 'Confession' in this context is meant a statement of faith, a solemn declaration of religious belief.

[3] *Μνημεῖα*, vol. ii, p. 564. Karmiris gives the Greek text of the *Confession* on pp. 565–70; English translation in J. N. W. B. Robertson, *The Synod of Jerusalem*, pp. 185–215.

After Lukaris' death attempts were made to defend his memory by arguing that the *Confession* was not really his work, but was falsely fathered upon him by the Calvinists. This was the view maintained by the Council of Jerusalem in 1672, and

touches, anyone who did not know who the author of the *Confession* was, would think that it was composed 'by Calvin himself or by one of his circle'. Karmiris reckons that only three out of the eighteen chapters of the *Confession* are fully Orthodox in teaching.

Among other things, Lukaris in his *Confession* follows the standard Calvinist theory of Predestination and Election; he states that the witness of Scripture is of far higher authority than that of the Church; he rejects belief in the infallibility of the Church, and stresses its invisible much more than its visible aspect; he rejects the veneration of icons; and he teaches that there are only two sacraments, not seven. The presence of Christ in the Eucharist, he says, is 'such as faith presents and offers to us, not such as the vainly invented doctrine of Transubstantiation (*metousiosis*) teaches':

> For we believe that the faithful who communicate in the Supper eat the Body of Our Lord Jesus Christ, not by physically pressing and dissolving the communion with their teeth, but by partaking through the perception of the soul. For the Body of the Lord is not what is seen and received visibly, but what faith, receiving spiritually, presents to us and bestows. Therefore it is true that we eat and partake and have communion, if we believe; but if we believe not, we are deprived of all benefit of the sacrament.[1]

In his letters Lukaris speaks with contempt of the doctrine of Transubstantiation, which 'out of a piece of bread or a crumb creates a Jesus Christ'.[2]

it is still occasionally upheld by Greek writers today. Even if Lukaris is not the author in the narrowest sense (perhaps the first draft was written by one of his Calvinist friends—presumably Léger), yet he certainly adopted the *Confession* as his own and appended his signature to it. There is a manuscript of the *Confession* in the Municipal Library at Geneva, written in Lukaris' own hand. On the authorship of the *Confession*, see Hadjiantoniou, *Protestant Patriarch*, pp. 100–7.

[1] *Confession*, xvii, in Karmiris, op. cit., vol. ii, p. 568. The last clause—'if we believe not, we are deprived of all benefit of the sacrament'—is of course acceptable from an Orthodox point of view; but the rest of the passage is evasive and misleading. According to traditional Orthodox teaching, the presence of Christ in the Eucharist is an objective presence, and does not depend for its reality upon the spiritual state of the communicant. Thus the unbeliever is certainly deprived of the *benefit* of the sacrament, yet he partakes none the less in the true Body and Blood of Christ: he receives them, however, not to remission of sins and life everlasting, but to his own damnation.

[2] Hadjiantoniou, *Protestant Patriarch*, p. 106.

To his Protestant friends Lukaris readily admitted the Calvinist inspiration of his teaching. In a letter to the Swiss pastor, Antoine Léger, he said:

> If I die, I wish you to be able to testify that I die an Orthodox Catholic, in the faith of Our Lord Jesus Christ, in the teaching of the Gospel as contained in the *Confessio Belgica*, in my own *Confession*, and in all the Confessions of the Evangelical Churches, which are all alike. I hold in abomination the errors of the Papists and the superstitions of the Greeks; I approve and embrace the doctrine of the most excellent teacher John Calvin and of all who agree with him.[1]

It is scarcely surprising that Roman Catholic residents in Constantinople viewed Cyril's activities with alarm and disapproval. The Comte de Césy, the French Ambassador at Constantinople, wrote to Louis XIII: 'This Patriarch was a most dangerous heretic, whose one aim was to weaken and ruin the Roman Church and to establish Calvinism in Greece and in all parts of the east.'[2] On the other hand, Protestants both in England and the Continent welcomed the *Confession* with great enthusiasm. Sir Paul Rycaut regarded Cyril as a would-be Anglican:

> I am perswaded that this *Cyrillus*, having spent some time in *England*, and there observed that purity of our Doctrine, and the excellency of our Discipline, which flourished in the beginning of the Reign of King *Charles* the Martyr, and viewed our Churches trim'd and adorned in a modest Medium, between the wanton and superstitious dress of *Rome*, and the slovenry and insipid Government of *Geneva*, entertained a high Opinion of our happy Reformation; intending thence perhaps to draw a Pattern, whereby to amend and correct the defaults of the *Greek* Church. . . . And had not this good Patriarch been thus malitiously prosecuted, and his life taken from him by unhappy Wiles, he might, with God's assistance, have accomplished a work of Reformation, and piloted the Church into that state of Apostolical Purity, which King *James*, *Erasmus*, *Cassander*, *Melancthon*, *Buçar* the Arch-Bishop of *Spalatro*, and others did design.[3]

[1] J. H. Hottinger, *Analecta historico-theologica*, Zurich, 1652, p. 560; quoted in A. Malvy and M. Viller, *La Confession Orthodoxe de Pierre Moghila*, pp. xxxi–xxxii.

[2] Malvy and Viller, op. cit., p. xxvi.

[3] *The Present State of the Greek and Armenian Churches*, Preface. Lukaris did not in fact visit England: perhaps Rycaut has confused him with Kritopoulos.

One suspects, however, that Lukaris took as his model the system of Geneva rather than the Anglicanism of Archbishop Laud.

The Orthodox reaction to Cyril's Calvinism was swift and unambiguous. His *Confession* was condemned by no less than six councils during the half century following his death (Constantinople, 1638; Constantinople, 1642; Jassy, 1642; Constantinople, 1672; Jerusalem, otherwise known as Bethlehem, 1672; Constantinople, 1691). 'As black is the opposite of white,' stated the Council of Jerusalem, 'and as darkness is the negation of light, so the *Confession* of Cyril is the opposite and the negation of the divinely inspired and evangelical truth held in the Eastern Church.'[1] Yet in a negative way Cyril's *Confession* exercised a decisive influence upon the development of Orthodox religious thought, for it forced many bishops and theologians, by natural reaction, into a Roman position. Faced by the inroads of Protestantism, Orthodox fought back with the weapons that lay most readily to hand—Latin weapons. Under the circumstances it was perhaps the only thing that they could do.

The Latinizing tendency is found most notably in two other seventeenth century Confessions, both intended as an answer to Lukaris, the one by Peter of Moghila, Metropolitan of Kiev from 1633 to 1647, the other by Dositheos, Patriarch of Jerusalem from 1669 to 1707. But although under Latin influence Peter and Dositheos deviate at some points from the main stream of Orthodox tradition, their deviation is far less radical than that of Cyril.

Moghila had been educated in his youth by the Jesuits. In his *Orthodox Confession*, which he wrote in Latin in the year 1640 or perhaps shortly before, he drew heavily on Roman works, particularly the Catechism of Canisius, so that in structure and arrangement, as also in its general approach and spirit, the work corresponds closely to Roman Catholic manuals current at the time. Nor is this all: on certain specific points of theology—especially of sacramental theology—where Rome and Orthodoxy differ, Moghila adopted the Roman view. In his section concerning the departed, he maintained the existence of a third place, distinct from heaven and hell, and identical with the Latin purgatory, save that he rejected the idea of purging by

[1] Karmiris, *Μνημεῖα*, vol. ii, p. 720.

fire. When discussing Baptism, he admitted affusion as a normal alternative to immersion.[1] In the part dealing with the Eucharist, he not only employed the word *transsubstantiatio*—he was not by any means the first Orthodox writer to do this, for the term had already been used as early as the middle of the fifteenth century by Gennadios, Patriarch of Constantinople—but he also taught that the 'moment' of consecration comes at the Words of Institution, not at the Epiclesis.

However, when Moghila's *Orthodox Confession* was submitted for approval to the Council of Jassy in 1642, these passages were modified. A Greek, Meletios Syrigos, was commissioned by the Council to translate the original Latin version into Greek and at the same time to make such emendations as should be necessary. In his revised version, Syrigos explicitly repudiated belief in a third place or purgatory, distinct from heaven and hell; he deleted the mention of affusion as an alternative to immersion; and he was careful to state that the Epiclesis is the moment of consecration in the Eucharist. In this revised form the *Orthodox Confession* was duly ratified by the Council.[2]

But Syrigos was himself something of a 'Latinizer' and there were many western elements in the *Orthodox Confession* which he failed to delete. He retained the term 'transubstantiation' (*metousiosis*); in the section on the sacraments the Scholastic distinction between matter and form was still employed; he left unchanged the passage on the *status innocentiae* of Adam before the Fall, where the normal Latin view is presented; he did not alter the remarks about Confession, in which Moghila adopted the Latin idea of 'satisfaction' and treated the penance as a necessary part of the sacrament.[3] The revision by Syrigos was thus not nearly as drastic as it might have been; but even so

[1] For the meaning of the terms 'affusion' and 'immersion', see below, p. 87.

[2] The Greek version of the *Orthodox Confession*, as revised by Syrigos and approved at Jassy, is given in Karmiris, op. cit., vol. ii, pp. 593–686 (English translation edited by J. J. Overbeck, *The Orthodox Confession of the Catholic and Apostolic Eastern Church from the version of Peter Mogila*, London, 1898). Moghila's original Latin version is now lost, but an intermediate Latin text survives which at some points follows the changes made in 1642, but at others still follows the first version of 1640 (edited by A. Malvy and M. Viller, *La Confession Orthodoxe de Pierre Moghila*, with an introduction analysing the alterations made in 1642).

On purgatory, see the *Orthodox Confession*, Part I, questions 61–68; on Baptism, Part I, question 102; on the Eucharist, Part I, question 107.

[3] *Orthodox Confession*, Part I, questions 23, 100, 107, and 112–13.

Moghila does not seem to have been wholly satisfied with the changes made at Jassy in his *Confession.* At any rate in the *Little Catechism* which he issued in 1645, he still continued to teach consecration by the Words of Institution. When discussing the Last Things, however, the *Little Catechism* is far more guarded than the *Orthodox Confession*, and does not go nearly so far in a Latin direction: but even though in the *Little Catechism* Moghila does not explicitly affirm the existence of purgatory, yet neither does he repudiate the doctrine.

The *Orthodox Confession* of Moghila represents the high-water mark of Latin influence upon Orthodox theology, for although Latinisms are also apparent in the *Confession* of Dositheos, they are less serious. Concerning the state of the departed Dositheos is more reserved than Moghila; but although he avoids the word purgatory and does not in so many words teach a third place between heaven and hell, yet in effect, if not in terminology, he comes very close to the Roman position, adopting in particular the idea of expiatory suffering after death. When discussing the Eucharist, he employs not only the term *metousiosis* but also the Scholastic distinction between substance (οὐσία) and accidents (συμβεβηκότα):

> After the consecration of the bread and wine, the bread is changed, transubstantiated, converted, and transelemented into the true Body of the Lord, which was born in Bethlehem of Mary, the Ever-Virgin and Mother of God, which was baptized in Jordan, suffered, was buried, rose, ascended, which sits on the right hand of God the Father and will come again upon the clouds of heaven; and the wine is converted and transubstantiated into the true Blood of Christ, which while he hung upon the Cross was poured out for life of the world.
>
> Furthermore we believe that after the consecration of the bread and wine the substance of the bread and of the wine remain no longer, but there is only the very Body and Blood of the Lord in the species and form (εἴδει καὶ τύπῳ) of bread and wine, that is to say, under the accidents of the bread and the wine.[1]

Dositheos adds, however, that the term *metousiosis* must not be taken to describe the *manner* of the change—'for this is altogether

[1] Karmiris, *Μνημεῖα*, vol. ii, p. 761. For the text of the *Confession* of Dositheos, see Karmiris, op. cit., vol. ii, pp. 746–73. For purgatory, see Decree xviii; for substance and accidents, Decree xvii. There is an English translation of the *Confession* in Robertson, *The Synod of Jerusalem*, pp. 110–62.

incomprehensible and cannot possibly be described': it simply indicates the *reality* of the change. The *Confession* of Dositheos was formally ratified by the Council of Jerusalem (1672), often called the Council of Bethlehem. In a later work Dositheos withdrew what he had said in his *Confession* concerning the state of the departed, but his views on the Eucharist remained unchanged.

The style of Eucharistic theology upheld by Dositheos is also found in many other Greek writers of the same period. For example, Nicholas Bulgaris (1634–?1684) in his *Holy Catechism* adopts the Scholastic distinction between matter and form in the sacraments, and uses the terms 'transubstantiation' and 'accidents'.[1] Early in the eighteenth century, when the Anglican Nonjurors entered into negotiations with the Eastern Patriarchs, the latter sent them a copy of the *Confession* of Dositheos, treating this as an authoritative statement of Orthodox teaching, which (so the Greeks insisted) the Nonjurors must accept before any union could be established.[2] When the Nonjurors expressed doubts about the wording of certain prayers to the Mother of God, the Patriarchs showed a surprising tolerance and did not press the matter;[3] but over the terminology used to describe the consecration in the Eucharist, the Patriarchs allowed them no latitude whatever, but demanded strictly that they adopt the formulae of Dositheos, including the terms 'transubstantiation' and 'accidents'.[4]

Such were the main issues over which the Protestantizing and the Latinizing wings within the Orthodox Church disagreed during the seventeenth century. Outwardly it was the Latinizing

[1] The *Ἱερὰ Κατήχησις* of Nicholas Bulgaris, first published at Venice in 1681, proved extremely popular and was many times reprinted. English translation: *The Holy Catechism*, edited by W. E. Daniel and R. Raikes Bromage. On matter and form, see pp. 8 and 13–18 of the English translation; on transubstantiation and accidents, p. 204.

Despite this popularity, the *Holy Catechism* was criticized by some for its 'Latinisms'. When, for example, it was reprinted at Constantinople in 1861, a number of notes were included warning the reader against various Romanizing features. It is interesting to observe that these notes appeal in particular to a book by Eustratios Argenti, *Treatise against Unleavened Bread*, and quote among other things Argenti's strictures upon the Latin distinction between matter and form in the sacraments.

[2] Letter of 1723: Karmiris, *Μνημεῖα*, vol. ii, p. 819; Williams, *The Orthodox Church of the East in the Eighteenth Century*, p. 119.

[3] Letter of 1718: Karmiris, op. cit., vol. ii, p. 810; Williams, op. cit., p. 53.

[4] Letter of 1718: Karmiris, op. cit., vol. ii, p. 813; Williams, op. cit., pp. 58–59.

party which won, since the *Confession* of Lukaris was firmly condemned, whereas the Councils of Jassy and Jerusalem, which approved the *Confessions* of Moghila and Dositheos, were accepted by the Orthodox Church at large. Yet the triumph of the Latinizers was by no means complete. Over the question of the departed (as we shall see in more detail in the fifth chapter) there was a very great divergence of opinion among Greek writers of the seventeenth and eighteenth centuries: many were unable to accept the doctrine expressed in Dositheos' *Confession* and ratified by the Council of Jerusalem, and Dositheos himself, as we noted, in later life had second thoughts on this subject. In the same way, not all Greek theologians employ the word 'transubstantiation';[1] and some—for example, Eustratios Argenti—although they use it, carefully avoid the closely related term 'accidents'. Thus while the extreme positions of Lukaris and Moghila (in the original version of his *Orthodox Confession*) were repudiated, discussion still continued in the Orthodox Church on many of the issues which they had raised.

Indeed, so long as Orthodox borrowed their theology from the west it was inevitable that these two tendencies should persist, with one school of thought drawing primarily on Scholasticism and the Counter-Reformation, the other primarily on Luther and Calvin. With varying success individual writers modified and adapted in an Orthodox direction what they had borrowed; but almost always the traces of its origin still remained. The tension between the two schools is particularly clear in Russia under Peter the Great, with Stephen Javorsky on one side and Theophan Prokopovich on the other. In Greek academic theology of the past hundred years, it is often easy to

[1] Among those who use the term *metousiosis* are the following: in the fifteenth century, Gennadios Scholarios; in the sixteenth, Meletios Pigas; in the seventeenth, Gabriel Severus, George Koressios, Peter of Moghila, Meletios Syrigos, Nektarios of Jerusalem, and Dositheos; in the eighteenth century, Chrysanthos of Jerusalem and Eustratios Argenti; also the Councils of Jassy (1642), of Jerusalem (1672), and of Constantinople (1691 and 1727). The following refrain from employing the term: Saint Mark of Ephesus; Patriarch Jeremias II of Constantinople in his *Answers* to the Lutherans; Mitrophanis Kritopoulos; the Councils of Constantinople in 1638, 1672, 1722, and 1838; the Letter of the Eastern Patriarchs to Pope Pius IX in 1848; and the Encyclical Letter of the Synod of Constantinople to Pope Leo XIII in 1895. Many Orthodox writers today still speak of 'transubstantiation', but others deliberately avoid the word, using in its place the older Patristic terms.

guess from a man's works whether the German university at which he studied was Protestant or Roman Catholic.[1]

(*iii*) *Greeks and Latins:*[2] *Hostility and Friendship*

We have spoken hitherto of the theological influence of the Latin west on Orthodox thinkers: but what, on a more personal and practical level, were the relations in the eastern Mediterranean between the two Churches during the seventeenth and eighteenth centuries? The Roman Catholics under Ottoman rule formed a small minority of the Christian population in the Levant, but they possessed a prominence out of all proportion to their actual numbers. There were two main reasons for this. First, they enjoyed powerful diplomatic patronage: when in difficulties the Latin minority could always appeal for help to the Catholic embassies at Constantinople, and in particular to the French ambassador. And in the second place, the position of the Roman Catholic congregations was greatly strengthened by the presence of missionary priests—Jesuits, Franciscans, and others—who came in large numbers from the west, particularly after the foundation of the *Sacra Congregatio de Propaganda Fide* in 1622.[3] In education and learning these western missionaries were far superior to the local Greek clergy

[1] Besides these Latin borrowings in the field of theology, Greek Orthodox of the Turkish period also drew upon Roman Catholic spiritual and devotional writings. One of the chief 'devotional classics' of the Greek seventeenth century—*The Salvation of Sinners*, by the Athonite monk Agapios Landos, first published at Venice in 1641—is taken almost entirely from Latin works, as Agapios himself admits in his preface! The main source is Cesarius of Heisterbach's *Dialogus Miraculorum*; the changes made by Agapios are very slight. (See I. Hausherr, 'Dogme et spiritualité orientale', in *Revue d'Ascétique et de Mystique*, vol. xxiii, Toulouse, 1947, pp. 26–29.) In the next century another Athonite monk, Saint Nicodèmus of the Holy Mountain, published editions of Ignatius Loyola's *Spiritual Exercises* and of Lorenzo Scupoli's *Spiritual Combat*; Nicodemus, however, is more reticent than Agapios about the Roman Catholic origin of his material. (See the introduction by H. A. Hodges to *Unseen Warfare*, translated by E. Kadloubovsky and G. E. H. Palmer, London, 1952; and M. Viller, 'Nicodème l'Agiorite et ses emprunts à la litterature spirituelle occidentale. Le Combat spirituel et les Exercises de S. Ignace dans l'Église byzantine', in *Revue d'Ascétique et de Mystique*, vol. v, 1924, pp. 174–7.)

[2] These words are used here to denote not language or nationality but religion. By 'Greeks' are meant members of the Orthodox Church and by 'Latins' Roman Catholics. Many Roman Catholics of the Turkish period were in fact Greek-speaking.

[3] Lukaris (who suffered much from the activities of the *Propaganda*), termed it 'the Congregation for the Propagation of Infidelity' (E. Legrand, *Bibliographie hellénique . . . au dix-septième siècle*, vol. iv, p. 487).

and hierarchy. As well as ministering to the Latin congregations they also worked among the Greeks.

Long before the end of the Byzantine Empire, Orthodox had come to regard the Roman Catholic Church with misgiving and suspicion. Quite apart from doctrinal questions, the sack of Constantinople by the Crusaders in 1204 was something (so it has rightly been observed) which 'Christians of the east could neither forgive nor forget'. The reunion Council of Ferrara-Florence in 1438–9 had in the end done more to widen than to bridge the gulf. Looking back on the Council, Greeks in later generations felt that they had somehow been tricked and deceived when they went to the west: they felt that the Latins had taken advantage of their political weakness in order to extract religious concessions from them; they felt that they had been forced against their better judgement into signing an act of submission in which they did not really believe. Historically this is certainly an over-simplification of what actually happened at the Council; but such was the 'legend' which later grew up among the Greeks. For them Florence was not an encouraging precedent for the future but an awful warning.

Yet if an underlying hostility towards Rome is never entirely absent, it is surprising how little it is in evidence in the Greek world of the seventeenth century. Despite occasional outbreaks of hostility, particularly at Constantinople and Jerusalem, encounters between Orthodox and Roman Catholics were often extraordinarily cordial. Mixed marriages were frequent; the two sides took active part in one another's services; western missionaries, with full permission from the Orthodox authorities, preached in Orthodox churches and heard the confessions of the Orthodox faithful; Orthodox received communion from Roman Catholic priests, while Greek converts to Rome were often told by the western missionaries to receive communion as before at Orthodox altars; a Roman Catholic was accepted as godparent at an Orthodox baptism, and vice versa. Both sides frequently acted as if the schism between east and west did not exist. The Latin missionaries, in the absence of any bishop of their own, behaved towards the local Orthodox bishop as though they recognized him as their ordinary; the Orthodox authorities for their part, so far from repudiating the missionaries as intruders, welcomed them as friends and allies, and encouraged them to undertake pastoral work among the Greek population.

Instances of common worship and *communicatio in sacris* during the seventeenth century are so frequent that only a few examples can be mentioned here.[1] Some of the most striking cases are found in the Ionian Islands, at this time under Venetian rule.[2] An anonymous Athonite monk of the sixteenth century has left a vivid description of the situation prevailing on Kerkyra (Corfu), where members of the two Churches lived side by side on terms of the utmost friendship. While the monk himself disapproved strongly of what went on—he entitles his work 'The Errors of the Corfiots, on account of which we excommunicate them'—it is evident that on Kerkyra itself these acts of friendship were accepted as a matter of course. The Greeks, so the monk writes, receive communion from Roman priests and go to them for confession. The clergy of the two Churches hold joint processions on Corpus Christi and on Holy Saturday, and even celebrate the Eucharist simultaneously in the same building, although at separate altars:

> The Latins hold a procession with the unleavened bread which they consecrate and call the Holy Gift. In front walk the Jews, then the Greeks, and after them the Latins—all of them together dressed up in their holy vestments; they sing together and all become one.
>
> The Latins observe a festival in their cathedral in honour of a certain Arsenius, a local saint; and the Greeks and Latins celebrate the Liturgy together in the same building, but at separate altars. The Greeks read the Epistle first, and then the Latins, and the same thing happens with the Gospel. As for the people, both nations stand mixed up together in front of the two altars, praying together and singing together. . . .
>
> On Holy Saturday the Greeks and the Latins assemble in one of

[1] The evidence is set forth in detail by P. Grigoriou, *Σχέσεις καθολικῶν καὶ ὀρθοδόξων*, and by G. Hofmann in numerous articles (see the bibliography). Compare also J. Hajjar, *Les chrétiens uniates du Proche-Orient*, pp. 200–61.

[2] It is sometimes argued that the common worship and *communicatio in sacris* between Orthodox and Roman Catholics were the effect of Venetian rule. While it is certainly true that in many cases the Venetians encouraged friendly relations, this was not the only factor involved. For in the first place, similar friendly relations also existed—though not perhaps to the same degree—in places not under Venetian rule; secondly, the policy of the Venetians towards their Orthodox subjects varied considerably at different times, and on a number of occasions, so far from encouraging closer relations between the two Churches, they were directly responsible for a growth in hostility (as in the Peloponnese and Chios).

the Latin churches, and the priests of both sides together carry upon their heads the *Epitaphion* or Lamb,[1] all together carrying the same *Epitaphion*, and they go with it to another church.[2]

When the Orthodox Archpriest at Kerkyra died, the Latin clergy of the island used to take part in his funeral procession, wearing vestments and carrying candles; the Orthodox clergy did the same at the funeral of the Roman Catholic bishop. The Orthodox clergy ceremonially attended the enthronement of a new Roman bishop, while the Roman bishop in turn paid ceremonial visits of courtesy to the Orthodox. On Saint Spiridon's day in the year 1724, for example, Cardinal Quirini went to the Liturgy in the Orthodox cathedral, clad in his *cappa magna* and preceded by a chaplain with a great cross of silver. He was received in procession on his arrival; after the reading of the Gospel the book was brought to him to be kissed; at the end of the service he was solemnly presented with the *antidoron*.[3]

Much the same things happened on nearby islands. On Zakynthos (Zante), as on Kerkyra, joint services were held, and at the end of these functions the clergy of both Churches sang the *Φῆμαι* (*Ad Multos Annos*) first in honour of the Pope of Rome and then for the Patriarch of Constantinople.[4] On Kephallenia, when an Orthodox procession with a miracle-working icon passed a Latin church, the Roman Catholic priest used to come out with incense and candles to cense the icon; Orthodox clergy did the same when the Corpus Christi procession went past their churches, and themselves took part in the actual procession. The liturgical arrangements for the Holy Saturday procession were even more remarkable on Kephallenia than on Kerkyra: on top of the Orthodox *Epitaphion* was placed the Latin Blessed Sacrament (whether in a monstrance or a ciborium is not stated), and the *Epitaphion* with the Sacrament was then carried processionally by the Roman Catholic Archbishop and the Orthodox Archpriest, walking side by side, assisted by two leading laymen of the respective Churches.[5]

Turning from the Ionian to the Aegean islands, we find similar instances of *communicatio in sacris*. On Andros, where the

[1] A figure, usually life-size, painted or embroidered on a stiff piece of cloth, representing the dead Christ laid out for burial.

[2] Athos, Iviron, Ms. 1340, quoted in Grigoriou, *Σχέσεις*, pp. 112–13.

[3] Grigoriou, op. cit., pp. 140–4. [4] Ibid., pp. 130–2. [5] Ibid., p. 116.

population was predominantly Orthodox, the Greek bishop and his clergy in full vestments, with candles and torches, took part in the Latin Corpus Christi procession;[1] the same thing occurred on Mykonos and Naxos,[2] and elsewhere. In some places—Naxos, for example[3]—the Roman Catholics were allowed to say Mass in Orthodox Churches, using a temporary altar in front of the *iconostasis*. Elsewhere—on Thera, for instance, and Paros[4]—there were 'mixed churches', with two permanent altars in adjacent sanctuaries, one for the Roman and one for the Byzantine rite. As late as the beginning of the nineteenth century, there were two Orthodox churches on Syros, containing Latin altars still used by Roman Catholic clergy.[5]

The Orthodox authorities gladly employed the Latin missionaries as preachers and confessors. 'I have received written permission from the Greek Metropolitan', writes a Jesuit from Naxos in 1641, 'to preach and catechise in the Greek churches.'[6] The Orthodox Metropolitan in Smyrna, so another Jesuit reports, 'has given his subjects complete freedom to go to our clergy for confession . . . and to our clergy he has given full power to hear confessions in his church both from Greeks and Latins.'[7] On Thera the nuns of the Orthodox convent of Saint Nicholas had Jesuit Fathers as their confessors;[8] at Athens a retired Orthodox Metropolitan went regularly for confession to a French Capuchin priest.[9]

Not only the higher authorities but the local population received the missionaries with great enthusiasm. 'During the seasons of Lent and Advent', a Jesuit priest relates, '. . . the preachers, on leaving the pulpit [of the Latin churches], are sometimes forced to go up again into those of the Greek and Armenian churches, to satisfy the desire which the people have to hear the word of God. . . . The missionaries often go to pay their respects to the [Greek] bishops and clergy, with whom we maintain a perfect understanding; the conversation is always on some religious topic, for several of them ask only to be in-

[1] Hilaire de Barenton, *La France catholique en orient*, p. 175.
[2] Grigoriou, op. cit., pp. 83, 329–30. [3] Ibid., p. 13.
[4] Ibid., pp. 25–26, 34–41, 57. [5] Ibid., p. 332.
[6] A. Carayon, *Relations inédites*, p. 116. Compare Grigoriou, op. cit., pp. 11–14, 71, 154–5.
[7] Carayon, op. cit., pp. 172–3. Compare Grigoriou, op. cit., p. 189–90.
[8] Grigoriou, op. cit., p. 34. [9] Ibid., p. 97.

structed.'[1] 'The Greeks and the Syrians', writes Père Besson in the middle of the seventeenth century, 'open their houses to the apostolic men; they open even the doors of their churches and their pulpits. The parish priests welcome our assistance, the bishops beg us to cultivate their vineyards.'[2]

The attitude of the Greek bishops is intelligible enough: they needed preachers and confessors; their own clergy were for the most part simple and ill-educated; the Latin missionaries were incomparably better qualified to give instruction and spiritual direction. But what was the attitude of the missionaries towards the Orthodox who came to them for confession? Sometimes they encouraged them to make an act of submission to the Roman Catholic Church, but more often—particularly when their penitents were ignorant and uneducated—they gave them absolution without embarking on any matters of religious controversy. And even when Greeks did make a formal act of adherence to Rome they were usually told by the missionaries to continue outwardly in their previous allegiance, receiving communion as before from Orthodox priests. If there was no Roman Catholic bishop available, the missionaries sometimes even allowed their converts to accept ordination from an Orthodox bishop. In practice they treated the Orthodox not so much as schismatics who required to be reconciled to the Church, but as if they were already Catholics, albeit Catholics who had fallen into certain corruptions and errors from which they required to be purged gently. It is to be noted, however, that throughout the seventeenth and eighteenth centuries the higher authorities at Rome itself adopted a far more rigorous position, in general forbidding all *communicatio in sacris* with Orthodox, although occasional exceptions were permitted. But the missionaries took little notice of the directives which they received, and persisted in their more tolerant attitude.[3]

[1] Carayon, *Relations inédites*, pp. 244–6.

[2] J. Besson, *La Syrie sainte*, p. 11.

[3] See the two articles by W. de Vries, 'Das Problem der "communicatio in sacris cum dissidentibus" ', in *Ostkirchliche Studien*, vol. vi, pp. 81–106, and 'Eine Denkschrift', in *Ostkirchliche Studien*, vol. vii, pp. 253–66. Compare Mansi, *Amplissima Collectio Conciliorum*, vol. xlvi, cols. 99–110.

Two typical directives by the *Propaganda* may be quoted. (i) 'Non debere missionarios divina celebrare in ecclesiis in quibus simul haeretici sua profana et sacrilega exercitia habent' (21 May 1627) (Mansi, vol. xlvi, col. 105). (ii) 'Non licere catholicis communicare cum haereticis et schismaticis et eorum confessiones

The Orthodox not only welcomed the western missionaries when they arrived, but frequently took the initiative and invited them to come. We may take as an example the relations between Athos and Rome during the second quarter of the seventeenth century. In 1628 Ignatius, Abbot of the monastery of Vatopedi on the Holy Mountain, visited Rome and asked the *Propaganda* to send a priest to set up a school on Athos for the monks. In answer to this request, Nicholas Rossi, formerly a student at the College of Saint Athanasius in Rome, was sent in 1635–6 to Athos, and opened a school at Karyes. In 1641, however, the Turkish authorities forced him to move with his school to Thessalonica; he died the following year and soon after the school came to an end. In 1643 the ruling synod of the Holy Mountain—the Great *Epistasia*—sent a letter to the Pope, asking that a church be given them in the city of Rome, in which monks from Athos could serve, while at the same time carrying on their studies; in return they offered a *kellion* or *skete* on Athos, for the use of Basilian monks from Italy who wished to live on the Holy Mountain. Although nothing came of this suggestion, it shows that the Athonite authorities at this date cannot have felt much hostility towards Rome.[1]

The same friendship and trust was displayed by Damaskinos, Greek Metropolitan of Aegina. In 1680 he wrote to Pope Innocent XI, asking that two Jesuits be sent to the island, qualified to teach and to hear confessions from the clergy and laity of his diocese. His letter begins:

> Most blessed ruler set up over us by God, Pope of Elder Rome, God-protected Shepherd of the true sheep of the Word, equal to the angels, honourable, holy, and true Head guarding the Apostolic Church, the boast of Orthodox Christendom, supreme bishop, guardian, *locum-tenens*, and vicar of Our Lord Jesus Christ.[2]

audire nec coram illis emittere nec iis sacramentum Eucharistiae conferre' (15 May 1709) (de Vries, *Ostkirchliche Studien*, vol. vi, p. 92).

Yet the authorities in Rome did not invariably forbid all *communicatio in sacris*. Pope Benedict XIV, for example, stated in a session of the Holy Office on 24 February 1752: 'Communicationem in divinis cum haereticis non posse nec debere tam facile ac tam generaliter pronunciari in omni penitus circumstantia de jure vetitam' (R. de Martinis, *Iuris Pontificii de Propaganda Fide*, Part II, Rome, 1909, p. 324).

[1] See Grigoriou, *Σχέσεις*, pp. 163–74, and Hofmann, *Athos e Roma*, pp. 5–6, 29–40. Compare also Hofmann, *Rom und Athosklöster* and *Rom und der Athos*.

[2] Hofmann, 'Byzantinische Bischöfe und Rom', *Orientalia Christiana*, vol. xxii, No. 70, pp. 19–20.

Specific though this declaration may appear, Damaskinos probably intended it not as a formal submission to Rome, but rather as a piece of diplomatic courtesy; yet when diplomatic courtesy is carried to such a point, it paves the way for a formal submission. And whatever precise weight be attached to the Metropolitan's words, the fact remains that he was fully prepared to use Roman Catholic religious for pastoral work in his diocese.

These are but a few examples out of many; but sufficient has been said to indicate something of the friendly relations prevailing during the seventeenth century between Orthodox and Roman Catholics in many parts of the Greek world. On the local level the fact of schism was in practice quietly ignored.

But around the year 1700 a number of factors combined to produce a sharp increase of hostility. Instances of friendship and *communicatio in sacris* became gradually less and less frequent, and by the middle of the eighteenth century, although they still occurred occasionally, they were altogether exceptional. What was the reason for this marked deterioration in relations?

It is not very easy to say. Of course there were always underlying difficulties which served to create tension between the two sides. Two such factors in particular may be mentioned. First, the Turks for political reasons had no wish to see too close a *rapprochement* between Greeks and Latins: if the Orthodox became reconciled to the Church of Rome, then perhaps the Catholic powers of western Europe would intervene far more vigorously to secure their liberation from infidel rule. (It is significant that when Mohammed II took Constantinople, he was careful to install as Patriarch a firm opponent of the Florentine Union—Gennadios Scholarios.) Secondly, the Protestant embassies at Constantinople, as well as individual Protestants visiting the Near East, were always glad to drive a wedge between Orthodoxy and Rome.

But apart from such permanently existing factors there were more particular reasons for a deterioration in relations around the end of the seventeenth century. The Venetian occupation of the Peloponnese (1685–1718) was in part to blame. In the areas which they took from the Turks, the Venetians, without actively persecuting the Orthodox, yet did all they could to promote the Roman cause. Orthodox churches, converted by the Turks into mosques, were now recovered for Christian worship, but instead of being restored to their previous Orthodox owners they were assigned to the Latins. Large numbers of Latin clergy were introduced and new Latin bishoprics were created; at the same time the Venetians interfered in the appointment of Orthodox bishops, prevented many of the sees from being filled, and tried to abolish the dependence of the Orthodox dioceses upon the Patriarchate of Constantinople.[1] The Greeks saw the Latin cause advanced, while their own was systematically undermined; they found themselves in a worse position under Christian Venetians than under infidel Turks, and like the Grand Duke Lukas Notaras before the fall of Constantinople, they not unnaturally concluded 'better the Moslem turban than the Latin mitre'.[2] When the Venetians were finally expelled, the Greeks of the Peloponnese felt little regret at their departure. The same kind of thing also happened elsewhere: as we shall note shortly, the Venetian occupation of Chios in 1694–5 had a disastrous effect on Orthodox-Catholic relations in the island.

But there was another and far more important reason for the hardening of the Orthodox attitude around this time. The Orthodox authorities, while prepared to make use of the Latin missionaries, had at the outset little desire to become Roman Catholics. But the missionaries were gifted and persuasive advocates for the Papal cause: friendship with them inevitably produced converts to the Roman Catholic faith, and the Orthodox gradually came to realize with alarm how numerous and influential these converts were. Here, then, was another factor which caused an increase in hostility—the success of Latin penetration and propaganda.

Matters were made worse by the policy of concealment which the western clergy adopted.[3] The missionaries, when they collaborated with the Orthodox, had naturally but one ultimate aim—the reconciliation of the Eastern Church to the see of Rome. But they realized that the best way to achieve their purpose was not to embark at once upon official negotiations, still less to undertake an open and aggressive proselytism among Orthodox congregations, but rather to win the confidence of

[1] See B. K. Stephanidis, *Ἐκκλησιαστικὴ Ἱστορία*, p. 642.

[2] Ducas, *Historia Byzantina*, 38 (Bonn ed., p. 264).

[3] See P. P. Argenti, *The Occupation of Chios by the Venetians*, pp. cii–cxv.

the Greeks, to infiltrate among them, and so work upon them from within. Converts, as we have seen, were told to continue outwardly as members of their previous Church, and to receive communion there as before. Thus in the course of the seventeenth century there was built up a powerful crypto-Roman party within the outward boundaries of the Orthodox Church —'un noyau catholique', as Father Charon terms it. The crypto-Romanists included a number of Greek bishops: the missionaries persuaded them to send professions of faith to Rome, but told them not to make their submission public, nor to cease from holding office as before in the Orthodox hierarchy. The missionaries naturally hoped that when this Papalist party had gained sufficient strength, the corporate union of a whole area, or even of an entire Patriarchate, could be proclaimed as a *fait accompli*. The Greeks, when they woke up to what was going on, viewed the missionaries with suspicion rather than friendship. The westerners, so the Greeks thought at first, had come to bring them light; now it turned out that they had brought fire to burn the Greeks' house about their ears.

This strategy of secret conversion had been used by the Jesuits with great success in the Ukraine during the decade preceding the Union of Brest-Litovsk (1595–6);[1] and during the following century it looked for a time as if it might succeed in the Patriarchate of Constantinople as well.[2] The Jesuits founded a house at Constantinople in 1609, and almost immediately they opened a school, which was attended by Greek children as well as Latin: naturally it served as a most valuable means for propagating 'unionist' ideas among young Orthodox.[3] The Jesuits and the other Latin missionaries, aided by the French and Austrian Embassies, aimed to create an 'alliance' between the Patriarch of Constantinople and the Pope of Rome, and so to counteract the Protestant tendencies of the Patriarch of Alexandria, Cyril Lukaris—'the forerunner of Antichrist, Cyril the Calvinist', as one of his enemies called him.[4]

[1] See Timothy Ware, *The Orthodox Church*, London, 1963, pp. 103–6.

[2] For developments at Constantinople during this period, besides the works of Hofmann cited below, see H. Musset, *Histoire du Christianisme*, vol. ii, pp. 134–43.

[3] See Hofmann, *Il Vicariato Apostolico di Constantinopoli*, pp. 40–41, 44, 70 (reports concerning the school in 1610, 1622, and 1648).

[4] Cyril Kontaris to the Austrian Ambassador Rudolf Schmidt, in 1638 (Hofmann, 'Neue Quellen', in *Revue des Études Byzantines*, vol. xi, p. 170).

Several Patriarchs of Constantinople were won over to the Roman cause. Even before the establishment of the Jesuits, in 1608 Patriarch Neophytos II sent a formal profession of faith to Pope Paul V, signed in his own hand: needless to say, this act of submission was not made public.[1] Timothy II, Patriarch from 1612 to 1620, was also very friendly towards the Roman Church: 'bene de fide catholica sentit, nos amat', as a Jesuit at Constantinople put it. In March 1615 Timothy wrote a letter to Paul V, in which he declared that he acknowledged the Pope as his 'head', and was willing to obey him in all things; he did not, however, make a formal profession of faith.[2]

During the reign of Cyril Lukaris at Constantinople, his opponents—as was only to be expected—appealed to Rome for assistance. Gregory IV of Amasia, who for a short time replaced Lukaris as Patriarch (12 April to 18 June 1623), was on friendly terms with the Roman Catholics.[3] Athanasius III Patellaros, who was Patriarch for forty days in 1634, after his deposition made a formal act of submission to Rome (21 October 1635): he occupied the Ecumenical Throne once more in 1652, but only for a few days.[4] The chief opponent of Lukaris, Cyril II of Berrhoia (Cyril Kontaris), on 15 December 1638 sent a formal profession of faith to Rome, while actually in office as Patriarch. Shortly after this he was deposed and sent into exile; while journeying to his destination he was strangled.[5] Joannikios II, four times Patriarch in less than ten years (1646–56), was very cordial towards Rome, but he avoided committing himself to any formal act of submission.[6]

A future Patriarch of Constantinople, Parthenios II, while Metropolitan of Chios, in 1640 wrote as follows to Pope Urban VIII:

[1] Hofmann, *Griechische Patriarchen und Römische Päpste, Orientalia Christiana*, vol. xxv, No. 76, pp. 43–46.

[2] Ibid., pp. 51, 55.

[3] Hofmann, op. cit., *Orientalia Christiana*, vol. xv, No. 52, p. 46.

[4] Hofmann, op. cit., *Orientalia Christiana*, vol. xix, No. 63, pp. 15, 43; see also 'Patriarchen von Konstantinopel', in *Orientalia Christiana*, vol. xxxii, No. 89, pp. 14–17.

[5] Hofmann, *Griechische Patriarchen und Römische Päpste, Orientalia Christiana*, vol. xx, No. 64, pp. 10–12, 37; 'Patriarchen von Konstantinopel', in *Orientalia Christiana*, vol. xxxii, No. 89, pp. 17–27.

[6] Hofmann, *Griechische Patriarchen und Römische Päpste, Orientalia Christiana*, vol. xxv, No. 76, pp. 69–70.

. . . To your Beatitude I render all due obedience and submission, acknowledging you to be the true successor of the leader of the Apostles, and the chief shepherd of the Catholic Church throughout the whole world. With all piety and obedience I bow before your holy feet and kiss them, asking your blessing, for with full power you guide and tend the whole of Christ's chosen flock. So I confess and so I believe; and I am zealous that my subjects also should be such as I am myself. Finding them eager, I guide them in the ways of piety; for there are not a few who think just as I do. . . .[1]

It seems likely that after his appointment to Constantinople, he continued to do all he could to 'guide his subjects in the ways of piety'!

The diary of John Covel, chaplain to the English Embassy at Constantinople from 1670 to 1677, supplies interesting information about Romanist activities at this date:

Feb. 7th, came a young priest—he wrote down his name himself, D. Hilarione Bubuli—to me from padre Jeremiah, to know if any letters were for Venice from my Ld., me, etc.; amongst other discourse he made a great discovery to me. He was a Basilian (a Greek), but in orders (by Rome), a Venetian, born and bred under the Greek Arch Bp. there. He was not informed well by Padre Jeremiah (who is a Greek of another stamp), and, taking me for a Romanist, told me there were many Metropolites now Romans in their hearts, and that some money wd. do anything amongst them; they question'd not but shortly to make Metropolites enough of their own way.

There was a plan afoot, so Covel continues, whereby the Ambassador of France and the other Roman Catholic Residents at Constantinople were to secure the removal of the present Patriarch: he was to be replaced by the Metropolitan of Paros, 'a true man in his heart to them'. 'The businesse', Covel states, 'is committed to the Italian Archbp. now at the new church (St. Francesco): he [Father Hilarione] told me the Jesuits and the Capuchins know of it.' As Covel put it in his diary, 'Though the Ch. of Rome boast their Emissaryes here (as, indeed, there are many, many), Jesuits, Dominicans, Franciscans, yet, believe me, they have other designes than converting of Turkes.'[2]

[1] Hofmann, 'Der Metropolit von Chios, Parthenios', in *Ostkirchliche Studien*, vol. i, pp. 297–300.

[2] J. T. Bent, *Early Voyages and Travels in the Levant*, pp. 149–150, 210. Bent dates the entry, 'Feb. 7th 1667'. This is impossible: Covel did not arrive in Constantinople until 1670.

The Latin missionaries secured illustrious converts at many other places besides Constantinople itself. Josaphat, Metropolitan of Lacedaemon, in 1625;[1] three Patriarchs of Ochrid between 1624 and 1658;[2] Meletios, Metropolitan of Rhodes (1645–51);[3] six Greek bishops in the Kyklades in 1662;[4] the monastery of Saint John, Patmos, in 1681 and again in 1725;[5] a convent of nuns on the island of Santorin in 1710;[6] an abbot from the monastery of Iviron, Mount Athos, in 1726;[7] the abbot of a monastery on Hydra in 1727;[8] Kallinikos, Metropolitan of Aegina, with many of his clergy, in 1727:[9] so the cases of submission continue. Even the Protestantizer Cyril Lukaris wrote to Pope Paul V in 1608, in terms which imply a recognition of Papal supremacy![10] This list is by no means exhaustive: no doubt there were many other conversions, for which the documentary evidence has perished, or remains unpublished. It must be kept in mind, of course, that the motive in many cases was not so much religious conviction as the hope of material aid and temporal advantage; in each instance the good faith of the 'convert' needs to be carefully examined. But whatever the motive, conversions undoubtedly took place.

Yet at Constantinople and in most areas these conversions remained the acts of individuals. They did not lead, as the missionaries had hoped, to the corporate reunion of whole dioceses and Patriarchates *en bloc*. In one place only was the process of infiltration more successful: the Patriarchate of Antioch.[11] During the seventeenth century a number of Patri-

[1] Hofmann, 'Byzantinische Bischöfe und Rom', in *Orientalia Christiana*, vol. xxii, No. 70, pp. 25–26.

[2] Ibid., pp. 12–17.

[3] Hofmann, 'Byzantina', in *Orientalia Christiana*, vol. xxvi, No. 78, pp. 74–75.

[4] Hofmann, 'Byzantinische Bischöfe und Rom', in *Orientalia Christiana*, vol. xxii, No. 70, pp. 22–24.

[5] Hofmann, *Patmos und Rom*, pp. 25–27, 53–55; 'Griechische Klöster und Rom', in *Orientalia Christiana*, vol. xx, No. 66, pp. 11–12.

[6] 'Griechische Klöster und Rom', pp. 13–14.

[7] *Rom und Athosklöster*, pp. 32–33.

[8] 'Griechische Klöster und Rom', p. 8.

[9] 'Byzantinische Bischöfe und Rom', pp. 24–25.

[10] *Griechische Patriarchen und Römische Päpste*, *Orientalia Christiana*, vol. xv, No. 52, pp. 15, 44–46.

[11] For the history of Antioch at this time, see Musset, *Histoire du Christianisme*, vol. ii, pp. 158–74; C. Karalevskij (*alias* Korolevsky or Charon), 'Antioche', *Dictionnaire d'histoire et de géographie ecclésiastiques*, vol. iii, cols. 641–9, 667–9; and C. A. Papadopoulos, *'Ιστορία τῆς 'Εκκλησίας 'Αντιοχείας*, particularly pp. 1028–30 and the Appendix.

archs here, as at Constantinople, came under Roman Catholic influence. In 1631 Ignatius III made what amounted virtually to an act of submission to the Pope, although nothing formal was concluded. His successor, Euthymios II (Patriarch from May to December 1634), negotiated secretly with Rome. The next Patriarch, Euthymios III (reigned 1634–47), was on friendly terms with the Latin missionaries, and assured them that he acknowledged the supremacy of the Pope; but he refused to sign any act of submission, however secret, saying that he was surrounded by spies, and that if he signed, he would as a result undoubtedly be poisoned.[1]

Macarius III (1647–72) was less timorous. In 1662 he sent a secret profession of faith to Rome; and at a dinner in the same year with the French Consul at Damascus, also attended by the Syrian and Armenian Patriarchs, he openly proposed a toast 'to the health of our Holy Father the Pope: and I pray God that there may be but one flock and one shepherd, as once there was in the past.'[2] Two later Patriarchs, Athanasius III around 1687 and Cyril V around 1716, also sent secret submissions to Rome, but the good faith of Athanasius was somewhat in doubt, since in practice he showed himself a fierce and active opponent of Roman Catholicism.

Matters eventually came to a head in 1724, when an open division occurred between the Romanist party within the Patriarchate and those who wished to continue Orthodox. In this year Patriarch Athanasius III died. The clergy and leading laity of the pro-Roman group at Damascus assembled in great haste and elected Seraphim Tanas as successor. Seraphim, who took the title Cyril VI, had been educated at Rome, and his attachment to the Roman Catholic cause was well known. Meanwhile, when news arrived at Constantinople of the death of Athanasius III, the Holy Synod promptly elected as Patriarch a young Greek monk aged twenty-eight, named Silvester. When the Synod at Constantinople learnt of the election of Tanas at Damascus, they refused to recognize it in any way. Thus from 1724 onwards there were two rival Patriarchs claiming the Antiochene throne, the one owing allegiance to the Pope and

[1] See the report for the year 1650 by Father Jean Amieu, S.J., in Rabbath, *Documents inédits*, pp. 401–2.

[2] Rabbath, op. cit., p. 466.

the other recognized at Constantinople by the Ecumenical Patriarchate.

Silvester, who reigned from 1724 to 1766, did his utmost to bring the schism to an end, displaying a pastoral zeal not always found in Orthodox prelates of the Turkish period. Eustratios Argenti, in a letter of 1751, terms him 'a second Athanasius', 'a truly apostolic man';[1] but he was unable to exercise any effective control over a great part of his nominal Patriarchate, which continued to recognize Cyril VI.[2] The two rivals made life equally unpleasant for one another. In 1725 Cyril was forced to flee from Damascus to the Lebanon. But Silvester in his turn encountered such lively opposition from the Roman party (supported by the French Consul) that he too was obliged to withdraw: leaving Aleppo, he went first to Tripoli and then to Macedonia and Rumania. After seven years outside his Patriarchate, Silvester returned to Syria in 1732 and tried to establish himself at Damascus, but the Roman party again caused him so much trouble that he retired to North Syria. So matters continued: with the help of the Turkish authorities, Orthodox and Roman Catholics harassed and persecuted one another, until both sides were utterly exhausted.

The débâcle at Antioch made the Orthodox realize once and for all the dangers to which they were exposed through infiltration and propaganda by western missionaries. A bishop in virtual exile from his own see, an ancient Patriarchate rent in two, and its very survival as part of the Orthodox Church seriously threatened: such were the results which the Greeks saw as following from Latin penetration. Is it astonishing that they should no longer extend the same welcome to the Latin missionaries?

[1] K. A. Uspenski, *The Patriarchate of Alexandria*, p. 342.

[2] To some extent Silvester had only himself to blame, for in his zeal for Orthodoxy he was often ill-advised and tactless. When he first arrived in Syria, for example, the chief citizens of Aleppo came to meet him outside the city, and a very elaborate and expensive meal was prepared in his honour. The day was a Wednesday, and so strictly speaking the eating of fish was forbidden; but as previous Patriarchs had dispensed their flock from this rule, the banquet included fish. But the new Patriarch was a rigorist in matters of fasting: 'Silvester, observing the fishes, kicked the table over with his feet and started to excommunicate them for eating fish.' This gesture alienated many of his supporters, who promptly turned to his rival: 'The Aleppans at once deserted and submitted to Popery; for the Papists allowed them to eat not only fish but meat whenever they wanted.' (Hypsilantis, *Τὰ μετὰ τὴν ἅλωσιν*, p. 326.)

But a number of years before the Antiochene schism Orthodox leaders had already begun to organize some degree of counter-propaganda. This was chiefly the work of Dositheos, Patriarch of Jerusalem from 1669 to 1707, whose *Confession* we have already mentioned. He was popularly known as *Λατινομάστιξ*, 'the scourge of the Latins': *infensissimus Latinae ecclesiae hostis*, as the Franciscans in the Holy City called him.[1] Like Silvester, he was only twenty-eight years old at the time of his appointment to the Patriarchate (he had been made deacon at the age of eleven, and a Metropolitan when twenty-five). In 1682 Dositheos established a press at Jassy in Rumania, at the expense of the Jerusalem Patriarchate; and during the years that followed he issued, from this press and from other places in Rumania, a formidable series of anti-Latin works, in most cases treatises composed by earlier writers but hitherto unpublished or little known. Books were printed not only in Greek but in Russian, Bulgarian, Turkish, and Arabic; copies were in many cases distributed free of charge. Dositheos is chiefly remembered for a series of three volumes, *The Book of Reconciliation*, *The Book of Love*, and *The Book of Joy*,[2] which include a wide range of controversial works by many different polemicists. Dositheos' own book, *The History of the Patriarchs of Jerusalem*, was not published until after his death. As much a polemical as an historical work, it could more truly be named, 'Concerning the continual Dissension between the Eastern and the Western Church since the Schism'.[3]

[1] In a memorandum of 1698: see J. de Hammer, *Histoire de l'Empire Ottoman*, vol. xii, Paris, 1838, p. 548.

[2] For the Greek titles see the Bibliography.

[3] So C. A. Papadopoulos (*Νέα Σίων*, vol. v, Jerusalem, 1907, p. 147), in allusion to the *De Perpetua Consensione* of Allatius.

One of the things which severely handicapped the Greeks during the Turkish period was the lack of printing presses. From 1626 onwards the *Propaganda* maintained a press at Rome, issuing books in Latin, Greek, and Arabic: the Orthodox had little means of replying in print. Outside the Ottoman dominions they had a press at Venice, which enjoyed the official approval of the Venetian authorities (who were very tolerant in religious matters); hence the inscription borne by books printed at this press, 'Con licentia de' superiori è privilegio'. But within the main part of the Turkish Empire during the seventeenth century the Greeks were permitted no presses at all; Dositheos, however, was able to print books in Rumania because here a greater measure of freedom prevailed *vis-à-vis* the Turks. In 1627, under the auspices of Patriarch Cyril Lukaris, Nicholas Metaxas set up a printing press at Constantinople, but it was closed by the Turks after six months, and not until the middle of the next century did the Ottoman authorities permit the re-

Dositheos, although influenced by Latin theology, did not look with favour upon the Latins at work in the Near East. Dr. Covel records:

In one letter of his, which I have now by me, he calls the Pope, *θηρίον, μονιὸν, τὸ βδέλυγμα τῆς ἐρημώσεως ἑστὼς ἐν τόπῳ ἁγίῳ, Savage Beast, wild Bear, the Abomination of Desolation standing in the Holy Place;* and in another Letter he saith, *οὐ πατὴρ ἀλλὰ φθορεὺς ἐστὶ τοῦ γένους τῶν χριστιανῶν, καὶ διώκτης τῆς ἐκκλησίας τοῦ χριστοῦ, he is not the Father, but the Corrupter of the whole race of Christians, and a persecutor of the Church of Christ.* He calls the Latin Friars there, *θηρία ἄγρια, ὠμωτάτους ἀνθρωποκτόνους, δαίμονας, wild Beasts, most unmerciful Murderers, Devils.*[1]

Dositheos disliked Jesuits just as much as Franciscans. He speaks in one place of 'four great Beasts, opposed and hostile to the Church of God', these 'beasts' being the heresy of Luther, the heresy of Calvin, the order of Jesuits, and the Gregorian or New Style calendar. Of the four Dositheos considers the Jesuits by far the most pernicious, terming them 'the most shameless and audacious of all the enemies of the Church'.[2]

Thus the Venetian occupation of the Peloponnese, the success of Latin missionary infiltration culminating in the schism at Antioch, and the increase of Orthodox counter-propaganda, together with other factors of lesser import, combined around the beginning of the eighteenth century to accentuate the separation between Rome and the Orthodox Church. In places, the older situation persisted: as late as 1749, for example, Patriarch Cyril V of Constantinople found it necessary to reprimand the Orthodox of Siphnos and Mykonos for sharing in worship and sacraments with the Latins, and for behaving in general as if there were no division between the Orthodox Church and Rome.[3] But while the attitude displayed here by the

establishment of a Patriarchal press. Greek works in the eighteenth century were often printed at Leipzig or Vienna.

On Greek printing presses, see A. Helladius, *Status Praesens Ecclesiae Graecae*, pp. 1–20; on Lukaris' press and its dramatic closure, see Hadjiantoniou, *Protestant Patriarch*, pp. 78–88. Compare also E. Turdeanu, 'Le livre grec en Russie', in *Revue des Études slaves*, vol. xxvi, 1950, pp. 69–97.

[1] John Covel, *Some Account of the Present Greek Church*, p. liv.

[2] From the Introduction to the edition of Moghila's *Orthodox Confession* published by Dositheos at Snagov in 1699 (see Legrand, *Bibliographie hellénique . . . au dix-septième siècle*, vol. iii, pp. 68–69).

[3] M. J. Gedeon, *Πατριαρχικοὶ Πίνακες*, pp. 642–3.

people of Siphnos and Mykonos was very common in 1650, by 1750 it had become exceptional; and whereas in 1650 it was widely tolerated by the Orthodox hierarchy, a hundred years later the Patriarch sharply condemned it. After 1700 the sharing of churches and pulpits, together with all forms of *communicatio in sacris*, became less and less frequent, although they did not entirely cease.[1] To an ever-increasing extent the Greeks came to regard the Latin missionaries no longer as fellow-workers whose collaboration they gladly accepted, but as enemies dedicated to the overthrow of the Orthodox faith.

(*iv*) *Chios*

In the whole of the Turkish Empire there was no place which enjoyed as great a degree of prosperity as Eustratios Argenti's native island, Chios—'the Paradise of all Greece', as Cornelis de Bruyn called it in 1678.[2] 'This island', says Jean de Thévenot, who visited Chios in 1656, 'is the only one to have preserved its liberty under the Turks. Its inhabitants live as they wish, and practise their religion with the greatest freedom imaginable. They are subject to the Turk and pay him tribute, but are not molested by him in any way, nor weighed down with taxes.'[3] Dapper, at the end of the same century, speaks highly of Chian courtesy: 'The inhabitants there are extremely polite, alike towards one another and towards strangers, so much so that one can say in their favour that they surpass all other peoples in kindness, civility, and gentleness.'[4] A hundred years later Olivier wrote with equal enthusiasm:

> After crossing a narrow stretch of water, I believed myself transported into another region, into a different clime. I had seen Greece bowed under the yoke of the most appalling despotism; it was per-

[1] Indeed, in parts of the Near East a measure of *communicatio in sacris* has continued right up to the present day.

[2] P. P. Argenti and S. P. Kyriakidis, *'Η Χίος παρὰ τοῖς γεωγράφοις καὶ περιηγηταῖς*, p. 330. Compare the vivid words of another French visitor, Georges de la Chapelle, at Chios in 1648: 'Il semble que ce soit un Paradis terrestre que l'Isle de Scio, tant elle est belle et delicieuse. Elle produit des fruicts excellens, sur tout des Raisins muscats; de la Soye en abondance, du Coton, du Benjoin, de la Therebente, et du Masticq, qui ne vient qu'en ce Païs-là. Il ya si grande quantité de Perdrix, que l'on peuple des colombiers; elles chantent à merveilles, et ne sont pas moins privées que nos Pigeons' (Argenti and Kyriakidis, op. cit., p. 1433).

[3] Argenti and Kyriakidis, op. cit., p. 223.

[4] *Description Exacte des isles de l'Archipel*, p. 225.

fidious, coarse, timid, ignorant, superstitious, and poor. But here in Chios it enjoys some shadow of liberty; it is upright, civil, full of courage, industrious, spiritual, well educated, and rich. Here I no longer found that mixture of pride and servility which characterizes the Greeks of Constantinople and of a great part of the Levant. . . . The Chiots are distinguished from other Greeks by a marked leaning towards commerce, a lively taste for the arts, a willingness to engage in ventures, and by a light-hearted spirit, playful and epigrammatic. . . . No other town in the Levant embraces such a wealth of learning; no other contains so many men exempt from prejudices, full of good sense and reason.[1]

Olivier speaks of the learning of Chios: there was in fact a celebrated school on the island, the *Χία Σχολή*, which was famous throughout the Greek world. Here Latin and Italian were taught, as well as grammar and philosophy.[2] From Chios as from other places, a succession of students travelled to places of learning in the west: of these, the most famous in the religious field—besides Argenti himself—were George Koressios, Leo Allatius, and Païsios Ligaridis.[3]

The freedom which the people of Chios enjoyed extended in particular to matters of religion. In 1567, a year after the Turks

[1] Argenti and Kyriakidis, op. cit., pp. 832–3. Olivier visited Chios in 1794.

[2] See V. Barsky, in Argenti and Kyriakidis, op. cit., p. 1649.

[3] The first and last of these were Orthodox, the second a Roman Catholic. Koressios (1554–1641), physician as well as theologian, wrote various works of controversy against the Latins, in particular a treatise on the Procession of the Holy Spirit. Allatius (? 1587–1669), the most distinguished of the three, was originally Orthodox, but was later converted to the Roman Catholic Church. He studied from 1600 to 1610 at the Greek College of Saint Athanasius at Rome; as well as studying theology, he took a degree in medicine in 1616. Although returning for a short period to his native Chios, he spent most of his later life in Rome. He published nineteen books, the most famous being the *De Ecclesiae Occidentalis atque Orientalis Perpetua Consensione*; he also left 150 volumes of notes in manuscript. He founded three scholarships in the Greek College for students from Chios (G. Hofmann, *Vescovadi cattolici della Grecia. I. Chios*, p. 18). Ligaridis (1610–78) was also a student at the Greek College. In 1641 he was sent back to the east to work for the Roman cause, but by degrees he became more and more closely associated with the Orthodox authorities, eventually being consecrated Orthodox Metropolitan of Gaza by the Patriarch of Constantinople in 1652. During the consecration ceremony he made a formal act of adherence to the four Eastern Patriarchs, but this did not prevent him from informing the Franciscans in Jerusalem shortly afterwards that he still considered himself subject to the jurisdiction of the Pope! Using his title as Metropolitan of Gaza, he wrote several times to the *Propaganda* in Rome, asking them for money. In 1661 he went to Russia, where he played a prominent part in the affair of Patriarch Nicon. He never resided in, and probably never visited, his episcopal see of Gaza.

had captured the island from the Genoese, the Sultan granted special 'Privileges' to the island, which allowed unusually favourable conditions to the Christian population.[1] In the words of Sir Paul Rycaut:

> In no place of the *Turks* Dominions do Christians enjoy more freedom in their Religion and Estates, than on the Isle of *Xio*, or *Scio*, to which they are entituled by an ancient Capitulation. . . . A *Turk* cannot strike or abuse a *Christian* without severe Correction: Here the Men wear Hats and Cloaths almost after the *Spanish* Mode; carry the Crucifix in procession through the Streets, and exercise their Religion with all freedom.[2]

A French visitor, Jean Dumont, remarked in 1694:

> Were it not that I saw a few turbans here and there, I would have thought that I was no longer in Turkey. It is enough to tell you that there are on this island more than two hundred Christian churches and at least thirty convents of men and women, both Latin and Greek, that carry out their worship without being molested in any way. They are free to hold processions in the open streets as in France or Italy, and they have bells in their churches.[3]

Elsewhere in the Ottoman Empire Christians were as a rule strictly forbidden to ring bells or hold public processions.

From 1304 to 1329 and from 1346 to 1566 Chios was under Genoese control, and even before the fourteenth century there had been a vigorous Genoese colony on the island. Many of the leading families, including that of Argenti, were Italian by origin. In consequence of the Genoese occupation Chios contained an unusually strong Roman Catholic minority.[4] The Roman Catholics enjoyed the same religious freedom as the Greeks; writing of the situation prior to 1695, Joseph Pitton de Tournefort says:

> The priests used to carry the Blessed Sacrament to the sick in broad daylight with banners; the Corpus Christi procession was

[1] For the text of the Chian 'Privileges', see P. P. Argenti, *Chius Vincta*, pp. 208–27; commentary on pp. cxxxvi–clxxiv.

[2] *The Present State of the Greek and Armenian Churches*, pp. 357–8.

[3] Argenti and Kyriakidis, *'H Χίος παρὰ τοῖς γεωγράφοις καὶ περιηγηταῖς*, p. 498.

[4] In the second half of the seventeenth century the Latin population of the town of Chios numbered about 8,000, out of a total of some 30,000 (P. P. Argenti, *Chius Vincta*, p. 249).

held with full solemnity, the clergy walking in copes with canopy and censers; in short the Turks called this island 'little Rome'.[1]

Dapper speaks of the educational work done by the religious orders:

> The Roman Catholics live there with freedom enough, in all that concerns their religion. . . . The Jesuits have a large and fine convent and a very beautiful church; they number more than twenty, all natives of the island. Following their usual practice, they devote themselves to teaching young Greeks, whom they seek by every kind of method to draw into the bosom of their religion.[2]

The Capuchins and Dominicans also ran schools.

Relations between Orthodox and Roman Catholics were much the same on Chios as in the rest of the Greek world.[3] There is evidence of the same tolerance and cordiality in the middle of the seventeenth century, followed by the same growing hostility. Here, as elsewhere, leading Greek Churchmen fell under Roman Catholic influence. We have already quoted part of the letter which Parthenios, Metropolitan of Chios, wrote to the Pope in 1640.[4] In 1670 another Metropolitan wrote in very friendly terms to the Pope, although without making a formal profession of faith: this missive was taken to Rome by the Latin bishop in Chios, Ludovico Balsarini. By way of reply the *Propaganda* entrusted two letters to Balsarini: both were courteous in tone, but one was addressed as to a schismatic bishop, the other as to a bishop subject to Rome. Evidently the Roman authorities distrusted the Greek Metropolitan; Balsarini was to use his discretion in deciding which letter to deliver. It is not clear what action he actually took.[5]

Friendship towards Roman Catholicism was displayed not

[1] Pitton de Tournefort, *Relation d'un Voyage du Levant*, vol. i, p. 367.

[2] *Description Exacte*, p. 226. Dapper writes as a Protestant. Another Protestant, Covel, comments somewhat drily on the Roman Catholic schools: 'There are severall schooles (the Jesuites have three) where Greekes goe as well as others, and afterwards they are removed to Italy to study: therefore you may expect that ye Romane tenets must needs by degrees be propagated. (Georgius Coresius. A Sciate)' (Argenti and Kyriakidis, op. cit., p. 311). Covel evidently suspects Koressios of Latinizing tendencies in his theology.

[3] On relations between the two Churches, see P. P. Argenti, *Diplomatic Archive of Chios*, pp. xxi–xxii, xxxvii–xliii, and 805–1062.

[4] See above, pp. 26–27.

[5] Hofmann, 'Byzantinische Bischöfe und Rom', in *Orientalia Christiana*, vol. xxii, No. 70, pp. 20–22.

only by the Greek Metropolitans but also by the monks of the leading Greek monastery on Chios, the *Nea Moni.* When Marco Giustiniani Massone, Latin bishop from 1603 to 1640 (or 1641), visited the community, he was allowed to celebrate pontifically in the church, using a portable altar in front of the icon of the Mother of God. The abbot and his monks attended the service and assisted the bishop. After a meal in the abbot's apartment, at which Massone said grace in Latin, the monks concluded by begging him, since he was shortly to go on a visit to Rome, to commend their monastery to the Supreme Pontiff's care.[1] An abbot of *Nea Moni* in the previous century wrote to Pope Gregory XIII to ask for help in rebuilding the monastery. 'Most holy Father of Fathers,' so the letter ends, 'we beg and beseech you, extend your hand in help and grant some alms to your servants; for we have nowhere to lay our head, save upon your Beatitude and Holiness.'[2]

In Chios, as elsewhere, there were 'mixed churches' shared by Roman Catholics and Orthodox, with one altar for each;[3] mixed marriages occurred frequently. The Orthodox treated the Roman Corpus Christi procession with reverence: Andrea Rendi, a Chian Jesuit, related how in 1630 the Orthodox Metropolitan went specially to a house from which he could conveniently observe the procession, while in front of the building he placed three of his priests in vestments, to cense the Blessed Sacrament when it passed by.[4] The great Dominican liturgist Jacques Goar, who was in Chios from 1631 to 1637, states that the Greeks often went to Latin churches to receive communion. He himself gave communion to two Orthodox deacons:

> I add, not something which I saw, but something which I myself did: with my own hands openly in the presence of all and in sight of the church, I gave Holy Communion—under one kind—to some Greek deacons; and when the Greek bishop learnt about it, he made no protest whatever.[5]

[1] Allatius, *De Perpetua Consensione*, p. 1059.

[2] Grigoriou, *Σχέσεις*, p. 109, Hofmann, 'Griechische Klöster und Rom', in *Orientalia Christiana*, vol. xx, No. 66, pp. 6–8.

[3] On these mixed churches see A. K. Sarou, *Περὶ μεικτῶν ναῶν ὀρθοδόξων καὶ καθολικῶν ἐν Χίῳ*, in *Ἐπετηρὶς Ἑταιρείας Βυζαντινῶν Σπουδῶν*, vol. xix, pp. 194–208; also Arnold Smith, *The Architecture of Chios*, London, 1962, p. 85.

[4] Grigoriou, *Σχέσεις*, p. 107.

[5] Allatius, *De Perpetua Consensione*, pp. 1659–62. See S. Salaville, *Studia Orientalia liturgico-theologica*, Rome, 1940, pp. 54–61.

But by the following century this peaceful situation had come altogether to an end. 'The Greeks and Roman Catholics have a great aversion to one another,' writes Richard Pococke, who stayed on Chios in 1739, 'and those of one profession are not Christians in the judgement of the other.'[1] Eight years later Julien Galland found the same: 'The schismatic Greeks adhere to their errors with an extraordinary stubbornness. Their hatred for the Latins exceeds all bounds, and is more bitter than that felt by the Greeks in any other part of the Levant.'[2]

The first serious outbreak of ill-feeling occurred in 1664–5. The Greeks obtained from the Ottoman authorities certain 'pretended regulations' (as the Latins put it), entitling them to take possession of twenty-four Latin churches. This they proceeded to do (so Andrea Soffiano, the Roman Catholic bishop, complained), 'with all the violence, fury, and sacrilege that can possibly be imagined', smashing altars, statues, and crucifixes. Their ultimate intention, he alleges, was to oust the Roman Catholics from such churches as still remained to them, and so to ensure that the Orthodox religion alone was practised on the island.[3]

The virtual suppression of the Roman faith, which Soffiano feared in 1665, actually came to pass thirty years later; but for this the Latins of Chios had largely themselves and their fellow Catholics to thank. In 1694 the Venetians occupied the island at the invitation of the Latin community; it seems that the Latin bishop, Ludovico Balsarini, acted as an informer and spy on the Venetians' behalf.[4] Once in power, the Venetians treated the Greeks of Chios with great severity. 'They shut up all their Churches,' states a contemporary historian, 'confiscate the goods of many, forbid the *Grecian* priests the exercise of their function and the administration of the sacraments, and will suffer none but *Latins* to confess dying *Greeks*, or to baptize infants.'[5] The Greeks of Chios reacted to Venetian rule in the

[1] *A Description of the East*, vol. ii, Part 2, p. 10.

[2] Argenti and Kyriakidis, *'Η Χίος παρὰ τοῖς γεωγράφοις καὶ περιηγηταῖς*, p. 696.

[3] P. P. Argenti, *Diplomatic Archive of Chios*, pp. 859, 868–70. For another account of this incident, see Rycaut, *The Present State of the Greek and Armenian Churches*, pp. 339–49.

[4] P. P. Argenti, *The Occupation of Chios by the Venetians*, p. lxxxviii.

[5] Demetrius Cantemir, *The History of the Growth and Decay of the Othman Empire*, p. 392.

same way as the Peloponnesians: better the infidels than the Papists. At an inquiry held subsequently in Venice, Lorenzo Giustiniani, a member of the leading Roman Catholic family in Chios, admitted explicitly that the Greeks preferred Turkish to Venetian rule. His testimony is the more significant, since as a Catholic he was likely to be prejudiced in the Venetians' favour.[1]

The Greeks had their revenge when the Venetian forces withdrew in 1695. They pointed out to the Turks that they had always been loyal subjects of the Sultan (which was true) and with some justification they placed the blame for the recent occupation upon the Latin community. The Turks promptly confiscated all the Latin parish churches, as well as the property and buildings of the religious orders; some of these churches were used as mosques, the remainder handed over to the Greeks. The sole place of worship left to the Latins was a chapel in the French Consulate, by itself totally inadequate; a visitor in 1706 found that as many as twenty masses were celebrated there daily.[2] The chief effect of the ill-advised Venetian invasion was therefore the almost complete ruin of Roman Catholicism in Chios. The Latins of the island suffered a blow from which they never recovered, and their numbers steadily dwindled: over 8,000 before 1694, they amounted to no more than 120 in 1938.[3]

The memory of the Venetian affair permanently poisoned relations between the two Churches in Chios. The Latins enjoyed little security after 1695, but were subject to constant annoyances from the Orthodox party, who watched carefully for any sign of a Roman Catholic revival. In 1707, for example,

[1] P. P. Argenti, *The Occupation of Chios by the Venetians*, p. lxxxix. Another Roman Catholic witness, Domenico Agnolo, remarked baldly that the islanders 'said they were better off under the Turks' (ibid.). Compare the comments of Du Palai, on Chios in 1696: 'D'ailleurs les grecs se sont si mal trouvés des Vénitiens dans le peu de tems qu'ils ont été sous leur puissance, qu'ils préféreront encore plus à l'avenir la domination du Turc à celle des Chrétiens Romains tant qu'ils seront aussy mauvais maitres que ceux cy.' (Argenti and Kyriakidis, op. cit., pp. 1486–7.)

[2] *Voyage du Sieur Paul Lucas, fait par ordre du Roy dans la Grèce*, vol. i, p. 297; compare Hofmann, *Vescovadi cattolici della Grecia. I. Chios*, pp. 24–25, 107–8. When the Dutch Consul was Roman Catholic, the Latin community could use his chapel as well.

In the years following the position improved slightly. By 1757 several churches had been reopened (Hofmann, op. cit., p. 118).

[3] P. P. Argenti, *Chius Vincta*, p. 251.

as a result of Greek machinations eight leading Roman Catholics, one a Jesuit priest, were arrested by the Turks and sent to the galleys.[1] The religious orders by degrees re-established themselves in the island, and opened 'places to read the Gospel in (as they call it) without giving them the names of Churches', as the British Ambassador at Constantinople put it; but the Turks, doubtless prompted by the Greeks, put a stop to this in 1722, destroying the new churches and imprisoning the Latin bishop.[2] But the Latins owed their troubles not only to the Greeks, but to themselves. 'If religion has anything to fear in this place,' wrote the French Ambassador in 1722, 'it is only from the rivalry and desire for self-aggrandizement that each religious order brings with it in coming to the missions.'[3] Besides the rivalry among the religious orders, there were quarrels between the Latin bishop and the leading Roman Catholic families; the latter even threatened in 1725 to have their own bishop banished and sent to the galleys.[4] If only the Roman Catholics would show themselves 'less vindictive and more moderate in their passions', the French Vice-Consul at Chios lamented, they could enjoy 'absolute tranquillity'.[5]

Relations between Greeks and Latins had not improved in 1756, when the French Vice-Consul reports:

> The Greeks, authorized by a *firman* from the Sultan, have thundered out an excommunication in all their churches against those of their rite who serve in Latin houses. Although the excommunication ought to apply only to fathers who entrust their children to the Latins, the malice of the *Gerontes*, the bishop, and the *papas* has extended it to all ages, and they have begun a most violent persecution against the Catholics; their plan being to deprive them not only of their servants and valets, but also of the peasants who work their land, and by this means to destroy them utterly.

He mentions certain acts of violence, and in particular a murderous attack by some Greeks on the Swedish Consul:

[1] Letter by the French Vice-Consul at Chios, in P. P. Argenti, *Diplomatic Archive of Chios*, p. 894.

[2] Despatch by Abraham Stanyan, in P. P. Argenti, *The Occupation of Chios by the Venetians*, pp. 228–9; compare the report by the French Ambassador, in P. P. Argenti, *Diplomatic Archive of Chios*, pp. 909–15.

[3] P. P. Argenti, *Diplomatic Archive of Chios*, p. 915.

[4] Ibid., p. 942.

[5] Ibid., p. 941.

For the rest, the assassins have not failed to make known the cause of their violence. They have informed the Swedish Consul that as he was a Frank, and excommunicated by their Patriarch, they thought less of killing him than a dog.[1]

So the cases of bitterness and ill-feeling continue. It is a melancholy story, little to the credit of either side. As Olivier rightly observed, the only people to profit from these 'scandalous incidents' were the Turks.[2] If we have dwelt at length upon the situation, it is to indicate something of the atmosphere in which Eustratios Argenti was brought up.

Corrupt and venal in its higher administration, ill-equipped intellectually to defend its traditions in the face of Roman Catholic pressure, there is much to pity in the state of the Orthodox Church during its prolonged and uninspiring subjection to Islam. Yet there is also much to admire. Beneath an outward decay, Greek Orthodoxy displayed a remarkable power of endurance, an unexpected spiritual strength. There was every worldly inducement for a Christian to turn Mohammedan, yet cases of apostasy, in Europe at any rate, are surprisingly infrequent; moreover, in every generation martyrs for the faith are to be found, in particular repentant apostates who were put to death for returning to Christianity.[3] Amid numerous discouragements, the Greek people—and above all the simple agricultural population—retained a persistent confidence in the promises of the Gospel. And this is surely an achievement not to be lightly dismissed, least of all by Christians in western Europe, who during recent centuries have practised their faith under incomparably easier conditions.

The Turkish government interfered in the superior organization of the Church, but one thing at least it left undisturbed—the celebration of the Holy Liturgy: and in this one thing the Orthodox possessed all. Thomas Smith wrote with more pene-

[1] Ibid., pp. 1006–8.

[2] Argenti and Kyriakidis, *'Η Χίος παρὰ τοῖς γεωγράφοις καὶ περιηγηταῖς*, p. 833. James Dallaway, an English visitor in 1794, writes: 'At this time, the Catholics do not exceed one thousand in number, yet these schisms are still maintained with indecent violence, and continue to interrupt domestic peace, and to disgrace a religion which professes meekness and forbearance' (ibid., p. 816).

[3] For stories of these 'New Martyrs' see A. Riley, *Athos or the Mountain of the Monks*, pp. 372–3, and R. M. Dawkins, *The Monks of Athos*, pp. 125–6, 314–17.

tration than many visitors from the west when he looked beyond the visible wretchedness of Greek Orthodoxy to inner glory of its liturgical life:

Next to the miraculous and gracious providence of *God*, I ascribe the preservation of *Christianity* among them to the strict and religious observation of the *Festivals* and *Fasts* of the Church. . . . This certainly is the chiefest preservative of Religion in those Eastern Countries against the poison of the *Mahometan* superstition. For Children and those of the most ordinary capacities know the meaning of these holy Solemnities, at which times they flock to Church in great companies, and thereby retain the memory of our *Blessed Saviour's* Birth, dying upon the Cross, Resurrection, and Ascension, and keep up the constant profession of their acknowledgment of the necessary and fundamental points of Faith, as of the doctrine of the *Blessed Trinity*, and the like. And while they celebrate the sufferings and martyrdoms of the *Apostles* of our Lord and Saviour *Jesus Christ*, and other great Saints, who laid down their lives most joyfully for his name, and underwent with unwearied and invincible patience all the Torments and Cruelties of their *Heathen* Persecutors, they take courage from such glorious examples, and are the better enabled to endure with less trouble and regret the miseries and hardships they daily struggle with.[1]

[1] *An Account of the Greek Church*, pp. 18–19 (quoted in part by G. Every, *The Byzantine Patriarchate*, pp. ix–x).

II

LIFE AND TRAVELS

THE house of Argenti has long been among the most eminent of the families of Chios. Italian by origin, the Argentis were already established on the island before it passed under Genoese sovereignty in the fourteenth century. In course of time they became Hellenized and predominantly Orthodox by religious faith; the name of Argenti is not often to be found in the Roman Catholic episcopal records. The family numbers among its members a martyr of the Orthodox Church, Saint Andrew Argenti, who was put to death at Constantinople in 1465, on 29 May—the precise date on which the city fell to the Turks twelve years before in 1453.[1] At the end of the eighteenth and start of the nineteenth century four other Argentis suffered violent death as *ἐθνομάρτυρες*, 'national martyrs' in the struggle for Greek independence. The most famous of these, Eustratios Argenti the Younger, the grandson of Eustratios the theologian, was an associate of the celebrated Riga and both were put to death by the Turks at the same time; they were strangled at Belgrade in 1798 and their remains thrown into the Danube.[2] Eustratios Argenti the Elder, the subject of the present study, is the only member of the family to have won prominence as a theological writer.

In his own works Eustratios refers only occasionally to his experiences, while from other sources little more than a bare outline of his life can be reconstructed, except during his last ten years, of which more detail is known. He was born between the years 1685 and 1690—perhaps in 1687—in the Enkremos quarter of the town of Chios.[3] His parents, Hadzi-Loukis and Viola Argenti, had six children, of whom Eustratios was the third.[4] The date of his birth must be kept in mind: the unhappy

[1] For his life, see A. K. Sarou, *Βίος Ἁγίου Ἀνδρέου Ἀργέντη*; compare E. Dalleggio d'Alessio, in *Archives de l'Orient chrétien*. I. *Mémorial Louis Petit*, Bucharest, 1948, pp. 64–77.

[2] See P. P. Argenti, *Ἱστορία τοῦ Χιακοῦ οἴκου Ἀργέντη*, pp. 142–57.

[3] G. I. Zolotas, *Ἱστορία τῆς Χίου*, vol. i, Part 2, p. 274; P. P. Argenti, *Ἱστορία τοῦ Χιακοῦ οἴκου Ἀργέντη*, pp. 123, 218–19.

[4] For his immediate family relationships, see P. P. Argenti, *Ἱστορία τοῦ Χιακοῦ οἴκου Ἀργέντη*, pp. 235–6; family tree on pp. 253–4.

period of the Venetian occupation was among his earliest memories, and he grew up amid the sharp bitterness and enmity which prevailed between the Roman Catholics and Orthodox of Chios after the events of 1694–5.

His early education was almost certainly at the chief Greek school on the island, the 'Chian School'. In view of the undoubted Orthodox connections of the family and the strong anti-Latin feeling at the time, it is not likely that he went to any of the Roman Catholic teachers on Chios. It is known that in due course he was sent to the Patriarchal School at Constantinople, the finest Greek Orthodox school in the Turkish Empire. Here he must have studied the Greek literature of antiquity, together with theology, philosophy, mathematics, and physics. In theology, he would have read not only the Old and New Testaments but also many of the Fathers, particularly the Cappadocians and Saint John of Damascus. Mathematics in the Patriarchal School at this period were taught mainly from Euclid, physics from Aristotle: it was not until the nineteenth century that the school's curriculum took any great notice of more recent developments in the natural sciences.[1]

An idea of Eustratios' theological reading at Constantinople can be gained from a notebook which he kept at this time. It bears the title, 'Expenses and work of Eustratios Argenti, 1708, in the month of August', and continues with the somewhat cryptic subtitle, 'You weave a spider's web, and your web shall not be a garment; for your works are works of iniquity. Those who desire to grow wealthy fall into temptation and snares and many irrational desires.' The notebook contains extracts from the Bible, from sermons, poems, and letters, which he copied out as part of his work at the Patriarchal School.[2] Among other items, there are two sermons on the Passion of Christ, with a 'Gospel of the Passion collected from the Four Gospels'; a

[1] On the teaching in Greek *gymnasia* at this time, Alexander Helladius writes: 'Studia Mathematica valde desiderantur: praeter enim Euclidem atque Archimedem nihil habent, ac valde raro iis incumbunt. Studia Physica et Metaphysica, si experimentalia excipias, non ita negligenter tractantur, quare et Aristotelis magni sunt Fautores Graeci. Medica studia in his Gymnasiis, vel universitatulis, ut ita loquor, si Bururestum excipies plane ignorantur.' (*Status Praesens Ecclesiae Graecae*, p. 60.) See also T. Evangelidis, *'Η Παιδεία ἐπὶ Τουρκοκρατίας*, vol. i, pp. 23–24.

[2] 'Libros quos supra in Gymnasiis tractare Graecos diximus, omnes, quamquam mediocri pretio comparare possint, propria tamen manu Juvenes transcribunt' (Helladius, op. cit., p. 57).

'Homily on the Monastic State'; and a 'Letter of Basil the Great to Saint Gregory concerning the Way of Life in Solitude'. The longest section is called 'Concerning the Works of Orthodox Christians', and there is also a series of sayings 'from different poets'.[1]

From Constantinople Argenti travelled to the west, as so many other Greeks have done before and since. Of his exact movements we have no detailed knowledge, but he remained abroad for some time—perhaps as long as ten years—and may even have paid more than one visit to Europe. He resided chiefly in Italy and in Germany. He mentions in one of his books that he was for some time in Leghorn (Livorno):[2] here there was a Greek church and a flourishing Greek community. He does not appear to have visited Rome; it is more likely that he studied at Padua. He certainly knew Venice, for he describes a journey from Venice through Austria, calling at Innsbruck, which he made in 1719;[3] and though he does not say what his destination was, he may have been on his way to Halle, in Saxony, where he is said to have studied.[4]

In the course of his travels he learnt Latin, Italian, and almost certainly German, while he also had some acquaintance with Hebrew and Arabic.[5] He continued in Italy and Germany the theological studies which he had begun at Constantinople, and acquired a thorough knowledge of post-medieval Latin theologians, from whom he quotes frequently in his writings. Besides theology he studied medicine (the University of Padua had a celebrated medical faculty); possibly he practised as a doctor at Halle. A combination of medicine and theology was

[1] On this manuscript see Zolotas, '*Ἱστορία τῆς Χίου*, vol. i, Part 2, pp. 276–7; also P. P. Argenti, '*Ἱστορία τοῦ Χιακοῦ οἴκου 'Αργέντη*, pp. 141–2, and A. K. Sarou, *Βίος Εὐστρατίου 'Αργέντη*, pp. 87–8. On p. 60 of the MS. there is a note, 'Written in the year of salvation 1708 at Constantinople'.

The 'Letter of Basil the Great' is in fact *Ep.* ii, in Migne, *Patrologia Graeca* (P.G.), xxxii. 224–33.

[2] *Σύνταγμα κατὰ 'Αζύμων*, p. 261.

[3] Ibid., pp. 85–6.

[4] K. N. Sathas, *Νεοελληνικὴ Φιλολογία*, p. 469; A. M. Vlastos, *Χιακά*, vol. ii, pp. 120–1.

[5] For his knowledge of Hebrew and Arabic, see the etymological *scholion* in *Σύνταγμα κατὰ 'Αζύμων*, pp. 23–24. Sarou, *Βίος Εὐστρατίου 'Αργέντη*, pp. 25–26 states that in later life he visited Antioch and taught the Arabic-speaking Orthodox there in their own language. This is not impossible, but Sarou provides no evidence.

It is possible that he learnt Latin, not on his travels, but in childhood at the Chian School.

by no means unusual: his fellow Chiot, George Koressios, was both doctor and theologian, as were Nicholas Bulgaris, Theophilos Korydalleus (1563–1646) (a follower of Cyril Lukaris), and John Kontonis (1723–1761) of Zakynthos, while Leo Allatius, after completing his theological studies at the Greek College, in 1616 took a medical degree at the Sapienza in Rome. Another such medical theologian was Stephen Karatheodoris in the nineteenth century, author (or part-author) of the important Letter of the Eastern Patriarchs to Pius IX in 1848. The Greek Orthodox Church has never regarded theology as a specialized matter of concern only to the clergy, but has a long and honourable tradition of 'lay theologians'. Those who combined medicine and theology were known as 'doctor-philosophers' (*ἰατροφιλόσοφοι*), a name applied to Eustratios on the title-page in several of his books.

Around 1720 Eustratios, now aged between thirty and thirty-five, returned to Chios, and here for the next quarter of a century he practised as a doctor. Chios was in fact particularly noted throughout the Turkish Empire for its physicians, as can be seen from the remarks of two western visitors to the island during Eustratios' life-time. The first of them, Julien Galland (on Chios in 1747), relates:

> Nowhere in the Levant are doctors more respected than on Chios. The Turks, in deference to their profession, allow them to wear boots of yellow leather and clothes of striking colour, in exactly the same way as they do themselves—a thing which they normally forbid to all their subjects. . . . The doctors of Chios are all native Christians of the island, and only practise medicine after completing their studies in Italy, whether they are Greeks or Latins.[1]

Thus the young Eustratios, in travelling westwards to study medicine, followed a course normal among his countrymen.

The botanist Frederick Hasselquist, who stayed on Chios two years after Galland, mentions that during his travels he met a number of Greeks 'who have studied physick, chiefly in Padua: most of them born on some island in the Archipelago. Scio, in particular, has a number of tolerable physicians, and also supplies other places with them'. At Smyrna Hasselquist met a doctor from Chios, 'Doctor Demetri' by name, who 'was born

[1] Argenti and Kyriakidis, *Ἡ Χίος παρὰ τοῖς γεωγράφοις καὶ περιηγηταῖς*, p.725.

in Scio, had travelled through England and Germany, practised nine years in St. Esprit, the chief hospital in Rome', and who possessed, to Hasselquist's delight, a good knowledge of botany.[1]

Of Eustratios' own activities as a doctor we know nothing in detail. There exists, however, in the library of Dr. P. P. Argenti in London, a manuscript dealing with medical matters, which probably belonged to Eustratios (it was found in the ruins of his house) and which family tradition believes to have been actually written by him. The manuscript, dated by its style of handwriting to the period 1700–50, is divided into two parts closely similar in character, the first entitled 'A Doctor's Manual' (*Iatrosophion*) and the second 'A Book of Remedies' (*Antidotarion*). There is no indication in the *Iatrosophion* who the author (or rather the compiler) may be. The *Antidotarion* is said to be a translation from the Italian, and the name of the translator is given—Nicholas Hieropais—but not that of the original author. This makes it on the whole unlikely that the second part is by Eustratios; of course he knew Italian and was presumably capable of writing in that language: indeed, he might actually have preferred to write about medicine in Italian, since his medical studies were carried out in Italy. But if Argenti were the author of the *Antidotarion*, we should on the whole expect him to make his own translation from Italian into his native Greek, particularly in a manuscript which actually belonged to him. Perhaps family tradition is correct in regarding the medical manuscript as Eustratios' work: but in default of more specific evidence it is impossible to speak with certainty.[2]

The *Iatrosophion* opens with sections on the four elements which compose man's nature, extracted chiefly from Hippocrates and Galen, but in a shortened and somewhat corrupt text. The rest of the *Iatrosophion*, and the whole of the *Antidotarion*, contain brief remedies and prescriptions, of the traditional 'folk-medicine' type current in Greece at the time. Some typical paragraphs may be given:

[1] Argenti and Kyriakidis, op. cit., p. 732.

[2] J. Dekigallas, *Σχεδίασμα κατόπτρου τῆς Νεοελληνικῆς Φιλολογίας*, p. 7, states that Argenti wrote 'certain short works on medicine'. But since Dekigallas gives no titles or further details, one cannot but suspect that he is merely guessing, and has inferred the existence of these medical works from the fact that Argenti was a doctor.

Good for a pain in the head. Take green ivy and pound it up, remove the gum which it produces, mix it with oil, throw it into a cloth, and anoint the forehead and temples; and it will provide relief. Another remedy: Take germander and pound it up, then mix it with vinegar, warm it in a pot, and throw it into a cloth; apply it to the forehead and to all the tender parts of the head and the pain will stop. Or else take raw quicklime and sulphur, with pepper, white frankincense, and cardamom seed, pound them all together and mix with vinegar, and anoint the temples. . . .

When teeth become loose: Take the leaves or the bark of the mulberry tree, boil with vinegar, and hold it in your mouth; and it will heal.

When a person's voice goes: Mix cabbage juice with honey, and let the patient go to the bath and drink the mixture while he is there; and he will recover.

For a purge: Rhubarb dr. 5, agaric dr. 3, korasan dr. 5, senna dr. 5, savory dr. 5, Latin sweetmeat dr. 5, cloves dr. 2, saffron dr. 2, colocynth dr. 1. Directions: mix the ingredients together with honey and make three pills, each the size of a pea. Take one in the evening and two in the morning. And when it stops, eat cabbage soup and drink some wine.

Pills of mercury for the French disease (? syphilis) and for salt phlegm. Take 6 parts mercury, 1 of lead arsenate, and 15 of flour. Two pills to be taken in the evening and six in the morning, for 40 days.[1]

So the remedies continue: 'How to purge phlegm and yellow bile', 'For the heart, when it has wind and the bowels rumble', 'Pills to send children to sleep', 'Tablets for gout and arthritis', 'A remedy made from dates, from John of Damascus', and so on. It is perfectly possible that Eustratios, in his practice as a doctor, combined the use of these 'folk' remedies with the more scientific methods which he had learnt in the west.

Soon after his return to Chios from Europe Eustratios married, but of his wife Leonou nothing is known except that she bore him two children, John and Neophytos. During these years (1720–45) Eustratios, besides his work as a doctor, may also have taught in the Chian School,[2] and perhaps he acted as a preacher in local churches. In Chios preaching seems to have

[1] *Iatrosophion*, sections 1, 2, 5, 10; *Antidotarion*, section 82.

[2] Patriarch Kosmas, in his letter of 1741, addresses Eustratios as 'teacher' (*didaskalos*). Zolotas, *'Ιστορία τῆς Χίου*, vol. iii, Part 1, p. 507, says that Eustratios taught at the Chian School from 1710 to 1750, but gives no evidence to support this statement.

been unusually frequent: the Russian traveller Vassili Barsky, during a visit to the island in 1732, comments specially on the 'excellent teachers and preachers', who 'preach the word of God every week'.[1] In how many other places in the Greek Orthodox world was a weekly sermon the rule at this date? Pitton de Tournefort says that in most Greek churches the pulpit no longer existed even as a piece of furniture, 'for the custom of preaching has been abolished';[2] but he is given to grave exaggeration. Perhaps during these years Eustratios also began to assume the role of controversialist and to engage in the debates, public and private, with Roman Catholics for which in later life he became famous.

It is uncertain when he began to compose his theological works, but they seem to belong to the later part of his life. The first of his books to be published was a short treatise on the Papacy, *Concerning the False Infallibility of the Pope of Rome*. An Arabic translation of this was made in 1740, and printed by the Orthodox press at Jassy in 1746. The original Greek remains unpublished, but is preserved in a manuscript at Budapest; this manuscript also contains two further pieces in Greek upon the Papacy, also by Argenti, *The Acts and History of the Council of Constance* and *A Manual concerning the Latin Pope and Antichrist.* Both these exist only in manuscript and are entirely unpublished; the concluding treatise is incomplete, since the manuscript contains only the first sixteen chapters, out of a total of fifty four chapters whose titles are given in the table of contents.[3]

[1] Argenti and Kyriakidis, *Ἡ Χίος παρὰ τοῖς γεωγράφοις καὶ περιηγηταῖς*, p. 1649.

[2] Pitton de Tournefort, *Relation d'un Voyage du Levant*, vol. i, p. 114.

In the Greek islands there exists in fact a striking number of Baroque pulpits, in gilded wood elaborately carved, dating from the seventeenth and eighteenth centuries (precisely the period to which Pitton de Tournefort refers).

[3] For the full Greek titles of these and other works by Eustratios Argenti, see the Appendix (pp. 176–9).

A note opposite p. 1 of the Budapest manuscript states that it belonged to the library of George Zaviras (1744–1804). A native of Siatista in Macedonia, Zaviras later settled in Hungary. He is the author of *Νέα Ἑλλὰς ἢ Ἑλληνικὸν Θέατρον*, which was edited by G. P. Kremos and first published at Athens in 1872. He left his fine collection of manuscripts and books to the Greek Church at Budapest; various additions were made to the collection after his death. The Zaviras Library is now in the hands of the Institute of Modern Greek at Budapest University. On the history of the Zaviras Library, see S. P. Lambros in *Νέος Ἑλληνομνήμων*, vol. viii, Athens, 1911, pp. 70–79, and A. Graf, *Jeórjiosz Zavírasz Budapesti könyvtárának katalógusa*, pp. 3–4.

For details of the Arabic translation and publication of *Concerning the False In-*

But even before any of his works had been published, Eustratios had acquired a reputation beyond Chios itself. In 1741 he received a letter from Kosmas III, Patriarch of Alexandria from 1737 to 1746. The Patriarch addresses him as 'most honourable, most learnedly erudite and noble, best among physicians, praiseworthy and holy teacher, Kyrios Eustratios Argenti, beloved son in Christ our God'. 'It is time for you to march out upon an expedition dear to God,' Kosmas continues, and he asks Argenti to expound the true Christian faith, enjoining him to 'proclaim it in writing for the salvation of many, and with good judgement set it forth plainly from the canonical books, both Greek and Latin'.[1]

The next Patriarch of Alexandria, Matthew, who held office from 1746 to 1766, was a personal friend of Eustratios.[2] Soon after Matthew's accession Argenti, accompanied by his son John, found himself in Egypt, and with Matthew's encouragement he devoted himself actively to the defence of the Orthodox faith. The exact date of his arrival in Egypt is not clear, but he was there by the spring of 1748,[3] if not earlier, and he stayed for more than three years.

Matthew had need of all the help that Eustratios could render, for his Patriarchate was in appalling confusion. The Orthodox Church in Egypt was small in size (since the schism

fallibility of the Pope of Rome, see G. Graf, *Geschichte der christlichen arabischen Literatur*, vol. iii, pp. 140–1. Argenti twice mentions these anti-Papal treatises in his other published writings: *Σύνταγμα κατὰ Ἀζύμων*, p. 347, and *Ἐγχειρίδιον περὶ Βαπτίσματος*, pp. 80–81.

[1] The text of this letter is given in C. Erbiceanu, *Cronicarii Greci*, Bucharest, 1888, p. 226; reprinted in K. I. Amantos, *Οἱ Ἀργένται τῆς Χίου*, pp. 91–92, and in P. P. Argenti, *Ἱστορία τοῦ Χιακοῦ οἴκου Ἀργέντη*, pp. 123–4. Some have understood the Patriarch's letter as a definite invitation to visit Egypt, and have assumed that Eustratios actually went to Alexandria in 1742–3; but may not the expedition of which Kosmas speaks be no more than metaphorical? He does not ask Argenti to preach in person, but to set forth the truth *in writing*.

Zolotas, *Ἱστορία τῆς Χίου*, vol. iii, Part 1, p. 514, states that Argenti had already visited Egypt in 1726. Vlastos, *Χιακά*, vol. ii, p. 121, says that he visited Egypt 'around 1719'.

[2] See the Introduction to *Σύνταγμα κατὰ Ἀζύμων*. For the career of Matthew, see D. P. Paschalis, *Ματθαῖος ὁ Ἄνδριος, πάπας καὶ πατριάρχης Ἀλεξανδρείας* (especially pp. 30–34, which refer to Argenti's visit); and C. A. Papadopoulos, *Ἀνέκδοτος ἀλληλογραφία τοῦ Πατριάρχου Ἀλεξανδρείας Ματθαίου Ψάλτου*, in *Ἐκκλησιαστικὸς Φάρος*, vol. xvii, pp. 401–35 (pp. 415–17 are concerned with Argenti).

[3] See the letter by James of Patmos, dated 15 April 1748, which speaks of Argenti as resident in Egypt: *Ἐκκλησιαστικὸς Φάρος*, vol. xix, Alexandria, 1920, p. 534.

after Chalcedon the great majority of Egyptian Christians have been Monophysite): in the seventeenth century there were only seven churches within the whole of the Patriarchate of Alexandria. The Russian monk Arsenios Sukhanov, visiting Cairo in 1651, found that the total Orthodox congregation there amounted to a mere 600 Greeks and Arabs.[1] Few in numbers, the Orthodox of Egypt were also poor in resources. Athanasius Hypsilantis (Ypsilanti) describes conditions on his arrival in 1744:

> There I found the Patriarch Kosmas in utter destitution, labouring under an exceedingly heavy debt, scarcely able to survive on account of the intolerable bankruptcy of the Throne. The income of the Patriarchate is insufficient even to pay the interest due on the debt, while the inns and other houses and workshops which belong to the Patriarchate as so decayed that they are in danger of falling down.[2]

It is scarcely surprising that many Patriarchs in the seventeenth and eighteenth centuries preferred to reside in Constantinople rather than Egypt.

Such was the situation which Matthew inherited. In one respect, however, Alexandria was better off than the sister Patriarchate of Antioch, for during the seventeenth century at any rate it suffered far less from Roman Catholic infiltration. The Orthodox there showed a distinct hostility to Rome; as early as 1562 a Latin missionary, the Jesuit Christopher Rodriguez, laments:

> The Greeks are so obstinate in their heresy and in their hatred of the Roman Church that, on their own admission, they would rather become Turks than submit to the obedience of the Holy Roman Church.[3]

The Patriarchs of Alexandria—for example, Lukaris and Kritopoulos—were more friendly towards Protestantism than towards Rome, and it seems that only one Patriarch, Samuel Kapasoulis (1710–24), made a secret act of submission to the Pope.[4]

[1] C. A. Papadopoulos, *Ἱστορία τῆς Ἐκκλησίας Ἀλεξανδρείας*, p. 709.

[2] *Τὰ μετὰ τὴν ἅλωσιν*, p. 352.

[3] Rabbath, *Documents inédits*, p. 302.

[4] Papadopoulos, *Ἱστορία τῆς Ἐκκλησίας Ἀλεξανδρείας*, pp. 739–44; Hofmann, *Griechische Patriarchen und Römische Päpste*, *Orientalia Christiana*, vol. xiii, No. 47, *passim*, and vol. xxxvi, No. 97, pp. 41–60. Matthew's immediate predecessor,

During Matthew's reign, however, Roman activity in Alexandria was suddenly intensified. Eustratios Argenti himself has left an account of what happened, in a long letter written from Egypt in April 1751.[1] He begins by describing the general state of affairs in the Patriarchate, fully confirming the gloomy picture presented by Hypsilantis. The throne of Saint Mark, he writes, once so highly exalted, is now in a condition altogether 'pitiable'. The standard of education has fallen deplorably low: 'I am ashamed to describe the barbarousness and ignorance of the bishops and priests here.'[2] Ill-taught and ill-organized, the Church in Egypt had fallen an easy prey to Uniates from Syria. There were close contacts between the Greeks and Arabs in Egypt and those in Syria, so that in due course the Romanizers of the Antiochene Patriarchate moved down to Alexandria and started to cause trouble.

Matthew's two immediate predecessors, Kosmas II and Kosmas III—so Argenti continues in his letter—did little to guard against this infiltration:

When he came to Egypt, Matthew found the churches in great disorder, both internally and externally; the church buildings fallen into decay; the poor crowded together and uncared for; the Patriarchal throne burdened with heavy debt; the Christians without a shepherd and in perplexity over religious questions; the sheep feeding together with wicked goats and wolves, frequently being plundered by them and daily consumed; the priests careless and inactive, on the excuse that it was the custom to be so.[3]

Kosmas III, wrote in friendly terms to the Pope at the time of his accession in 1737, but he does not appear to have made any formal act of submission (*Orientalia Christiana*, vol. xxxvi, No. 97, pp. 20–40).

[1] Text in K. A. Uspenski, *The Patriarchate of Alexandria*, pp. 340–7; Russian translation with comments by K. V. Kharlampovitch, in the *Journal of the Ministry of Public Instruction*, New Series, Part xxix, Saint Petersburg, 1910, pp. 69–73, 370–2. Large parts of Argenti's letter were used by Matthew (without acknowledgement!) in an account of the affairs of his Patriarchate which he composed in this same year, 1751 (for the text, see G. G. Mazarakis, *Συμβολὴ εἰς τὴν ἱστορίαν τῆς ἐν Αἰγύπτῳ Ὀρθοδόξου Ἐκκλησίας*, pp. 612–18); this account Matthew sent to various Orthodox Churches, especially the Russian, in an attempt to raise money (see C. A. Papadopoulos in *Ἐκκλησιαστικὸς Φάρος*, vol. xvii, Alexandria, 1918, p. 417, and G. Papamichael in *Ἐκκλησιαστικὸς Φάρος*, vol. vii, Alexandria, 1911, pp. 185–6). Thus Argenti's letter enjoyed a wide circulation, although passing under the name of another.

[2] K. A. Uspenski, op. cit., pp. 340–1.

[3] Ibid., pp. 343–4.

Matthew at once set to work with great energy, paying off the debts, repairing the churches, and looking after the poor. To combat the prevalent ignorance, he established proper schools and appointed teachers. In hopes of checking the Romeward movement, he forbade any ecclesiastical relations between his own people and the Roman Catholics, banning all mixed marriages and all *communicatio in sacris*. His clergy were forbidden to administer the sacraments to Papists, to accept Papist alms, or to hold services in Papist houses; the laity were not permitted to attend the Papists' worship or to receive their sacraments.

Matthew was not a man to be easily defeated but (as Argenti relates) he encountered formidable opposition. Seraphim Tanas (Cyril VI), since 1724 the Roman claimant to the Patriarchate of Antioch, consecrated as 'Bishop of Alexandria' an Arab, Joseph Babilas. This Joseph pretended to be an ordinary priest when he first arrived in Egypt, but suddenly created a great sensation by appearing in public without previous warning, arrayed in the vestments of an Eastern Orthodox bishop. He began various intrigues, bribing the Turks and using the influence which he could command among the wealthy Latin citizens and the foreign consuls at Alexandria. His object, Argenti claims, was to oust Matthew from his see and to obtain from the Ottoman government official recognition as Patriarch in his place. In this way the Patriarchate of Alexandria would be 'reconciled' to the Church of Rome.[1]

At this point in his letter, Argenti makes some sharp comments on the Greek College at Rome. The conduct of Babilas, he writes, is but one example out of many: the Roman Catholics are always using deceit to gain their ends, and one of their 'snares' is the College of Saint Athanasius. Thither (so he complains) they lure youthful and unsuspecting Orthodox who have travelled to the west to study; then they turn them into Papists and send them back to the east as secret agents for the Roman cause. They do not confer the priesthood on them in Rome, but tell them to seek ordination from Orthodox bishops, so that they will be accepted by Orthodox congregations.[2] These remarks by Argenti show how the policy of concealment pursued by the western missionaries in the end proved the cause of great bitterness and ill-feeling.

[1] K. A. Uspenski, op. cit., pp. 345–6. [2] Ibid., p. 345.

Argenti concludes his letter by describing the desperate condition of Orthodoxy: there is an imminent prospect that three out of the four remaining Patriarchates will be lost, and the Orthodox Church reduced in outward appearance to a 'sect', on a level with Copts, Armenians, and Jacobites.

To put it briefly, the Papists have set up in Egypt a Patriarch of Alexandria, and the Orthodox throne is breathing its last; the church of Saint Nicholas is in danger of being taken away from the Orthodox and seized by the Papists. For they are rich, more powerful, and agreed in wickedness; and if the Great Church of Constantinople and the Ecumenical Patriarch will not help, they will lose this second throne as well as the first throne of Rome; the other two, Antioch and Jerusalem, have almost been destroyed; and we shall be as the Armenians and Maronites, the Copts and Syrians, with only one Patriarch, of Constantinople, whom the Papists will afterwards expel root and branch with little trouble, when he is left alone and without his brethren.[1]

Argenti was no idle alarmist; although his gloomy predictions were not in fact realized, they seemed amply justified by the threatening outlook at the time. The picture which he here presents helps to explain the severity and violence of much anti-Latin polemic. The Orthodox felt that they were fighting for their life. They spoke harshly because they saw around them the devastating effects of Roman activity, and because they feared still greater devastation in the future. Argenti's letter should be compared with the evidence cited on the first chapter, to which it forms an illuminating supplement.

Argenti's despondency was shared by the Patriarch Matthew, who wrote in a pathetic letter of August 1753:

The trials brought upon us by the heretics and schismatics, like the blazing heat of midsummer, have worn us out. In the burdensome journey of this vain life with its course of tribulations, no other consolation have we save converse with our spiritual friends, whether far away or near.[2]

Religious feeling ran high in Alexandria at this time: one young Greek who had turned Roman Catholic tried to strangle his mother because she would not do the same.[3] But despite certain

[1] Ibid., p. 346.
[2] Papadopoulos, *'Ιστορία τῆς 'Εκκλησίας 'Αλεξανδρείας* p.766.
[3] Papadopoulos, op. cit., p. 777

losses the Greeks of Egypt on the whole remained firm in their Orthodoxy. Around 1765 they wrote to Matthew, who was abroad: 'All of us, great and small, men, women, and children, would gladly accept death rather than undergo disgrace at the hands of the Frankish fathers.'[1] Yet Matthew had little reason for complacency when, at the end of twenty years in office, he surveyed the condition of his flock. In 1766 the Orthodox of Egypt sent him a depressing appeal:

> Everywhere the Patriarchal throne shows the marks of its downfall. As is known to all, there is scarcely enough money to support the Patriarch with his synod and to pay the royal levies [i.e. to the Ottoman authorities]. All the Orthodox of Egypt are completely poverty-stricken . . . the merchants who live here have now grown few in numbers and have fallen on bad days.[2]

For all their energy and enthusiasm Matthew and Eustratios could do little to relieve the sad condition of the Alexandrian Church.

Argenti says nothing in his letter of 1751 about his own activities in Egypt. Perhaps he helped to reorganize the schools and taught in them. His main work, however, was in the field of controversy and propaganda. He strove unceasingly to combat and refute the Latin teaching, sometimes in small, private gatherings—he describes one argument at an inn, as the travellers sat together in the evening[3]—while on other occasions he engaged in public disputations of a more formal character. He has left a spirited description of one of these public debates:

> We held a discussion in Egypt with two missionaries or false apostles of the Pope of Rome, Father Gabriel and Father Cyril, in the presence of many Arab and Syrian Christians who had been led astray,[4] and of a few Orthodox. The subject chanced to be the Holy Chalice. We proved clearly from Christ, from the Apostles, from the Councils and Fathers both eastern and western, and above all from the holy and orthodox Popes of Old Rome in the past, that the later Popes of Rome had acted unlawfully in depriving the laity of the Chalice. . . . When this, I say, was clearly and plainly demonstrated, Father Cyril remained speechless, groaning and trembling in his perplexity; and being an ardent partisan of Popery, and feeling an excessive pride in his empty methods of scholastic reasoning, he

[1] Papadopoulos, op. cit., p. 776.
[2] Papadopoulos, op. cit., p. 778.
[3] *Σύνταγμα κατὰ Ἀζύμων*, p. 116.
[4] *πεπλανημένοι*, i.e. Uniates.

could not endure his defeat; but he contracted an attack of asthma, which turned after not many days into consumption, accompanied by fever; and so he died.[1] At the time, both of them withdrew in shame and discouragement. Those of the deceived who were present gnashed their teeth; but the few Orthodox who were there sang a hymn of victory in honour of Orthodoxy.[2]

After two days, Father Gabriel called on Argenti and tried to prove his case by appealing to John vi. 35, 'I am the bread of life': Christ did not say that he was the wine of life, and therefore the laity were to be given communion under the form of bread alone. He was mortified to find that Argenti did not take this argument seriously.

This debate is of particular interest, since it led to the composition of Argenti's most substantial work. The Patriarch Matthew and others were so impressed by his victory that they asked him to put down his arguments in writing. Argenti complied, and making use of some earlier material that he had with him,[3] he produced a book not only on the Chalice but on the whole question of the Eucharist, so far as it entered into disputes with the Roman Catholics. He called it *Concerning the Lord's Supper*, and divided it into three parts: the first part, on the matter (ὕλη) of the sacrament, attacked the Latin use of unleavened bread; the second, on the consecration (ἁγιασμός), maintained the necessity for an Epiclesis; the third, on the use (χρῆσις) of the sacrament, reproached the Latins for denying communion to young children, and for not giving it to the laity under both kinds. The finished work is thus much wider in scope than the debate from which it took its origin. When published, the whole book occupied more than 370 closely printed pages. Although it is primarily polemical in purpose, Argenti also included in it some straightforward teaching on the plan of the church building, the different orders of the clergy, the history of Christian worship, and the structure of the Holy Liturgy. For a time the book circulated in manuscript, and a copy came into the hands of Silvester of Antioch, who found it precisely what he needed in his combat with the Roman

[1] The editors of the *Σύνταγμα κατὰ Ἀζύμων* are more specific, stating in their Introduction that 'he went down to hell'.

[2] *Σύνταγμα κατὰ Ἀζύμων*, pp. 310–11.

[3] Part of the book was written as early as 1743: see *Σύνταγμα κατὰ Ἀζύμων*, p. 13.

Catholics of his own Patriarchate; he therefore had an epitome of the work translated into Arabic and printed. The original Greek was later published by a group of Argenti's friends; it appeared in 1760, when the author was already dead, as *Treatise against Unleavened Bread*, a title which strictly speaking applies only to the first part.[1]

About this same time, Argenti composed another, far briefer anti-Latin work, on the Roman doctrine of Purgatory: *Short Treatise against the Purgatorial Fire of the Papists*. This remained unpublished until 1939.[2]

While in Egypt, Argenti may also have engaged in work of less polemical character. According to George Zaviras, a reliable authority writing only a few years after Argenti's death, he drew up 'A List of the Patriarchs of Alexandria', as well as two other historical works of a more general character, 'A Chronological Epitome concerning the Martyr Saints' and 'A

[1] Details of how the book came to be written, and of its publication in Arabic and Greek, are supplied by the editors in the Introduction to the 1760 edition. This, the first Greek edition, was published at Leipzig; a second Greek edition, with the text unchanged, appeared at Nauplia in 1845.

The original title, *Περὶ τοῦ κυριακοῦ δείπνου*, is found in the manuscripts of the work both at Athens (National Library, 395; Benaki Museum, 199) and at the Monastery of Saint Catherine, Mount Sinai (Beneševič, Sin. gr. 526 a-c, otherwise numbered 2021–2). The original title does not appear on the title page of the 1760 printed edition, but it is found on p. 5 as a subtitle.

At the end of the Athens manuscript is the date 1755, which supplies a *terminus ad quem* for the completion of the work.

Both the Greek editions accidentally omitted a short passage at the opening of the third part of the book; this missing section is to be found in A. K. Demetrakopoulos, *Προσθῆκαι καὶ διορθώσεις εἰς τὴν Νεοελληνικὴν Φιλολογίαν Κωνσταντίνου Σάθα*, pp. 83–4.

G. Graf, *Geschichte der christlichen arabischen Literatur*, vol. iii, pp. 141 and 145, describes two Arabic translations of the *Treatise* in manuscript, but he mentions no printed edition. One of these manuscripts is dated 1740 and the other 1742. These dates raise some difficulty, for (1) a passage on p. 13 of the *Treatise* was not written until 1743; and (2) the debate with Fathers Gabriel and Cyril, which gave rise to the book in its present form, took place during Argenti's visit to Egypt during 1748–51. It would therefore seem that either (1) the dates on the Arabic manuscripts are for some reason incorrect, and these manuscripts are in fact later than 1748; or else (2) the Arabic manuscripts are not translations of the *Treatise* in its present form, but of some earlier essay by Argenti on the same subject.

[2] The editor was Michael Constantinides, Great Archimandrite at the Greek Cathedral in London (subsequently Metropolitan of Corinth and Archbishop of North and South America). The text is taken from a manuscript at Jerusalem (Patr. Bibl. 386). This is dated 12 February 1752, which provides a *terminus ad quem* for the composition of the work; there is no evidence to fix the date more precisely. Argenti refers to the *Short Treatise* in *Σύνταγμα κατὰ Ἀζύμων*, pp. 283–4.

Chronological Epitome from the birth of Christ to the present time'. These last two works might have been written at any time in his life, but it is natural to assume that the first was composed during his stay in Egypt. All three works have remained unpublished, and I have not managed to trace them in manuscript.[1]

It would be natural for a man of Argenti's scholarly interests, during a long visit to Egypt, to work in the Patriarchal Library at Alexandria; and it is possible that, besides drawing up a list of the Alexandrian Patriarchs, he also constructed a catalogue of the books in the Patriarchal Library. At any rate, in the library of the Greek Community at Kecskemét, Hungary, there exists an interesting list of books in a manuscript dating from the middle of the eighteenth century. This manuscript con-

[1] These three works are mentioned by G. Zaviras, *Νέα 'Ελλὰς ἢ 'Ελληνικὸν Θέατρον*, p. 302. Zaviras adds that a manuscript of the third work is to be found in the library of Gabriel Kallonas (1724–95), who was the Greek priest at Budapest and the owner of a fine collection of manuscripts (see Zaviras, op. cit., pp. 239–41).

G. I. Zolotas, *'Ιστορία τῆς Χίου*, vol. iii, Part 1, p. 514, refers to a manuscript in the Patriarchal Library at Cairo, containing a list of the Patriarchs of Alexandria. According to Zolotas the first five chapters of this list were compiled and written down by Eustratios Argenti during a visit to Egypt in the year 1726. Unfortunately Zolotas gives no catalogue number or further description of this manuscript, and it has not proved possible to trace it. This work may well be the same as the List of the Patriarchs of Alexandria to which Zaviras refers.

Ms. 101 in the Patriarchal Library (T. D. Moschonas, *Κατάλογοι τῆς Πατριαρχικῆς Βιβλιοθήκης*, vol. i, Alexandria, 1945, p. 97) contains on ff. 461–7 a list of the Patriarchs of Alexandria, which is attributed by Moschonas to Eustratios Argenti; but this attribution seems open to question on several grounds. The relevant pages of the manuscript consist in (1) the list proper, divided into five chapters; (2) numerous interlinear and marginal additions. (2) is in a different hand from (1), but all the annotations in (2) seem to have been made by the same person. The main text of the list continues to the year 1783, while the annotations mention the resignation of Patriarch Matthew in 1766 and his death in 1775. Since Argenti was dead before 1760, the list as it stands cannot be by him. It is of course possible that the list, as we now have it, is not in its original form, but has been recopied by someone else after Argenti's death and brought up to date; but this is a pure conjecture, since the list itself contains nothing to suggest that this is in fact what has happened. Furthermore, the list nowhere bears the name of Argenti. It is in any case little more than a bare series of names with a few general remarks on each, and there are no special details about events which occurred while Argenti was in Egypt. We may note that this list is in five chapters, while Zolotas also speaks of five chapters in connexion with the list which he saw. Is this in fact Zolotas' list? If so, it is not clear (1) why he attributed the list to Argenti; or (2) whence he derived the date 1726, for the relevant pages of the manuscript nowhere bear this date.

It would appear, therefore, that the ascription of Ms. 101, ff. 461–7 to Argenti is merely a conjecture by Moschonas.

tains the greater part of Argenti's work *Concerning the Lord's Supper*, together with other theological material of much the same character, in particular a tract on the Epiclesis: this further material may be wholly or in part by Argenti, although this is not certain. But bound up with these theological pieces there is a 'Catalogue of the Books of the Library of the Most Holy Throne of Alexandria'. Unfortunately there is no indication whatever who compiled the list; but it is curious that it should be bound up with a theological work by Eustratios Argenti, and one wonders if there may not be some connection between the two. Whether he is in fact the compiler of the catalogue it is impossible to say; but certainly he was resident in Egypt for long enough to examine the Patriarchal Library with care.[1]

Argenti left Egypt in 1751, having learnt in the previous year of the death of John, his elder brother. John had taken monastic vows in 1723 on the death of his wife, and changed his name to James. He joined the monastery of Saint John Moundon, which was—after the *Nea Moni*—the most celebrated religious house in Chios.[2] The community granted James the lease of one of the four lesser houses dependent on the monastery, the *metochion* of Saint George at Zartoulida. James devoted most of his fortune to redecorating the chapel of the *metochion* and to repairing the rest of the property. Within a few years he came to occupy a leading position in the community, and he was abbot (*kathigoumenos*) from 1738 to 1740, and again from 1748 until his death in 1749 (as in many Greek monasteries at this time, the abbot was not elected for life, but for a limited period only—in this case for a year). The family connection with Saint John Moundon was further strengthened in 1738, when Eustratios' son John entered the community: he paid the *ἀδελφᾶτον*, the fee of money required from those who wished to become

[1] The Catalogue of Books is in Ms. 5 of the Kecskemét collection, ff. 131r–139r. It is written on shiny paper of an oriental character.

[2] Details of dealings between the Monastery of Saint John and the Argenti family are contained in the *Moundon Codex*, in which the official business of the community was recorded. For extracts from the Codex, see Zolotas, '*Ἱστορία τῆς Χίου*, vol. iii, Part 2, pp. 287–322; P. P. Argenti, '*Ἱστορία τοῦ Χιακοῦ οἴκου Ἀργέντη*, pp. 168–76; and J. M. Andreadis, '*Ἱστορία τῆς ἐν Χίῳ Ὀρθοδόξου Ἐκκλησίας*, pp. ccxxvii–ccxxxiii. For the history of the monastery, consult K. I. Amantos, '*Ἡ Μονὴ τῶν Μουνδῶν ἐν Χίῳ*.

brethren, but he was not actually professed as a monk.[1] John stayed in the monastery until 1747, when he travelled to Egypt with his father.

James bequeathed the lease of the *metochion* to his brother Eustratios, the latter being required to pay the sum of 150 *aslania* to the monastery, in order to make good his right of succession. On hearing of James' death, Eustratios and his son John wrote from Egypt, sending the 150 *aslania*, and asking that the *metochion* should be given to them 'that they might settle there for the remainder of their lives in quiet and peace'. Eustratios was now over sixty, and was perhaps feeling the strain of continual controversy in Egypt; presumably his wife was already dead. Some embarrassment was caused by the presence of three penniless young monks whom James had befriended and given a home in the *metochion*; but it was agreed that these should remain in Zartoulida and act as servants to Eustratios.[2]

It was more than twenty months later when Eustratios actually arrived at the monastery. The entry in the monastic records for 2 January 1752 states: 'Today the most celebrated and best of physicians, Kyrios Eustratios Argenti, came and gave his fee of 25 *aslania* into the hands of the *kathigoumenos* in the presence of the Fathers, and from today he undertakes to perform the services, great and small, as the other fathers do, according to the order of the monastery.'[3] He was not professed as a monk. His son John was not with him, but had perhaps remained in Egypt.

But Eustratios' hopes of spending the rest of his life at Zartoulida in peace and quiet were not to be realized. Little more than a year after his arrival, on 26 April 1753, he took back the 150 *aslania* which he had paid and left the monastery,

[1] *Moundon Codex* B, f. 83. P. P. Argenti and Andreadis give the date as 1738; Zolotas, followed by Sarou, *Βίος Εὐστρατίου 'Αργέντη*, pp. 63–4, gives 1743.

It may seem strange that John should become a member of the community, yet take no vows; but such a practice was not unusual at this period. There are several instances in the *Codex* where a man pays the fee, and then after living for a time in the community, takes back his money and returns to secular life. Compare Richard Pococke on one of the female convents of Chios: 'Some live in the convent without ever taking the vow, or at least not till such time as there is little danger of being induced to break it' (*A Description of the East*, vol. ii, Part 2, p. 5).

[2] *Moundon Codex* B, f. 157 (entry for 23 April 1750).

[3] Ibid., f. 162. Zolotas gives the date as 12 January.

relinquishing both his own and his son John's claims to the *metochion*. The reason given in the monastic records is that he was a layman, 'and there is no such custom, that laymen should be found in the *metochia* of the monastery'; the monks therefore asked him to withdraw, and 'of his own free will' he agreed to do so.[1] While it is true that Canon Law requires a *metochion* to be in the charge of a priest monk, we may doubt whether the records of the monastery tell the full story; for this rule was frequently disregarded, and if it was the custom in this particular community to apply the rule, why did the monks institute Eustratios in the *metochion* in the first place? Possibly, then, there was a disagreement of some kind between him and the community, and for this reason he thought it prudent to withdraw.[2] John was not present at the agreement of 26 April, and he never in fact returned to the monastery. He married, and became the father of Eustratios the Younger, the *ἐθνομάρτυς*.[3]

Shortly after he left Zartoulida Eustratios was once more drawn into active controversy, at the invitation of another Patriarch, Cyril V of Constantinople.[4] Cyril was entangled in a savage quarrel with his Synod concerning the validity of Latin Baptism, denied by Cyril but upheld by his Metropolitans. So far as is known, Argenti did not actually go to Constantinople in person; but at any rate he supplied Cyril with valuable theological support in the form of a tract against Latin baptism entitled *Manual concerning Baptism*. This he probably wrote in 1754 or 1755; it was published by the newly established Patriarchal Press at Constantinople in 1756, and reprinted in

[1] Ibid., f. 169.

[2] Sarou suggests that Argenti's withdrawal may be in some way connected with the disputes being carried on at this time between the Metropolitan of Chios and the Ecumenical Patriarch, in which the Monastery of Saint John was involved: *Βίος Εὐστρατίου Ἀργέντη*, pp. 46–47; see also Andreadis, *Ἱστορία τῆς ἐν Χίῳ Ὀρθοδόξου Ἐκκλησίας*, pp. 201–7.

[3] Although he never returned to live at Zartoulida, John does not seem to have relinquished all his claims to the *metochion*, for he appears as its legal owner in an entry in the *Moundon Codex* for 28 April 1776. The family connection with Moundon was continued by Anthimos Argenti, *kathigoumenos* on numerous occasions between 1785 and 1822. Anthimos inherited the *metochion* from John.

[4] For Argenti's part in the Baptism Controversy, see Athanasius of Paros, *Ἐπιτομή*, p. 351; English translation in W. Palmer, *Dissertations on subjects relating to the 'Orthodox' or 'Eastern-Catholic' Communion*, pp. 199–201.

the following year at Leipzig under the title *Flower of Piety or a Short Treatise concerning Rebaptism.*[1]

A letter written in 1756 by the French Vice-Consul at Chios to the French Ambassador at Constantinople shows that Argenti was as active in anti-Latin activities in his native Chios as he was abroad. After complaining of the religious and other disturbances on the island during that year,[2] the Vice-Consul continues:

> One of the most effective ways of restoring tranquillity in this country would be to seize *Zanni Petrocokino son of Strati Petrocokino*, *Zanni Skaramanka*, and the doctor *Strati Argenti*, and have them hanged. The country is under the leadership of these three sworn enemies of Catholicism, they are jealous of the French trade, which it would be to their interest to destroy; and it is only by their downfall that it will be possible to avoid that of our religion. . . . Your Excellency will allow me to insist on the punishment of the three chief authors of the persecution; and if you cannot have them punished as rigorously as they deserve, it will at least be necessary to have them exiled to Cyprus.[3]

'It is only by their downfall that it will be possible to avoid that of our religion': the position of Roman Catholicism in Chios at this date must indeed have been precarious, if the activities of three Greek laymen were sufficient to threaten it with extinction!

As far as is known, neither the threat of hanging nor that of exile was carried into effect; although Argenti died not long

[1] The variation in title between the two editions has naturally deceived many bibliographers, who list them as two separate works (see for example P. P. Argenti, *Bibliography of Chios*, pp. 552–3). Argenti's treatise is followed in the second edition (the *Flower of Piety*) by an anonymous letter: a note on p. 90 states, 'The present letter was sent to the Orthodox who are in Serbia by a certain Orthodox teacher'. The letter is not in Argenti's style of writing, and Legrand attributes it to Eugenios Bulgaris (*Bibliographie hellénique . . . au dix-huitième siècle*, vol. i, p. 469).

Sarou, *Βίος Εὐστρατίου Ἀργέντη*, p. 35, suggests that Argenti wrote the *Manual concerning Baptism* between the years 1743 and 1747, but this seems too early a date. The Baptism Controversy did not arise until 1750; and since on p. 85 of the book Argenti refers specifically to 'the inquiry about baptism which has recently arisen', a date after 1750 would appear to be necessary.

The *Manual concerning Baptism* is mentioned by the Roman Catholic Archbishop of Naxos, Apostolic Visitor to Chios in the year 1757, in his official report (Hofmann, *Vescovadi cattolici della Grecia. I. Chios*, p. 122).

[2] For the earlier part of this letter, see pp. 40–41.

[3] P. P. Argenti, *Diplomatic Archive of Chios*, pp. 1010–11.

after this letter was written, there is no reason to believe that his end was anything but natural. The exact date of his death, like that of his birth, is uncertain, but it may have been in 1757;[1] it was certainly before 1760, since the title-page of *Treatise Against Unleavened Bread*, published in that year, speaks of him as 'the *late* Eustratios Argenti'. He bequeathed his library to the hospital at Chios, where it constituted the first public library in the island. It remained there until 1822, when in the course of the massacres by the Turks it was ruthlessly burned.[2]

Argenti's theological activity, as can be seen from the titles of the books which we have mentioned, was limited to a particular field: polemics against the Roman Catholic Church. Even within these limits he considered only certain topics. The Council of Florence, in its *Decretum pro Graecis* (1439), singled out five issues which came later to be known in Orthodox-Catholic polemics as the 'Five Differences': the Procession of the Holy Spirit; unleavened bread; purgatory; the blessedness of the Saints; and the Primacy of the Pope. On the first of these topics, Eustratios makes but a few remarks in passing;[3] he may have felt that it had already been treated so thoroughly in earlier discussions that there was no need for a new book on the subject. It is also true that after the fall of the Byzantine Empire, far less attention was paid to the *Filioque* issue, although Orthodox have never ceased to regard it as an *impedimentum dirimens*. To three of the other points he devoted particular works: on the second he wrote *Treatise against Unleavened Bread* (although here he considers much more than the question of unleavened bread alone); on the third he wrote *Short Treatise against the Purgatorial Fire of the Papists*; and on the fifth he wrote *Concerning the False Infallibility of the Pope of Rome*, and the two other tracts in the same manuscript. (The fourth Difference he does not treat in detail, but it is of course closely related to the question of purgatory.) He also discussed a matter which had not figured as a major topic at Florence: Baptism, which formed the subject of *Manual concerning Baptism*.

[1] See Zolotas, *Ἱστορία τῆς Χίου*, vol. i, Part 2, p. 275; Sarou, *Βίος Εὐστρατίου Ἀργέντη*, p. 50.

[2] A. M. Vlastos, *Χιακά*, vol. ii, p. 122, note 2; P. P. Argenti, *Bibliography of Chios*, p. xvii.

[3] *Σύνταγμα κατὰ Ἀζύμων*, pp. 172, 229, 234.

In the succeeding chapters, we shall consider each of these works in turn. Baptism takes logically the first place; for the rest we shall follow the order adopted by the Council of Florence. As a preliminary, something more must be said about the Baptism Controversy of the 1750s and its antecedents.

III

THE BAPTISM CONTROVERSY

One Lord, one faith, one Baptism. EPHESIANS iv. 3.

(*i*) *The Reception of Heretics*

When in 1750 Patriarch Cyril V insisted that Latin converts should undergo a fresh Baptism on entering the Orthodox Church, he was attacked not only by the Roman Catholic residents in Constantinople, but also—more surprisingly—by many of his own Orthodox flock, who denounced his action as an innovation, contrary to the Canons and the tradition of the Church. Yet in fact the matter was by no means as straightforward as most of Cyril's opponents imagined. The Patriarch, so far from flouting the tradition of the past, could quote weighty precedents on his side, both from the ancient Fathers and from more recent history. It was not the first time since the great schism between east and west that Orthodox had demanded the rebaptism of western converts.[1]

From the fourth century onwards heretics and schismatics who are reconciled to the Church have been divided into three classes:

(1) Some are received into communion without further formality, once they have made an abjuration of their errors and a profession of faith.

(2) Others are required not only to make an act of abjuration and a profession of faith, but to be anointed with the Holy Chrism.

(3) Others again are not only chrismated but baptized, their previous Baptism at the hands of heretics being rejected as invalid.[2]

[1] On the reception of converts into the Orthodox Church, see L. Petit, 'L'entrée des catholiques dans l'Église orthodoxe', *Échos d'Orient*, vol. ii, pp. 129–38; C. A. Papadopoulos, *Περὶ τοῦ βαπτίσματος τῶν ἑτεροδόξων*, in *'Εκκλησιαστικὸς Φάρος*, vol. xiv, pp. 469–83; M. Jugie, *Theologia Dogmatica Christianorum Orientalium*, vol. iii, pp. 103–25; J. N. Karmiris, *Μνημεῖα*, vol. ii, pp. 972–1000, 1009–24; J. Kotsonis, *'Η κανονικὴ ἄποψις περὶ τῆς ἐπικοινωνίας μετὰ τῶν ἑτεροδόξων* , pp. 112–34.

[2] For this threefold division, see the First Canonical Letter of Saint Basil the Great (*Epistle* clxxxviii. 1), written in 374. Basil calls the first group *παρασυναγωγαί*, the second schismatics, and the third heretics, his usage of the term 'schismatic' being somewhat different from that which is normal today.

With an inconsistency more apparent than real, the Orthodox Church has sometimes placed Latin converts in the first class, and sometimes in the second or the third. As an added complication, the practice of the Russians at any given moment has usually differed from that of the Greeks: when the Russian Church rebaptized the Latins, the ancient Patriarchates of the east did not, and vice versa.

Until the fall of Constantinople the Byzantine Church made no specific enactments concerning the reception of Latin converts. Cases of rebaptism were not entirely unknown. As early as 1054 we find Cardinal Humbert protesting that the Greeks 'rebaptizant in nomine sanctae Trinitatis baptizatos, et maxime Latinos';[1] and in 1215 the Lateran Council accused the Greeks of rebaptizing western Christians.[2] But it seems that, at any rate until the fourteenth century, as a general rule neither Baptism nor Chrismation was considered necessary. Writing around 1190, the Byzantine canonist Theodore Balsamon says that a Latin may be admitted to communion 'provided he first declares that he will abstain from Latin doctrines and customs, and provided that he has been instructed according to the Canons, and is willing to be treated in all things as an Orthodox.'[3] There is no suggestion that he must also be chrismated or baptized: evidently Balsamon placed western Christians in the first of the three classes mentioned above, not in the second or the third. But by the fifteenth century many Greeks had become more rigorous, and Saint Mark of Ephesus states that in his day Latins were received by Chrismation.[4] This was not, however, the invariable practice, for even in the fifteenth century instances occur in which Latins were received by simple profession of faith.

The matter was first regularized by a Council held at Constantinople in 1484. The practice described by Mark of Ephesus was formally ratified and a special order drawn up in which Chrismation was required as well as an abjuration and a profession of faith.[5] These regulations remained officially in force for the next three hundred years throughout the four

[1] Migne, *Patrologia Latina* (P.L.), cxliii. 1003B. But can Humbert's statement be relied on? Elsewhere in this same document he is wildly inaccurate.

[2] Canon IV (Mansi, *Amplissima Collectio Conciliorum*, vol. xxii, col. 990).

[3] P. G. cxxxviii. 968B.

[4] Karmiris, *Μνημεῖα*, vol. i, 2nd edition, p. 425.

[5] See Karmiris, op. cit., vol. ii, pp. 987–9.

Patriarchates of Constantinople, Alexandria, Antioch, and Jerusalem.

It seems, however, that in the seventeenth century some Greeks, not content with the regulations of 1484, were not only chrismating Latins but baptizing them. Caucus, Latin Archbishop of Corfu, begins his long list of the 'Errors of the Modern Greeks' (there are thirty-one items in all) by stating, 'They re-baptise all the *Latins* that embrace their Communion.'[1] Leo Allatius, anxious as ever not to exaggerate the divergences between east and west, argues that Caucus has confused Chrism with Baptism: the Greeks chrismate Latin converts but do not baptize them.[2] Father Richard Simon, however, writing later in the same century, maintains that there is more truth in Caucus' charge than Allatius was prepared to allow:

> As to the re-baptising of the *Latins*, it is certain that they have done it in other Places, besides Corfou; and that because of the Enmity they bear towards them, looking upon all their Ceremonies as abominable.[3]

Simon's testimony is confirmed by another French priest, Father François Richard, writing in 1657:

> A number of Greeks do not regard our baptism as good and valid; and although this heresy does not prevail so much on the islands of the Archipelago as in the towns of the mainland, none the less some are to be found who rebaptize those of us Franks who wish to pass over to their rite. But others are content to have them rechrismated (this, however, is another heresy).[4]

It should be mentioned in passing that the Greeks were not the only ones to practise rebaptism. In the middle of the fourteenth century, for example, when the Byzantine Emperor John V Cantacuzene went to Hungary to negotiate an alliance, King Louis of Hungary demanded as a preliminary condition that the Emperor and his suite should undergo Baptism at the

[1] R. Simon, *The Critical History of the Religions and Customs of the Eastern Nations*, p. 5. Simon gives Caucus' list at length: it is a curious document, worth reading in full. Compare M.-J. le Guillou, *Mission et Unité*, vol. ii, pp. 49–51.

[2] *De Perpetua Consensione*, pp. 1262–4.

[3] *The Critical History*, p. 10. But see the criticisms of Simon in *La Perpétuité de la foi de l'Église catholique touchant l'Eucharistie* (by J. Nicole, A. Arnauld, and others), vol. v, Paris, 1782, pp. 108–9, 622–34.

[4] F. Richard, *Relation*, p. 139.

hands of Roman clergy. And when Louis conquered large tracts of Bulgaria, Latin missionaries proceeded systematically to rebaptize the Orthodox there: it is said that eight Franciscan friars administered Baptism to no less than 200,000 persons in the course of fifty days.[1] Similar instances, on a less spectacular scale, seem to have occurred in the eastern Mediterranean during the seventeenth century: Nektarios, Patriarch of Jerusalem, describes a strange case in which (so he alleges) an Orthodox priest was rebaptized by the Franciscans in the Holy City.[2]

From 1484, then, the Greeks normally chrismated Latin converts, although instances of rebaptism occasionally occurred. Affairs in Russia had meanwhile taken a different course. Up to the middle of the fifteenth century there was the same variation there as in the Byzantine Church: sometimes rebaptism, more usually reception by Chrismation or simple profession of faith. But after the Council of Florence (1438–9) rebaptism became more and more frequent, until in 1620 a Council at Moscow formally decreed that all converts must be baptized on embracing Orthodoxy, whatever the previous Baptism which they had received. This decision was reversed by a further Council held at the same city in 1667, which laid down that Russia should henceforth follow the Greek ruling of 1484.[3]

But in the south of Russia the Church of Kiev, which fell under the jurisdiction of the Ecumenical Patriarch, had always followed the 1484 regulations, so that while the Orthodox of Great Russia were rebaptizing converts, the Orthodox of Little Russia merely chrismated them. In the middle of the seventeenth century Kiev went even further than Constantinople: the

[1] See J. Meyendorff, 'Projets de concile oecuménique en 1367', *Dumbarton Oaks Papers*, vol. xiv, p. 154. Father Meyendorff comments: 'Il semble donc que l'usage de rebaptiser les orthodoxes qui embrassaient la foi romaine était courant en Europe centrale et orientale, les souverains de ces pays se souciant assez peu des usages canoniques acceptés à Rome même' (p. 155, note 30).

[2] See the chapter *Περὶ ἀναβαπτισμοῦ τῶν ἐν 'Ιεροσολὴμ φρατόρων*, at the end of his book, *Πρὸς τὰς προσκομισθείσας θέσεις*, pp. 241–55. Possibly there has been some misunderstanding here, and the priest was not actually rebaptized but only sprinkled with holy water.

For further evidence of Latins rebaptizing Greeks, see Simon, *The Critical History*, p. 11, and *Voyage du Mont Liban*, Paris, 1675, p. 226; also Malvy and Viller, *La Confession Orthodoxe de Pierre Moghila*, pp. 156–7.

[3] An extract of the Acts of the Council of 1667 is given in English by Palmer, *Dissertations*, pp. 188–97.

Metropolitan Peter of Moghila, in the Ritual or *Trebnik* which he issued in 1646, laid down that Roman Catholic converts should be received without Chrismation. The *Trebnik* divides converts into the three classes with which we are already familiar: (1) Socinians and Anabaptists (for these, both rebaptism and Chrismation are required); (2) Lutherans and Calvinists (chrismated, but not baptized); (3) apostate Orthodox, Roman Catholics, whether of the eastern or the western rite, and Armenians (received without Chrismation, after an abjuration of their previous heresy). As we should expect, the sacramental theology which Moghila's *Trebnik* presupposes is Latin rather than Greek.[1]

Lutheran and Calvinist converts were for a time treated more rigorously than Roman Catholics. In 1644 Parthenios II, Patriarch of Constantinople, laid down that they must be baptized as well as chrismated.[2] But in 1672 the Council of Jerusalem stated in general terms that heretics who join the Orthodox Church are not baptized;[3] and since no distinction is drawn between Roman Catholics and Protestants, the Council presumably intended this ruling to apply to the latter as well as the former. In Russia the Council of 1667 merely decreed that Latins were to be accepted without rebaptism, but said nothing of Protestants, who continued to be received by Baptism as before. But in 1718 Peter the Great wrote to Jeremias III of Constantinople inquiring about Protestant Baptism, and the Patriarch replied that Lutherans and Calvinists who are received into the Orthodox Church, 'ought to be perfected merely by unction with the Holy Chrism, and not rebaptized.'[4] This ruling was followed henceforward in Russia.

The Greek and Russian Churches, therefore, after two hundred years of divergent practice were once more in substantial agreement at the start of the eighteenth century. Neither Roman Catholics nor Protestants (apart from members of certain extremist sects) were received by Baptism, but they were merely chrismated. The Church of Kiev alone deviated slightly from this general pattern, since here from 1646 onwards

[1] On the *Trebnik* of 1646, see A. Wenger, 'La réconciliation des hérétiques dans l'Église russe', *Revue des Études Byzantines*, vol. xii, pp. 144–75.

[2] Jugie, *Theologia Dogmatica Christianorum Orientalium*, vol. iii, p. 95.

[3] Dositheos, *Confession*, Decree xv.

[4] Karmiris, *Μνημεῖα*, vol. ii, p. 1019; Palmer, *Dissertations*, p. 198.

Roman Catholics—but not, of course, Protestants—were received without Chrismation.

So matters continued until the accession of Cyril V to the throne of Constantinople in 1748.[1] The troubled course of events during his two periods of office illustrates only too well the manifold difficulties of the Ecumenical Patriarchate which we mentioned in the first chapter: suspicion and hostility between the Patriarch and his Synod; unceasing intrigues among the Metropolitans; interference by the Turkish authorities in the affairs of the Church; intervention by diplomatic representatives of the western powers. But in Cyril's career there was an unusual feature: he was very popular with the common people, who played an exceptionally prominent part in the Baptism Controversy of the 1750s.

An active and able administrator, Cyril showed himself from the start a determined opponent of Roman Catholicism. He made his attitude plain in his letter to the citizens of Siphnos

[1] The main sources for Cyril's reign are: S. Makraios, '*Ὑπομνήματα Ἐκκλησιαστικῆς Ἱστορίας*, in Sathas, *Μεσαιωνικὴ Βιβλιοθήκη*, vol. iii, pp. 203–27 (favourable to Cyril; on the whole the most reliable contemporary account); A. K. Hypsilantis, *Τὰ μετὰ τὴν ἅλωσιν*, pp. 365–73; Pankratios Demaris, *Κατάλογος Χρονολογικός*, extracts of which are given by A. P. Palmieri in *Revue Bénédictine*, vol. xxiii, pp. 220–31, and by L. Petit in Mansi, *Amplissima Collectio Conciliorum*, vol. xxxviii, col. 577–81, 585–6 (Demaris writes from the viewpoint of the Metropolitans and is strongly critical of Cyril); the anonymous poem *Destroyer of Errors* (*Πλανοσπαράκτης*), edited by T. H. Papadopoullos, *The History of the Greek Church and People under Turkish Domination*, pp. 275–364 (the poem is violently prejudiced in the Metropolitans' favour); K. Daponte, *Καθρέπτης γυναικῶν*, vol. ii, pp. 178–82, and '*Ἱστορικὸς Κατάλογος*, in Sathas, *Μεσαιωνικὴ Βιβλιοθήκη*, vol. iii, pp. 129–31 (on the monk Auxentios); G. Vendotis, *Προσθήκη τῆς Ἐκκλησιαστικῆς Ἱστορίας Μελετίου*, pp. 87–88 (not reliable). Accounts by western observers: François de Tott, *Mémoires*, vol. i, pp. 50–55; Comte Desalleux, cited by A. P. Palmieri in *Revue de l'Orient chrétien*, vol. viii, pp. 129–32. Accounts by more recent writers: K. Oikonomos, *Τὰ σωζόμενα ἐκκλησιαστικὰ συγγράμματα*, vol. i, pp. 477–80; B. Georgiadis, *Ἀνέκδοτος ἐπιστολὴ τοῦ πρώην Κωνσταντινουπόλεως Καλλινίκου τοῦ Γ'*, in *Ἐκκλησιαστικὴ Ἀλήθεια*, vol. iii, pp. 601–4, 617–20, 633–4; M. J. Gedeon, '*Ἑτεροδιδασκαλίαι ἐν τῇ Ἐκκλησίᾳ Κωνσταντινουπόλεως μετὰ τὴν ἅλωσιν*, in *Ἐκκλησιαστικὴ Ἀλήθεια*, vol. iii, pp. 774–80; A. P. Palmieri, 'La rebaptisation des Latins chez les Grecs', *Revue de l'Orient chrétien*, vol. vii pp. 618–46, and vol. viii, pp. 111–32; A. P. Palmieri, 'Un document inédit sur la rebaptisation des Latins', *Revue Bénédictine*, vol. xxiii, pp. 215–31; L. Petit, in Mansi, *Amplissima Collectio Conciliorum*, vol. xxxviii, cols. 575–634 (gives texts of the official decrees and other documents); E. Savramis, '*Ἡ πρώτη καθαίρεσις τοῦ Οἰκουμενικοῦ Πατριάρχου Κυρίλλου Ε' τοῦ Καρακάλου*, in *Ἐπετηρὶς Ἑταιρείας Βυζαντινῶν Σπουδῶν*, vol. x, pp. 161–86; T. A. Gritsopoulos, '*Ὁ Πατριάρχης Κωνσταντινουπόλεως Κύριλλος ὁ Καράκαλλος*, in *Ἐπετηρὶς Ἑταιρείας Βυζαντινῶν Σπουδῶν*, vol. xxix, pp. 367–89; T. H. Papadopoullos, *The History of the Greek Church and People under Turkish Domination*, pp. 159–264.

and Mykonos in 1749,[1] and in his letter of the following year to the Orthodox of Aleppo, warning them against a certain Maximos, the Roman Catholic claimant to the see.[2] Not content with this, in 1750 he adopted a further method of attack against the Latins: when some Roman Catholics in Galata applied to be admitted into Orthodoxy, he laid down that they were to be received by Baptism. This step was at once attacked by many leading Orthodox as an unjustified innovation, and not unnaturally it provoked a great outcry among the Latins at Constantinople, whether private citizens or official representatives of the Catholic powers. After the usual bribery and intrigue, Cyril's Orthodox and Latin opponents succeeded in expelling him from the Patriarchal throne (May or June 1751).[3]

Cyril's successor, Païsios II, who now became Patriarch for the fourth time, found himself in a precarious position. He had the support of the Metropolitans of the Synod, but was not liked by the common people, who longed for Cyril to return and suspected Païsios of being a secret agent for the Roman Church. Agitation among the people was increased by the preaching of Auxentios, a monk at Katirli (near Nicomedia), who was widely reverenced as a saint and miracle-worker. Soon after Cyril passed into exile, Auxentios began to attack Latin Baptism. Compared by his supporters to the saints of old, Antony and Pachomius, he was reviled by his enemies as 'the instrument of Satan', 'fake monk and false hermit, fake ascetic and false saint', 'an impostor whose past life deserved punishment'.[4] He seems in fact to have been honest and sincere enough, though perhaps used by others less simple than himself for their own ends. Païsios and the Synod tried to dissuade Auxentios from attacking Latin Baptism, but without success; they then proceeded, in July or August, 1752, to issue a formal letter, framed in moderate and courteous terms, which condemned his preaching and confirmed the previous practice, that Latin converts should not be rebaptized. The Synod take their stand

[1] M. J. Gedeon, *Πατριαρχικοὶ Πίνακες*, pp. 642–3. See above, p. 32.

[2] K. Delikanis, *Τὰ σωζόμενα ἐπίσημα ἔγγραφα*, pp. 195–200.

[3] Makraios, *Ὑπομνήματα*, pp. 203–5.

[4] For the favourable comments, see Daponte, *Ἱστορικὸς Κατάλογος*, p. 129. For the views of Auxentios' enemies, see *Planosparaktis*, especially lines 703, 734–5; and Desalleux, in Palmieri, *Revue de l'Orient chrétien*, vol. viii, p. 129.

upon Canon 47 of the Apostolic Canons, which states that a person, once baptized, must not be baptized again; and upon Canon 7 of the second Ecumenical Council (A.D. 381), which divides heretics into two classes, those whose Baptism may be recognised as valid, and those for whom rebaptism is necessary.[1] The Latins, so the letter argues, fall beyond doubt into the first of these two classes.[2] Auxentios took no notice of this letter.

It was an explosive situation, and the Turkish government decided that it was time to intervene. Considering Auxentios a disturbing element in the peace of the Church, they arrested him and put him out of the way.[3] A large crowd of the monk's supporters, thinking that he had been taken to the capital, made their way to Constantinople, and on the morning of Sunday, 6 September 1752—the day after Auxentios' arrest—a serious riot broke out, more by chance than by design. A mob forced its way into the Patriarchate and attacked Païsios, shouting: 'We do not want you! You are an Armenian! why do you not re-baptize? You are a Frank! why do you not rebaptize? We do not want you!'[4] The unlucky Patriarch was dragged from his room, pulled through the market place, and, but for a timely rescue by the Turkish troops, he might well have been killed.

The civil authorities, who had never before faced such an uprising of the populace, were anxious at all costs to calm the mob. They asked the rioters whom they wanted as Patriarch in Païsios' place. The rioters asked for Cyril, who was promptly summoned from his place of exile in Halki and enthroned on

[1] Though no doubts were expressed concerning the authenticity of this canon in the eighteenth century, it is today regarded as a fragment of a fifth-century letter, and not the work of the Council of 381. This, however, does not affect its canonical authority for the Orthodox Church, since (whatever its origin) it was adopted—with slight alterations—by the Council *in Trullo* (A.D. 692) as its 95th Canon.

[2] Text of the letter in Mansi, vol. xxxviii, cols. 587–606.

[3] Accounts differ concerning his fate. Some say that he was strangled, others that he was exiled to Mount Athos but returned to Katirli and lived there in secret. At any rate he took no further part in the Baptism Controversy.

The importance of Auxentios has been somewhat over-emphasised by certain Roman Catholic writers, mostly notably Palmieri and Petit, who rely too much on the evidence of the avowed enemies of Cyril. No doubt the preaching of Auxentios helped to secure Cyril's return to the Patriarchate in 1752, but there is nothing to prove that it was Auxentios who originally inspired Cyril's rebaptism policy; it would rather seem that it was Auxentios who followed Cyril's lead. Whatever the motives of Cyril's anti-Latin measures, he was not merely yielding to pressure from a fanatical monk.

[4] Demaris, in Mansi, col. 578.

the following day, to the unbounded joy of the common people. It was a new thing for the Greeks to impose their will in such a way upon their Turkish masters. The French Ambassador, Comte Desalleux, says that there were more than ten thousand in the mob: 'an insurrection of this sort among the Greeks—something unparalleled, so they say, since the capture of Constantinople—caused such terror in the Seraglio, that the Sultan sent message after message to the Grand Vizier telling him to pacify the riot at any price.'[1] The Turks, regarding Cyril as responsible for the disturbance, planned to execute him when order had been restored, but they were mollified by a large payment of money.

The struggle between Patriarch and Synod was now resumed. Cyril, unchanged by exile and undeterred by opposition, continued his attack on Latin Baptism; in the words of a contemporary, 'he rightly judged an insincere friendship more harmful than open hostility.'[2] On the whole, the Turks were pleased by his hostility to the Roman Catholic Church, 'for the Ottomans think that the Greeks prove more subservient to themselves, the more they are alienated from the Franks.'[3] The Metropolitans maintained that the question of Latin Baptism must be settled not by the Patriarch alone, but by a council of bishops; but to this Cyril would not agree, for he knew that the voting at such a council would not be in his favour.

The Metropolitans at length decided to take the matter into their own hands, without further reference to the Patriarch. On 28 April 1755 they published a Synodical Decree, not aimed explicitly at Cyril, but condemning a book against Latin Baptism by a certain Christopher the Aetolian. In their Decree, they state that this book is contrary to their letter of 1752, as well as to the Fathers and Tradition; they accuse Christopher of misinterpreting Scripture and misrepresenting the teaching of the Roman Catholic Church; and they conclude by calling his work 'loathsome, unlawful, uncanonical, and blasphemous'. The Metropolitans appeal as before to the second Ecumenical Council. They argue that the defects and innovations in Latin Baptism of which Christopher complains have long been known to all; this, however, did not prevent the Council of 1484 and

[1] Palmieri, *Revue de l'Orient chrétien*, vol. viii, p. 131.

[2] Makraios, *Ὑπομνήματα*, p. 217. [3] Makraios, op. cit., p. 219.

later writers such as Dositheos from accepting the Latins into Orthodoxy without rebaptism. The Synodical Decree of 1755 is far more outspoken than the letter of 1752, and it is evident that during the three intervening years the opposed parties had hardened in their attitudes. The Metropolitans were becoming exasperated. In their condemnation of Christopher's book, they also condemned all who accepted his arguments—a direct challenge to the Patriarch.[1]

Cyril retorted with two formal pronouncements. The first, issued in June 1755, took the form of an Anathema against the Synodical Decree of 28 April and against all who accepted it. The traditional curses are invoked against any who should prove recalcitrant and continue to uphold the Decree:

> May they be cut off from the Lord God Almighty, and accursed, and without forgiveness, and may their corpses remain undissolved and swollen.[2] Rocks and iron shall be dissolved, but not they. May they inherit the leprosy of Gehazi and the noose of Judas; may they lament and tremble upon earth, as Cain did; may the wrath of God be upon their heads and their portion with the traitor Judas and the Jews who fought against God; may the earth gape apart and swallow them up, as once it swallowed Dathan and Abiram; may the Angel of the Lord persecute them with the sword all the days of their life; may they be subject to all the Patriarchal and Synodal curses, and under judgement of the eternal Anathema, and condemned to the fire of Gehenna. Amen.

[1] Text of the Decree in Mansi, vol. xxxviii, cols. 609–18.

[2] Bodily incorruptibility is double-edged. According to popular Greek thought not only the bodies of saints but also those of sinners are sometimes miraculously preserved from dissolution. But while the saints' bodies remain in their natural state, sinners' corpses become hideously discoloured and swollen; thus an incorruptible body is evidence either of great holiness or of its exact opposite, according to the character of the incorruption. As an example of the second type, see the story current on Mount Athos concerning the three Latinizing monks: their bodies, so it is said, refused to decay after death; eventually they were placed in a cave, and there the blackened corpses remain to the present day, the hair and nails still growing. Similar stories circulate on the Holy Mountain concerning the fate of the Greek abbot of Saint Panteleimon, who in the early nineteenth century allowed the monastery to pass into the hands of the Russians; when his grave was dug up so that his bones could be stored in the mortuary chapel, the body had to be hastily reburied, since it was entirely undissolved. A book by an Athonite monk published in 1903 states that this is 'unfortunately an incontrovertible fact, which those living at the Russian monastery confess with horror'! To avoid embarrassment on another such occasion, so the Greeks alleged, the Russians had the corpse boiled: this at any rate would get the bones clean. See Riley, *Athos or the Mountain of the Monks*, pp. 246–7; Dawkins, *The Monks of Athos*, pp. 305–7.

These curses, it should be remembered, were directed not against the Latins but against the Greek Metropolitans and their party. A note is subjoined to the Anathema, recording its reception by the people:

Let everyone know for certain that when this letter was read at the pulpit in the holy churches of Christ, then the chosen people of God, the holy nation, the royal priesthood, that is, the pious and Orthodox Christians, with one accord cried out *Anathema* three times. And the voice of the people, when it thundered, was as the voice of many waters thundering mightily, according to the Scripture.[1]

A month later, in July 1755, Cyril followed this up with a second pronouncement, entitled *A Definition of the Holy Church of Christ defending the Holy Baptism given from God, and spitting upon the baptisms of the heretics which are otherwise administered.* The Definition opens with a preamble upon Baptism, its necessity, its symbolism, and its inner meaning. It next states the exclusive character of the Orthodox Church; she is the one true Church, and therefore she alone possesses the divine sacraments:

We know only One, our own, Holy, Catholic, and Apostolic Church, and acknowledge only her sacraments, and consequently only her divine Baptism; but as for the baptisms of the heretics, which are not administered as the Holy Spirit commanded the holy Apostles, and as the Church of Christ has ever continued to administer them up to the present day, but are the inventions of corrupted men, we judge them to be utterly at variance with the whole Apostolic tradition and alien to it, and we reject them by common decision; and those who join us from the heretics, we receive as unordained and unbaptized.

The conclusion follows:

Therefore we also, following the holy and divine ordinances, judge that the baptisms of heretics are to be rejected and abhorred, as disconsonant with the Apostolic and divine commandment and alien to it, and as waters which cannot profit (as Saints Ambrose and Athanasius the Great say), nor give any sanctification to such as

[1] The Anathema was first printed in 1756 in Ῥαντισμοῦ Στηλήτευσις, pp. xxv-xxix. It has been several times reprinted: for example in Mansi, vol. xxxviii, cols. 605–9, and in Papadopoullos, *The History of the Greek Church and People under Turkish Domination*, pp. 440–3. There is some disagreement whether the Anathema should be dated January or June 1755: see Papadopoullos, op. cit., pp. 192–4.

receive them, nor avail at all to the washing away of sins. And such of the heretics as are baptized with a baptism which is no baptism we receive as unbaptized when they join the Orthodox faith, and without any risk we baptize them, according to the Canons of the holy Apostles and Councils, on which rests firmly the Holy, Apostolic, and Catholic Church of Christ, which is the mother of us all.[1]

The Definition is signed not only by Cyril but by two other Patriarchs, Matthew of Alexandria and Parthenios of Jerusalem. Silvester of Antioch refused to sign, not because he disagreed with the Definition as such, but because Cyril lacked the support of his Metropolitans.[2]

The Anathema and the Definition differ markedly in style and character. The Anathema is impressive chiefly as a piece of vituperation; the Definition displays a firm grasp of theology. The Anathema sometimes employs popular Greek rather than the strict ecclesiastical style; the Definition is far purer and more elevated in its diction. There is a possible explanation for this. In the earlier stages of the Baptism Controversy Cyril, although supported by the people, had no learned theologians on his side. His opponents the Metropolitans used Kritias, the Grand Ecclesiarch, to draft their statements, but Cyril had no such scholar on whom he could rely. Matthew of Alexandria—a close supporter of Cyril—advised him to seek the help of Eustratios Argenti; this Cyril did, and Argenti—as we have seen—in answer sent his *Manual concerning Baptism*, a concise and trenchant tract on the controversy, which the Patriarch printed at Constantinople without delay.[3] Perhaps Argenti helped Cyril in other ways as well: at any rate the difference in quality between the Anathema and the Definition is easily explained, if we supposed that Argenti had no hand in drafting the

[1] The Definition, like the Anathema, was first printed in 1756 in '*Ραντισμοῦ Στηλήτευσις*, pp. 173–6; reprinted in Mansi, vol. xxxviii, cols. 617–22; Papadopoullos, pp. 444–7; Karmiris, *Μνημεῖα*, vol. ii, pp. 989–91; and elsewhere. English translation in Palmer, *Dissertations*. pp. 199–202.

[2] K. Karnapas, *'Ιάκωβος ὁ Πάτμιος*, pp. 238–40. Silvester and Cyril seem in fact to have been on close and friendly terms with one another.

[3] Athanasius of Paros, *'Επιτομή*, p. 351. The other leading Greek theologian of the time besides Argenti, Eugenios Bulgaris, also supported Cyril over the question of rebaptism, although he does not seem to have played an active part in the actual controversy (doubtless he had troubles enough of his own at the Athonite School). Athanasius of Paros relates that he heard Eugenios commend Argenti's book on Baptism very highly indeed.

Anathema, but drew up the Definition or at least assisted in its composition.

But the promulgation of an Anathema from the Ecumenical throne, followed by a Definition bearing the signatures of three Patriarchs, was insufficient to suppress opposition. Since spiritual sanctions had failed, Cyril invoked the civil arm and secured from the Turkish authorities an order that the Metropolitans leave Constantinople forthwith and retire to their dioceses.[1] Although contrary to precedent, it was scarcely in itself unreasonable to ask that they should look after their own flocks rather than engage in intrigues at the capital. A few Metropolitans were firmly escorted to their destinations, but the leaders of the opposition succeeded in defying the order: they escaped into hiding and continued their operations underground, with active assistance from the Roman Catholics in Constantinople.[2] Their efforts were eventually rewarded in January 1757 when Cyril was deposed, once more the victim of an alliance between Latins and Orthodox.

But now the populace again took an active part in the course of events. They remained loyal to the memory of the deposed Cyril, and rendered entirely ineffective the rule of his successor, Kallinikos IV, a man of some learning and Cyril's chief opponent among the Metropolitans. So unpopular was the new Patriarch that he could neither preside at the Liturgy nor appear in public without heavy protection from the Turkish police. On the day after his accession, the feast of Saint Antony the Great, the congregation set upon him in church with cries of 'Out with the Frank!' and nearly killed him. Kallinikos for his part did little to conciliate the people, and concluded his sermon on one occasion by telling his flock that they could all go to the Devil.[3] He was widely regarded as a traitor to the Orthodox cause and a secret Papist; the fact that he was friendly

[1] It had long been normal for the Metropolitans to reside not in their eparchies but in the capital, where they composed the *synodos endimousa* or permanent synod. It is interesting to compare Cyril's action with that of a Byzantine Patriarch, Athanasius I (1289–93, 1303–9). A strict reformer, Athanasius suppressed the *synodos endimousa*, sending the bishops off to their dioceses, and restored the ancient practice whereby the bishops met only once a year. (J. Meyendorff, *Introduction à l'étude de Grégoire Palamas*, Paris, 1959, p. 35.)

[2] For a vivid picture of the Metropolitans in hiding, see the second part of *Planosparaktis*; for Roman Catholic help, see F. de Tott, *Mémoires*, vol. i, pp. 51–53.

[3] F. de Tott, *Mémoires*, vol. i, p. 55.

with many of the Roman Catholics in Constantinople naturally gave colour to this charge. Strongly though he disapproved of Cyril's Definition, Kallinikos did not venture to repeal it: with popular feeling already tumultuously aroused against him, he dared not exacerbate it further. He soon fell out of favour even with his former supporters in the Synod, and was deposed in July 1757 after a reign of no more than six months. He was exiled to Sinai, but left secretly in 1762 and settled at his native town of Zagora in Thessaly, where his library is still to be found.[1] Bitter feelings subsided under the next Patriarch, Seraphim II, who pursued a policy of conciliation. But Cyril's Definition remained in force, and although it was not always strictly applied, officially it was neither revoked nor modified for more than a hundred years.

(ii) *Strictness and Economy, Sprinkling and Immersion*

What were Cyril's motives for condemning Latin Baptism? A passage towards the end of the *Manual concerning Baptism* supplies the answer, or at any rate part of the answer. Having completed his discussion of the theological issues involved, Argenti suddenly turns to the religious situation in his own time, and launches into a vehement protest against Latin 'aggression':

> So far as they are able, the Papists persecute and make war upon the Orthodox. Without any fresh cause or open justification they have seized the churches of Saint Anne at Ancona, of Saint Athanasius at Rome, of the *Panagia* at Leghorn, the three churches at Messina, and others elsewhere in the west, which the Orthodox in their poverty had founded with great trouble and expense; they have seized the Holy Places at Jerusalem; resorting sometimes to direct attacks and sometimes to deceit, they have utterly destroyed three of the Patriarchal Thrones; they have compelled the Orthodox

[1] The Zagora collection contains a number of manuscript tracts relating to the Baptism Controversy, in most cases the work of Kallinikos himself. See the catalogue of the Library in *Νέος Ἑλληνομνήμων*, vol. xiv, Athens, 1917, pp. 80–85, 90 (Mss. 102–5, 108–10, 114, 122). Two works are directed specifically against Argenti:

(1) Ms. 110: *Ἔκθεσις συναπτική* (*sic*) *περὶ τῶν ἑπτὰ μυστηρίων καὶ ἀπάντησις εἰς τὰ κεφάλαια τοῦ Ἀργέντη*.

(2) Ms. 114: *Καλλινίκου πατριάρχου Ἀντίρρησις εἰς τὰ Ἀργέντου* (*sic*).

Unfortunately I have not been able to see the special study on Kallinikos IV by C. Dyovouniotis (published at Athens, 1915).

in Hungary and Poland to subscribe to Popery; and what further harm could they have done to the Orthodox, which they have not done?[1]

Complaints such as this are frequent in Greek writers of the Turkish period. Deeply conscious of their inferiority to Rome in worldly power and outward organization, the Greeks looked round them and saw on all sides a progressive erosion. Brest-Litovsk in 1596, Antioch in 1724, and now Alexandria: how much further would the Latin advance be carried? Orthodoxy seemed to be losing ground continually before the 'cruel and bloodthirsty wolves of the west', as one Greek historian at this time calls them.[2]

Such is the context in which the Baptism Controversy and Cyril's Definition of 1755 must be seen, as part of the general struggle between Orthodoxy and Rome. Doubtless Cyril feared that at Constantinople, as at Antioch, a crypto-Roman party would grow up among the Orthodox and finally try to seize control. Perhaps these fears had some foundation: Cyril's great opponent, Kallinikos, as we have seen, was friendly with Roman Catholics, while several of the banished Metropolitans (Kallinikos included) were sheltered by Latin residents in Constantinople. Cyril was therefore anxious at all costs to curtail Roman Catholic influence in his Patriarchate and to prevent further infiltration by the Latins.

Such must have been the end which he had in view when he declared Latin Baptism entirely invalid. He wanted to underline the gulf between Orthodoxy and Rome, to draw a sharp line of demarcation between the two; he wanted to make it absolutely clear to his flock that the Orthodox Church, and it alone, was the true Church of Christ. Surely prospective converts would reflect more carefully before seceding to Rome, if it were forcibly emphasized that the Orthodox Catholic Church was the sole treasury of valid sacraments; surely waverers would think again, when they reflected that the Pope, for all his vaunted infallibility, had never even been baptized! Faced by Latin encroachments and infiltration, Cyril answered by setting up a wall of partition between Orthodoxy and the west. Aware of his weakness on the temporal level, he took refuge in an inflexible and uncompromising assertion of the spiritual claim

[1] *'Εγχειρίδιον περὶ Βαπτίσματος*, pp. 85–6.
[2] Makraios, *'Υπομνήματα*, p. 217.

of the Orthodox Church to be the exclusive possessor of Baptism.

Yet to treat the whole incident simply as a matter of ecclesiastical politics would be a grave injustice to Cyril V and Eustratios Argenti. Certainly Cyril had practical motives for condemning Latin Baptism, but his action was not merely a piece of religious opportunism, for he could also defend it on serious theological grounds. To these points of theology we must now turn.

First, something must be said about the term 'rebaptism', which for convenience we have used on the preceding pages. Strictly speaking such a word begs the whole question at issue. Orthodox believe, just as firmly as Roman Catholics, that Baptism is conferred once for all, and cannot be repeated without grave sacrilege and blasphemy. Thus when Greeks and Russians insisted on baptizing converts, they did not think of this as a second Baptism, but argued that the converts in question had never been truly baptized in the first place. They would have said that they were not 'rebaptizing' but 'baptizing' them.

But on what grounds did Cyril V and his party reject all western baptism as null and void? Their basic position is clearly stated in the Definition of 1755, quoted above. 'We know only One, our own, Holy, Catholic, and Apostolic Church, and acknowledge only her sacraments, and consequently only her divine Baptism.' The line of thought is evident: there is only one Church—the Orthodox Catholic Church; the sacraments are God's gift to the Church, and therefore cannot be conferred by any who are outside her; heretics and schismatics are outside the Church, and so cannot possess the sacrament of Baptism or any other. Since, then, their previous Baptism is invalid, converts from the west on embracing Orthodoxy must undergo the true Baptism of the Church.

This view of sacramental validity is usually termed the Cyprianic, for it finds its classic expression in the works of Saint Cyprian of Carthage. Some fifty years before Cyprian, the same view had already been expounded by another African writer, Tertullian, in the *De Baptismo* (a work belonging to his Catholic period, probably composed around 198–200):

> For us there is one, and only one Baptism, since there is only one God and one Church in the heavens. . . . But the heretics have no participation in our teaching: the very fact that they are excluded

from communion proves them to be outsiders. . . . We and they do not have the same God, nor the one—that is to say the same—Christ; and so we cannot both have the one Baptism, for it is not the same.

So Tertullian draws his conclusion: since heretics do not possess the one Baptism, they lack the power to confer Baptism on each other.[1]

Tertullian is closely followed by Saint Cyprian:

> Baptism cannot be common to us and the heretics, for we do not have God the Father in common, nor Christ the Son, nor the Holy Spirit, nor the faith, nor the Church itself. Therefore those who come from heresy to the Church ought to be baptized, so that they may be made ready for the Kingdom of God by divine regeneration in the lawful, true, and unique Baptism of Holy Church.[2]

'The Church is one,' Cyprian argues, 'and only those who are in the Church can be baptized';[3] 'we say that no heretic or schismatic whatsoever has any power or right' (*nihil habere potestatis ac iuris*).[4] 'No heretic or schismatic whatever possesses the Holy Spirit . . . and he who does not possess the Holy Spirit cannot in any sense baptize. . . . All without exception who come over to the Church of Christ from the adversaries and the antichrists are to be baptized with the Baptism of the Church.'[5]

Such was the sacramental theology which lay behind Cyril's Definition of 1755. The Cyprianic view can be summarized in a syllogism:

> True sacraments cannot exist outside the Church;
> Heretics and schismatics are outside the Church;
> Therefore, heretics and schismatics do not possess true sacraments.

But the west since the time of Saint Augustine has normally adopted a somewhat different position. Augustine accepted Cyprian's minor premise but denied his major. Unlike Saint Cyprian, he distinguished between *validity* and *regularity*: a sacrament performed by heretics or schismatics, while irregular and illegitimate, is none the less technically valid provided that certain specified conditions are fulfilled. Whereas Cyprian denied heretics both the *ius* and the *potestas* to perform the

[1] *De Baptismo*, 15.
[2] *Epistle* lxxiii. 21.
[3] *Epistle* lxix. 2.
[4] *Epistle* lxix. 1.
[5] *Epistle* lxix. 10–11.

sacraments, Augustine denied them the first, but not necessarily the second. A number of Orthodox theologians, particularly in Russia during the past three centuries, have inclined towards the Augustinian view; but in general the position of the Orthodox Church has been Cyprianic and non-Augustinian. The Cyprianic view was taken for granted by most Greek writers in the eighteenth century, Argenti included; and the Cyprianic view is still followed by the standard Greek manuals of theology in use today.

Two qualifications must be added here. First, although the Augustinian theory predominates in the west, it is not accepted universally: in some Roman Catholic writings an approximation can be found to the Cyprianic position.[1] Secondly, while most Orthodox continue in the main to hold the Cyprianic theory, many of them today would slightly modify the austerity of Cyprian's conclusion. Augustine accepted Cyprian's minor premise but denied his major; it is equally possible to accept the major but deny the minor, and it is this that many Orthodox at the present moment have chosen to do. They continue to claim that the Orthodox Church is the one, true Church; they still uphold the basic Cyprianic principle that outside the Church there can be no sacraments; they make no use of the Augustinian distinction between validity and regularity. But they would yet add that many non-Orthodox Christians are still in some sense members of the Church,[2] so that it is possible that in certain cases these non-Orthodox Christians possess true sacraments. But Greek Orthodox in the eighteenth century such as Cyril V and Eustratios Argenti were less lenient in their reasoning: like Cyprian—and for that matter, like most of the Fathers—they would simply have said that heretics and schismatics are outside the Church, and left the matter at that.

But if Orthodox on the whole follow a Cyprianic view of sacramental validity, why do they not *invariably* baptize all converts? How can we explain the apparent inconsistency over the reception of Latins? If western sacraments are invalid, why is it that western Christians have often been accepted without Baptism?

[1] See F. Clark, *Anglican Orders and Defect of Intention*, London, 1956, p. 10, note 1.

[2] Compare the *vestigia* theory of the Church propounded by recent Roman Catholic writers.

Greek Orthodox of the eighteenth century, and of the present day, answer by invoking the double principle of 'strictness' or 'exactness' (ἀκρίβεια) and of 'economy' (οἰκονομία). 'Two kinds of guidance and correction are observed in the Church of Christ,' wrote Saint Nicodemus of the Holy Mountain in the *Pidalion* (the standard modern Greek work on Canon Law, originally published in 1800). 'The first is named strictness, the second economy and condescension. With these two the stewards of the Spirit guide souls to salvation, sometimes with one and sometimes with the other.'[1] From the point of view of strictness all non-Orthodox sacraments are null and void, but in virtue of her power of stewardship or economy the Church in particular cases, when receiving members of other communions, can decide to treat these sacraments as valid. From 1620 to 1667 the Russians followed the way of strictness and baptized all converts; after 1667 they applied economy and received Roman Catholics by Chrismation. The Church of Kiev, on the other hand, from 1646 exercised a still more generous measure of economy and admitted Roman Catholics without Chrismation. Constantinople applied economy from 1484 to 1755, when it was decreed that henceforward the way of strictness should be adopted.

What is meant by 'economy'? The Greek word *oikonomia* signifies literally 'the management of a household or family' (so Liddell and Scott), *oikonomos* meaning 'a steward'. In a religious context economy can be exercised either by God or by the Church. It indicates God's management of His creation, His providential ordering of the world, and in particular the supreme act of divine providence, the Incarnation, which the Greek Fathers call 'the Economy' without further qualification. But since the activity of the Church is integrally connected with the action of God in Christ, the term economy can be used not only of what God does but of what the Church does. In a wider sense it covers all those acts whereby the Church orders the affairs of her own household and provides for the needs of her members. In a narrower sense it signifies the power to bind and loose, conferred by the risen Christ (John xx. 21–22); and so it covers any departure from the strict rules of the Church, whether in the direction of greater rigour or (as is more usual) of greater

[1] *Pidalion*, p. 34.

leniency. Economy therefore includes much of what is covered by the western term 'dispensation', but it extends to many other things as well and is not simply a term in Canon Law.

To understand the application of economy to non-Orthodox sacraments, three points should be kept in mind:

(1) The basic principle underlying its use is that the Church has been endowed by God with authority to manage the affairs of her own household. She is therefore in a full sense the steward (οἰκονόμος) and sovereign administrator of the sacraments; and it falls within the scope of her stewardship and economy to *make valid*—if she so thinks fit—sacraments administered by non-Orthodox, *although such sacraments are no sacraments if considered in themselves and apart from the Orthodox Church.* Because a person's Baptism is accepted as valid—or rather made valid by economy—when he becomes Orthodox, it does not therefore follow that his Baptism was valid *before* he became Orthodox. The use of economy implies no recognition of the validity of non-Orthodox sacraments *per se*; it is something that concerns only the sacraments *of those entering the Orthodox Church.*

(2) Economy is only exercised where the formal conditions necessary for validity are present. The Church, when she makes valid a sacrament originally administered outside her borders, naturally demands that the external requirements essential for the accomplishment of the sacrament shall have been previously fulfilled: that is to say, those actions must have been already performed which, had they been carried out within the Church, would have sufficed to ensure a valid sacrament. Orders, for example, could not be recognized if the Christian body in question had lost the outward elements of the Apostolic succession.

(3) The aim of all the 'economic' activities of the Church is practical—the salvation of souls. The Church has rules, but unlike the Old Israel she is not rigidly bound to them; it lies within her power of household management or economy to contravene the strict letter of the law if the purpose of the law will thereby be more fully achieved. (Closely linked with the concept of economy is the idea of *philanthropia*, loving kindness towards men: the Church, following the example of Jesus her Head, makes allowance for the weakness of men and seeks never to lay on them a burden too heavy for them to bear.) Because

economy is something practical, its application need not be everywhere the same, but may be changed according to circumstances. Its exercise in one way at a particular time and place creates no binding precedent for the future, and does not commit the Church to following the same practice in other places and at other times. 'He who does something by economy', wrote Theophylact of Bulgaria, 'does it, not as good in an unqualified sense, but as profitable on a particular occasion.'[1]

This helps to explain the apparent inconsistency of Orthodox when receiving converts. From the viewpoint of modern western sacramental theology, the variations in the Greek and Russian attitude towards Latin Baptism indicate a state of intolerable vagueness and confusion. But once the principle of economy is taken into account—so Orthodox argue—it will be realized that there has been no change in Orthodox ecclesiology or sacramental theology, but simply a change in disciplinary practice. The Orthodox Church has sometimes been willing to use economy, and sometimes not; but this does not mean that her sacramental teaching as such has varied.

Guided always by practical considerations, Orthodoxy has exercised economy when this aided the reconciliation of heterodox without obscuring the truths of the Orthodox faith; but when leniency seemed to endanger the well-being of the Orthodox flock, exposing them to infiltration and encouraging them to indifferentism and apostasy, then the Church authorities resorted to strictness. Thus the Orthodox Church—so it can be argued—accepted Latin Baptism by economy or refused to do so, depending on how far Orthodox were in danger from Latin propaganda.[2] It is understandable that the Russians should have employed strictness in 1620: they remembered what had happened to the Orthodox of Little Russia a short time before in 1596; Moscow itself had recently been occupied by a Roman Catholic nation, the Poles; Church and State were weak and disorganized after the Time of Troubles. Fifty years later the danger had passed and the use of economy could safely be decreed. In 1484 the Greeks could afford to exercise economy,

[1] Quoted in *Pidalion*, p. 36.

[2] Compare C. Androutsos, *Δογματική*, pp. 332–3: 'This difference [viz., between the Greeks and Russians in the matter of receiving converts] can be explained on historical grounds, since it is to be attributed to the scandalous proselytising efforts of the Papists at different times in Turkey and Russia.'

for the Union of Florence had been firmly repudiated and there was little danger of its revival. But in the eighteenth century, confronted with the inroads made by western missionaries and with a grave schism at Antioch, they felt it necessary to follow the way of strictness. Even if this explanation slightly over-simplifies the historical facts, it is by no means entirely invalid. Seen in this way, the Definition of 1755 is not as revolutionary as it appears at first. Whereas economy had previously been exercised, three Patriarchs now decided that its use within their spheres of jurisdiction should be suspended.[1]

Hitherto we have considered the Orthodox attitude towards the Baptism of heretics in general, and we have seen how the Cyprianic position can be modified in practice by the principle of economy. But there is another side to the question. Orthodox objected (and still object) to Latin Baptism not only on the ground that it is ministered by heretics, but also because—so they maintain—the rite itself is not properly performed. Even if the Latins administered the sacrament in the correct way, as the Orthodox do, it would not follow that their Baptism is valid; but in fact (so Orthodox argue) it is *not* administered in the

[1] In the account given above of economy in its application to non-Orthodox sacraments, I have followed for the most part the conclusions of the *Pidalion*. This is, however, an exceedingly intricate subject over which many Orthodox writers disagree; and there are a large number of connected problems which it has not been possible to discuss here. Certain Russian theologians altogether reject the idea of a sacrament being 'made valid' by economy.

For Greek views on economy, see the elaborate discussion by Jerome Kotsonis in his two books, '*Η κανονικὴ ἄποψις περὶ τῆς ἐπικοινωνίας μετὰ τῶν ἑτεροδόξων*, and *Προβλήματα τῆς 'Εκκλησιαστικῆς Οἰκονομίας*. In English, see the following: J. A. Douglas, *The Relations of the Anglican Churches with the Eastern-Orthodox*, London, 1921, pp. 55–69; J. A. Douglas, 'The Orthodox Principle of Economy, and its Exercise', *The Christian East*, vol. xiii, London, 1932, pp. 99–109; F. Gavin, *Some Aspects of Contemporary Greek Orthodox Thought*, pp. 262–7, 292–305. Compare also the interesting and perceptive letter by Ephrem of Athens, dated 9 August 1755, which discusses the Baptism Controversy in terms of strictness and economy (Mansi, vol. xxxviii, cols. 629–34).

For two sharply contrasted Russian points of view, see: (1) Metropolitan Antony (Khrapovitzky), Presiding Bishop of the Russian Church in Exile, 'Why Anglican Clergy could be received in their Orders', *The Christian East*, vol. viii, London, 1927, pp. 60–69 (accepts the Greek idea of economy, much as presented in the *Pidalion*); (2) Patriarch Sergius (Starogorodzky), 'The Meaning of the Apostolic Succession in non-Orthodox Faiths', in E. R. Hardy, *Orthodox Statements on Anglican Orders*, New York, 1946, pp. 52–70; and 'L'Église du Christ et les communautés dissidentes', *Messager de l'Exarchat du Patriarche russe en Europe occidentale*, No. 21, Paris, 1955, pp. 9–32 (Sergius vigorously criticizes the Greek position and the views of Metropolitan Antony).

correct way, and this constitutes a further reason for repudiating Latin Baptism.

In Christendom today there are three different ways in which Baptism is performed:

(1) immersion (κατάδυσις);

(2) affusion or infusion (ἐπίχυσις), when water is poured over the candidate's forehead;

(3) aspersion (ῥαντισμός), when water is not poured but sprinkled on the candidate's forehead.

Immersion may be total or partial: in total immersion the body is completely submerged in the water; in partial immersion it is usually submerged only as far as the waist, but water is at the same time poured over the head, so that it flows down over the entire body and 'envelopes' it. Thus what distinguishes partial immersion from affusion is the fact that in partial (as in total) immersion the water flows over the *whole* body, as it were 'burying' the candidate (an important point to which we must shortly return); in affusion the water flows only over a part of the body (the forehead).

Baptism by immersion was the normal practice in the early Church, while Baptism by affusion was allowed in cases of necessity.[1] The Orthodox Church today continues to follow the original practice of immersion, and Baptism by affusion is only permitted in exceptional cases—for instance, if the candidate is seriously ill or in danger of death; Baptism by aspersion is not recognized by Orthodoxy. But from the twelfth century onwards the Latins have come by degrees to abandon the rite of immersion, although the practice persisted in some places at least until the end of the Middle Ages. It is not very clear why immersion was abandoned in the west: presumably affusion was preferred, because it is more convenient.[2] According to the present regulations of western Canon Law, both immersion and affusion are valid forms of Baptism. Affusion is the normal practice, but immersion is not forbidden. Baptism by aspersion is

[1] For immersion in the early Church, see *Didache*, vii, 1–3; *Hermas*, *Sim*. IX. xvi. 4; Tertullian, *De Corona*, 3 (P. L. ii. 79A); Basil, *De Spiritu Sancto*, xv (35); Jerome, *In Ep. ad Eph. comm*. II. iv. 5–6 (P. L. xxvi. 496B), etc. For infusion, see *Didache*, vii. 3.

[2] Some western writers defend the innovation by arguing that immersion has lethal effects: 'Graeci hac sua nimia copia aquae Baptismi aegros infantes suffocant, et illis mortem accelerant.' (Petrus Arcudius, *De Concordia*, p. 24.)

condemned as strictly irregular, but it may still on occasion be valid.[1]

It was in the fourteenth century that Orthodox first began to notice the abandonment of immersion by the west,[2] and henceforward this became a standard topic in Greek works against the Latins. Mitrophanis Kritopoulos in his *Confession* presents the normal Orthodox arguments:

> When people are baptized, it is necessary for them to be immersed three times in the water, since the Saviour, when he was baptized, in the same way 'went down' into the water on our behalf. 'And immediately *coming up* out of the water, he saw the heavens rent asunder' (Mark i. 10). He 'came up' because he had first gone down. The Apostles also followed the same practice when baptizing. Philip and the eunuch '*went down* into the water, . . . and when they *came up* out of the water, the Spirit of the Lord carried Philip away' (Acts viii. 38–39). Furthermore Baptism is an icon and likeness of the death of the Saviour: 'For if we have become united with him through the likeness of his death . . .' and so on (Romans vi. 5). How else shall we be likened to him in his death, unless we be hidden three times in the water, just as he was hidden three days in the earth? 'We were buried with him through Baptism' (Romans vi. 4): that is, by being hidden in the water we were buried with the Lord. At Baptism, therefore, the priest immerses the candidate three times in the water.[3]

Kritopoulos thus regards immersion as a necessary, not merely an optional, part of the baptismal sacrament, basing his case upon the evidence of Scripture (the Baptism of Christ in the Jordan; Baptism as administered by the Apostles; the inner meaning of the sacrament, as a mystical death and resurrection in Christ). These are arguments which we shall find more fully developed in Argenti's *Manual*.

On the necessity of immersion, Dositheos is much more emphatic than Kritopoulos:

> The three immersions form an essential part of the rite of Baptism, as handed down by the Apostles and the Holy Fathers. If any are not

[1] See *Rituale Romanum*, tit. II, cap. i, *De sacramento baptismi rite administrando*, sect. 10.

[2] See a tract dating from this century by Matthew Angelos Panaretos, *On the Absurdities of the kakodox Latins*, *Περὶ τῶν ἀτοπημάτων τῶν κακοδόξων Λατίνων*, cited in Jugie, *Theologia Dogmatica Christianorum Orientalium*, vol. iii, p. 63.

[3] Karmiris, *Μνημεῖα*, vol. ii, pp. 530–1.

baptized in this way, unless it be for some necessary cause, then they run the risk of being altogether unbaptized. Thus the Latins, who perform Baptism by sprinkling and omit the three immersions, are guilty of mortal sin.[1]

According to Orthodox sacramental theology, therefore, immersion constitutes an integral part of Baptism, not to be omitted save in emergencies (and even then only in virtue of the principle of economy). Orthodoxy believes that Christians of the west have done wrong to adopt as their normal practice a special exception intended only for emergencies. Even during periods when they have recognized by economy the Baptism of western converts, Orthodox have never ceased to protest against what they regard as its defects.

It should, however, be mentioned that in many parts of Russia during the seventeenth and eighteenth centuries affusion was permitted as a *regular* alternative to immersion, even when no sickness or special emergency was involved. Peter of Moghila's *Orthodox Confession* (in the original version of 1640), together with his *Little Catechism* of 1645, both treat immersion and affusion as alternatives, standing on the same level as one another.[2] This regular usage of affusion seems originally to have crept into the Orthodox Church from mere carelessness and ignorance; in the few instances where it received some degree of official recognition (as with Peter of Moghila), this was the result of direct western influence. As late as the beginning of the last century, some Russian manuals still spoke of affusion as a normal alternative to immersion; but today the regular usage of affusion is generally condemned by Orthodox authorities as an abuse.[3]

Such is the theological background to the Baptism Controversy of the 1750s. It is now time to look more closely at Argenti's *Manual*.

[1] *'Ιστορία περὶ τῶν ἐν 'Ιεροσολύμοις πατριαρχευσάντων*, p. 525. Roman Catholics in the west normally baptize by infusion, not aspersion; here Dositheos falls into an error common among Orthodox controversialists. This, however, does not affect his argument, for Orthodoxy objects just as much to infusion (save in emergencies) as to aspersion.

[2] The passage in the *Orthodox Confession* was corrected by Syrigos, so that the Greek version of 1642 speaks only of Baptism by immersion: see above, p. 12.

[3] For further evidence, see Jugie, *Theologia Dogmatica Christianorum Orientalium*, vol. iii, pp. 74–76.

(iii) Manual concerning Baptism

Argenti is concerned to write a short tract for the times, and so he deliberately limits his discussion to certain particular topics. He does not raise the wider question of the invalidity of all non-Orthodox sacraments *per se*, presumably because he takes this point for granted; he simply discusses the defects in the actual rite of Baptism, as administered by the Latins. These defects, he argues, are so serious that they make any legitimate exercise of economy impossible. Latin Baptism could be recognized by economy only if the essential conditions of Orthodox Baptism were observed in the Roman Church: it is Argenti's conviction that these essential conditions are lacking. Some Orthodox, he writes in his opening chapter, 'wish to vindicate the false baptism (ψευδοβάπτισμα) used by the westerners of the present time, defending it with empty and vain arguments, and with unlawful acts of economy and condescension. But when we exercise economy, we must not break the law.'[1] In other words, economy has its limits: as Eulogios, Patriarch of Alexandria, expressed it in the ninth century, 'Acts of economy can rightly be employed only when no harm is thereby done to the dogma of piety.'[2] Gregory VI of Constantinople wrote to the same effect in 1837:

> We can use economy in particular circumstances, but we must not break the law: such is the teaching which we have received. God has entrusted us with the strict observance of His holy laws, and we are not permitted, on the pretext of economy, to bring them into contempt, nor to alter the ancient rulings of the Fathers.[3]

This, then, is Argenti's theme—to show that the defects and corruptions of Latin Baptism are such as to place it outside the scope of any lawful application of economy. The corruption to which he devotes his main attention is, as we should expect, the omission of the act of immersion. Some Orthodox controversialists laid special emphasis on the threefold repetition of the immersion, but Argenti insists not on the number of immersions but on the fact of immersion as such; nor does he say anything about the form of words used in the Latin baptismal rite, another feature attacked by many Orthodox. Limiting himself,

[1] Ἐγχειρίδιον περὶ Βαπτίσματος, pp. 6–7.

[2] P. G. ciii. 953B.

[3] Quoted in Kotsonis, Προβλήματα, p. 35.

then, to this question of immersion, he argues its necessity on three grounds: the first, philological (the meaning of the word 'baptism'); the second, theological (the symbolism of the sacrament); the third, historical (the practice of the Church).

The first ground is briefly expounded in a single chapter. The Greek term 'baptize' (*βαπτίζειν*) is linked philologically with the word 'dip' (*βάπτειν*). Both alike necessarily carry the idea of plunging or sinking something in water, an idea also implied by the Latin equivalent *immergere*. A person who has merely had water poured or sprinkled on his forehead has in no sense been 'dipped' or 'plunged' in the water: how then can it be claimed that he has been baptized? If we look no further than the meaning of the word 'baptism', we can yet see at once that the Latins are unbaptized.[1]

In his second section, on the symbolism of the sacrament, he begins with the usual distinction between the two elements in every sacrament: what is outward and visible (*τὸ αἰσθητῶς ὁρώμενον*) and what is inward and invisible (*τὸ νοητῶς καταλαμβανόμενον*).[2] He later defines a sacrament as 'an action of the Catholic Church, ordained by God, in which through visible things and actions we are raised to the apprehension of things intelligible and spiritual; for visible things, as Saint John of Damascus says, are the symbols of things intelligible.'[3] What then is the inward meaning of Baptism and what outward symbols does it employ? Argenti answers that a whole range of inner meanings can rightly be given to the sacrament—washing, rebirth, renewal, enlightenment, the forgiveness of sins, sanctification; but beyond these there is another meaning, more fundamental than them all, which provides the key to the understanding of the rest:

> In its primary and general signification Holy Baptism means burial and resurrection with Christ. This is the meaning on which our Lord, his Apostles, and the Catholic Church primarily insisted, and which they primarily teach. For through the visible action of Baptism, the believer, who sees a man being buried in the water and coming out of the water, is raised to a more divine apprehension, so that he conceives the person baptized as buried and rising with Christ. Hence Jesus Christ called his own burial a 'baptism', saying to the sons of Zebedee in the tenth chapter of Mark, 'Can you drink

[1] *Ἐγχειρίδιον περὶ Βαπτίσματος*, pp. 7–8. [2] Ibid., p. 8. [3] Ibid., p. 28.

the cup which I drink, and be baptized with the baptism with which I am baptized?' And again, 'You shall indeed drink the cup which I drink, and be baptized with the baptism with which I am baptized.' By the cup, Our Lord here hints at his death by martyrdom, as he made absolutely clear shortly before his Passion, and by baptism he refers to his own burial. Such is the conception that he wishes us to have concerning Christian Baptism: that being baptized in the water we are buried with Christ, and going up or coming out of the water we are raised with him.[1]

Baptism, then, symbolizes burial and resurrection with Christ, and the outward acts whereby this is represented are the descent or immersion into the water and the ascent or emersion out of it. But Latin Baptism, by omitting immersion, has destroyed that correspondence between outward act and inward meaning which is essential to the nature of a sacrament.

To support his interpretation of baptismal symbolism, Argenti appeals to Scripture, to the Church's liturgical observance, and to Tradition in general. From Scripture he cites the obvious texts: Mark x. 38–39, Luke xii. 50, Romans vi. 3–13, and Colossians ii. 12.[2] Turning next to the Church's liturgical observance, he argues that one would expect the sacrament of Baptism to be celebrated above all upon the feast of Epiphany, which commemorates Christ's Baptism in Jordan at the hands of John, but in fact this is not so: the baptismal Liturgy *par excellence* is the Liturgy of the Paschal Vigil on Holy Saturday, when the Church is concerned with the burial and resurrection of Christ. This was the time in the primitive Church when the catechumens were baptized, and the texts for the day are still full of references to Baptism: in place of the *Trisagion*, for example, are sung the words, 'As many of you as were baptized into Christ . . . ', and the Epistle is from Romans vi. 3–11. On Easter morning the connection between burial and Baptism is again suggested in the words of the *Troparion*, 'Yesterday I was buried with thee, O Christ. . . .'[3] In the third place, Argenti

[1] *Ἐγχειρίδιον περὶ Βαπτίσματος*, pp. 9–11.

[2] Ibid., pp. 11–14. See particularly Romans vi. 3–4: 'As many of us as were baptized into Christ Jesus were baptized into his death; we were buried with him by baptism into death, so that as Christ was raised from the dead by the glory of the Father, we also might walk in newness of life'; and Colossians ii. 12: 'You were buried with him in baptism, in which you were also raised with him.'

[3] Ibid., pp. 14–15, 57–61.

continues, there is the evidence of Tradition in general—of the Canons, the Councils, and the Fathers of the Church; but this is so abundant that detailed citation would be out of the question. As one example out of many he quotes in full the second *Mystagogical Catechesis* of Saint Cyril of Jerusalem.[1]

Scripture, Liturgy, and Tradition all insist that Baptism signifies burial and resurrection with Christ; and this cannot be symbolized save by immersion. Furthermore, if we consider a second and subsidiary aspect of baptismal symbolism, we shall again be confronted with the necessity for immersion. Whatever language we use about Baptism—whether we call it washing, rebirth, renewal, regeneration, forgiveness of sins—these are things which concern the whole man, not some single member or part of the man. But if the spiritual effects of Baptism concern the whole man, then its outward application ought to involve the whole body. Only so can we preserve the vital correspondence between visible sign and inward meaning.[2] Immersion is therefore indispensable:

> Since, then, we have shown in the second chapter that westerners are unbaptized so far as the normal usage of the word 'baptism' is concerned, so now . . . we see that they are also unbaptized from the viewpoint of what is signified by the sacrament.[3]

In his third section Argenti turns to the actual practice of the Church: how, as a matter of historical fact, has the Church administered Baptism? He takes three examples from the practice of the New Testament. Christ, at his Baptism in Jordan, is distinctly said to have 'come up' from the water, and if he 'came up' he must also have 'gone down', that is, been immersed. John required 'much water' when baptizing at Aenon (John iii. 23), but much water would scarcely be necessary for Baptism in the Latin manner. Philip, when he baptized the eunuch (Acts viii. 36–39), required a pool: the eunuch, a person of consequence, accompanied doubtless by a retinue of servants, would have travelled with supplies of drinking water in skins—but this was not sufficient for Baptism.[4]

From later history Argenti selects a description given by

[1] Ibid., pp. 17–25, quoting Cyril, P. G. xxxiii. 1077–84.

[2] Ibid., pp. 48–49, 56–57.

[3] Ibid., p. 28.

[4] Ibid., pp. 30–36.

Alcuin of the baptismal rites at Rome on Holy Saturday around the year 800. Alcuin's narrative shows that the custom of Rome in the days of her orthodoxy, before she separated herself from the Catholic Church, was very different from her present practice.[1] Baptism by immersion, once observed by Rome, is still (so Argenti adds) the universal practice of eastern Christians, not only Orthodox but Nestorian and Monophysite. The appeal to history therefore substantiates the Orthodox case:

> We see therefore that westerners are also unbaptized so far as the practice of the Church is concerned; and let this be the third conclusion.[2]

The appeal behind the present customs of the Roman Church to her earlier observance is frequently found in Argenti, as in other Orthodox writers. The Orthodox Church, so they argue, is the *Church of Tradition*, the Church which continues loyal to the ancient ways and preserves the Apostolic faith unchanged. The Roman Church, on the other hand, is a *Church of innovation* (καινοτομία), alike in faith and in worship. The Latins have inserted a new phrase in the Ecumenical Creed; they have tampered with the administration of the sacraments; arbitrarily and unilaterally they have made changes which, if permissible at all, would require the approbation of the whole Church and not only of a single Patriarch; they have set their own judgement above the practice of antiquity and the common mind of primitive Christendom. Argenti would have appreciated Khomiakov's view of the Pope as the first Protestant, the father of German rationalism.[3]

The word 'baptism', the symbolism of the sacrament, and the

[1] Ἐγχειρίδιον περὶ Βαπτίσματος, pp. 36–39, quoting *De divinis officiis*, 19 (P. L. ci. 1219CD).

[2] Ibid., p. 41.

[3] See A. Khomiakov's pamphlet, published under the pseudonym 'Ignotus', *Quelques mots par un chrétien orthodoxe sur les communions occidentales*, Paris, 1853 (reprinted in *L'Église latine et le Protestantisme*, Lausanne, 1872).

This 'argument from innovations' is, of course, also used by Roman Catholics against Protestants. See Owen Chadwick, *From Bossuet to Newman. The Idea of Doctrinal Development*, Cambridge, 1957, p. 13: 'Anyone who reads in the little handbooks of controversy, lively little handbooks published by the troopers of the Counter-Reformation, will see that, howsoever the argument may be adorned and illustrated, the key apologetic weapon is the appeal to an unchanging tradition. Protestants have varied in the faith: you have changed the doctrine and practice of a thousand years. You are a new religion. Where was your church before Luther?' *Mutatis mutandis*, Orthodoxy says much the same to Rome.

history of its administration have all been examined, and the conclusion is everywhere the same: Baptism without immersion is no Baptism. The exercise of economy therefore cannot be allowed:

> Since this partial Latin Baptism is to be rejected as an invention of heretics, . . . the Catholic Church never having accepted it as Baptism, for this reason the Orthodox of the Eastern Church baptized the Latins who came to Orthodoxy. But subsequently the Orthodox, assailed by war on every side, lacking strength, finding neither relief, nor freedom, nor the chance to refuse, abandoned this practice, and the zeal of Orthodoxy grew cold; hence some of the Orthodox baptized Latins secretly, while others—using economy as an excuse—thought it enough merely to anoint them with Chrism.[1]

It is thus Argenti's belief that the exercise of economy towards a Baptism not performed by immersion (save in cases of emergency) cannot under any conditions be theologically justified, and if economy has in fact been used in regard to such Baptisms during the past, this is to be explained by cowardice, human weakness, and pressure from foreign enemies. He rejects the more moderate view set forth above, according to which economy is sometimes admissible and sometimes not, depending on variations in the historical situation; on the contrary, he regards economy as always inadmissible.[2] But can this extreme thesis be reconciled with past history? Two important councils, at Constantinople in 1484 and at Moscow in 1667, gave special consideration to the question and were fully aware of the defects in Latin Baptism which Argenti has emphasized. Neither of these councils was exposed to foreign pressure or acted from fear of Papist reprisals; why then did they reach conclusions so different from those of Argenti?

In the *Manual concerning Baptism*, Protestant baptism falls under the same condemnation as Latin:

> The Latins can perhaps urge as an excuse the monarchy and tyranny of the Pope of Rome, under whom as prisoners they are compelled to serve; for the Greeks are enslaved in body, the Latins in soul as well; and therefore they are afraid to correct their Baptism and the rest of their corrupted sacraments. But as for the offshoots of the Latins, who are free throughout the world, the Lutherans and

[1] *'Εγχειρίδιον περὶ Βαπτίσματος*, pp. 49–50.

[2] Since the time, that is to say, when the west abandoned immersion.

the Calvinists, what convincing excuse can *they* urge in their defence? Thus they deserve ridicule and utter derision when they boast and make great claims, the Lutherans calling themselves 'Evangelicals', on the ground that they are governed and believe according to the Gospel, while the Calvinists have taken the name 'Reformed', claiming to have reformed and improved their faith. . . . But the Evangelicals ought first of all to have made their Baptism agree with the Baptism of the Gospels. . . . and the Reformed Christians should first have reformed their Baptism. . . . You will find nothing else evangelical or reformed in either of them, except empty names only and a presumptuous imposture; for the rest they have been transformed from bad to worse, and therefore they are both (with their parents the Latins) unbaptized.[1]

In their revolt from Rome, the Protestants were at times too conservative, and inherited uncritically many things which they would have done better to reject![2]

While condemning Latin and Protestant Baptism, the *Manual* says nothing of the Armenians and other Monophysites, who stood in a peculiar position; for although Armenian Baptism was administered by heretics, yet it retained the use of immersion. The Definition of 1755 condemns the Baptism of all heterodox without distinction, and makes no exception of the Armenians. But on Argenti's principles there would be no insuperable objection to the exercise of economy in their case.

Orthodox and Latin Baptism are so different, Argenti concludes, that either one or the other must be rejected; it is impossible to accept both:

One Lord, one faith, one Baptism, the Apostle says; and the Apostolic Church teaches us to confess one Baptism to remission of sins; if, then, Baptism is one, it follows that either the Baptism of the Catholic and Eastern Church is correct, or else the other Baptism of the west; since the two are not one, because they have no relationship and likeness with one another, so that one of the two must be rejected. For they cannot both be worthy of acceptance.[3]

Compare the words of Cyprian:

A strange presumption has led certain of our colleagues to maintain that those who have been dipped (*tincti*) by the heretics ought not to

[1] Argenti, op. cit., pp. 53–56.

[2] Compare E. L. Mascall on 'going behind the Middle Ages': *The Recovery of Unity*, London, 1958, pp. 2–3, 40, *et passim*.

[3] Argenti, op. cit., pp. 77–78.

be baptized when they join us. They state as their reason, that there is *one* Baptism: but this one Baptism is in the Catholic Church, for the Church is one and there cannot be Baptism outside the Church. For since there cannot be two Baptisms, if the heretics truly baptize, they themselves (and not we) have the one Baptism.[1]

Argenti adds:

From what has been said throughout this short treatise, we conclude correctly that westerners who come to Orthodoxy require to be baptized. This practice is not called 'rebaptism' (ἀναβαπτισμός), for we do not baptize them because we think that they have been badly baptized, but because they are entirely unbaptized. For what they call 'baptism' is falsely so named, and is a false baptism.[2]

Once again he is following Cyprian closely:

There is one Baptism, that of the Catholic Church, and in consequence we do not 'rebaptize' but baptize all those who, coming as they do from adulterous and unclean water, require to be washed and sanctified by the true water of salvation.[3]

Argenti, intending the *Manual* primarily for popular reading, does not deal specifically with the question of Canon Law. But it is not difficult to imagine his probable explanation of the two Canons to which the Metropolitans had appealed in their letter of 1752. Canon 47 of the Apostolic Canons he would have found irrelevant. It says that a person *if already baptized* must not be baptized again; but the Latins in Argenti's opinion have not been baptized. It is also beside the point to introduce the division of heretics into two classes as laid down by Canon 7 of the second Ecumenical Council. For none of the heretics in the first class, whose Baptism is recognized, had changed the manner of administering Baptism. On the other hand the Eunomians are placed in the second class, and it is surely significant that they had tampered with the baptismal rite, using only one immersion instead of three. If Eunomian Baptism is rejected, how much more that of the Latins who have omitted immersion altogether!

In addition to the *Manual concerning Baptism* there is a second book, published anonymously at Constantinople in the same year (1756), under the title *Sprinkling Pilloried*,[4] which since the

[1] *Epistle* lxxi. 1. [2] Op. cit., p. 86. [3] *Epistle* lxxiii. 1.

[4] The first edition was printed at Constantinople in 1756 on the newly established Patriarchal Press; a second edition appeared at Leipzig in 1758, with Greek

middle of the last century has been ascribed to Eustratios Argenti.[1] There is a general similarity between the two works, as is to be expected since they were written at the same time and with the same situation in mind; but as soon as they are compared in detail the attribution of *Sprinkling Pilloried* to Argenti appears exceedingly improbable. The *Manual* is written in correct ecclesiastical Greek, it is clearly arranged, logical in argument, and relevant in its quotations. *Sprinkling Pilloried* is a tedious and incoherent compilation, marred by mistakes of grammar and spelling, sometimes lapsing into popular language, ill-arranged, repetitive, and inclined to quote texts which have nothing to do with the immediate point. It is hard to believe that the same man wrote both books.

Phrases characteristic of the one work are largely or entirely absent from the other. The *Manual* often speaks of 'false baptism' (ψευδοβάπτισμα) or 'baptism falsely so called' (ψευδώνυμον βάπτισμα), terms which do not occur in *Sprinkling Pilloried*. While the *Manual* naturally uses the word 'sprinkling' (ῥαντισμός, ῥάντισμα), it does not couple it with the epithets in which the other book delights: 'papic', 'satanical', 'foul-smelling' (παππικός, σατανικός, δυσώδης). One of the favourite phrases in *Sprinkling Pilloried* is 'salt-water sprinkling and saliva with salt' (ἁλμυρὸς ῥαντισμὸς καὶ σὺν ἅλατι σίελος); the nearest that the *Manual* comes to this is a single reference to 'saliva, salt, and spittings',[2] while it offers no parallel to the expression in *Sprinkling Pilloried*, 'the deadly foul smell and worms in the Papic sprinkling'. This last expression is typical of the violent and futile abuse which

and Latin in parallel columns and an Italian version at the foot of the page. There is some confusion over the number and dates of the editions: see P. Lambros, 'Ἱστορικὴ πραγματεία περὶ τῆς ἀρχῆς καὶ προόδου τῆς τυπογραφίας ἐν Ἑλλάδι, in Χρυσαλλίς, vol. iv, pp. 169–72; Sarou, Βίος Εὐστρατίου Ἀργέντη, pp. 92–101; Papadopoullos, *The History of the Greek Church and People under Turkish Domination*, pp. 395–8.

[1] The earliest authorities to ascribe *Sprinkling Pilloried* to Argenti, so far as I can discover, are the Editor of the 1848 edition of S. Vlasopoulos, 'Ἡ ὑπεράσπισις τῆς Γραικικῆς Ἐκκλησίας, in the Foreword, pp. κδ'-κε'; and K. Oikonomos, Τὰ σωζόμενα ἐκκλησιαστικὰ συγγράμματα, vol. i, pp. 477, 511 (written in 1850, though not published until 1862). William Palmer, in his *Dissertations*, published 1853, also attributes the book to Argenti. A. K. Demetrakopoulos, Ὀρθόδοξος Ἑλλάς, p. 182, regards the work as Argenti's, as do most subsequent bibliographers. The question is discussed in full by T. H. Papadopoullos, op. cit., pp. 398–403, who does not consider Argenti the author; his arguments seem to me conclusive.

[2] Ἐγχειρίδιον περὶ Βαπτίσματος, p. 39.

disfigures every page of *Sprinkling Pilloried.* Argenti was no friend to the Church of Rome, but he wrote with a dignity and restraint entirely lacking in *Sprinkling Pilloried.*[1]

But who then, if not Argenti, is the author of the book? The most likely person is Christopher the Aetolian, whose writings, as we have seen, were condemned by the Metropolitans in April 1755; unfortunately the Synodal Decree does not mention them by title, but there is nothing in its language which would exclude *Sprinkling Pilloried.* Two pieces of evidence support this attribution. First, the poem *Destroyer of Errors* (*Πλανοσπαράκτης*) tells how Christopher shut himself up in the house of a wealthy woman and after five months produced a book 'like himself', which the poet then describes as follows: 'it begins with saliva, and having filled it up with saliva, he ends it with saliva again. . . . He has saliva dribbling all down his beard.'[2] This is highly appropriate as a characterization of *Sprinkling Pilloried*, which constantly alludes to the use of saliva in Latin Baptism. Secondly, Zaviras—who on the whole is trustworthy and accurate, and who was writing not long after the events—says of Christopher: 'He wrote a well-known book on the rebaptism of the Latins, which was published in Greek, Latin, and Italian, perhaps at Leipzig, in quarto. This book was written in a spirit of such animosity against the Latins as even Caiaphas himself would not have used in writing against Christ our Lord.'[3] The only book connected with the Baptism Controversy which was published in Greek, Latin, and Italian was the second edition of *Sprinkling Pilloried*, issued at Leipzig in 1758.

Thus the attribution to Christopher the Aetolian, although

[1] Three lesser points may be mentioned:

(1) Is *Sprinkling Pilloried* perhaps an early work, written by Argenti before he had acquired his later theological skill and discretion of speech? This is not a satisfactory solution. The book was obviously written with the Baptism Controversy in mind, and in any case it quotes from a work only published in 1750 (see P. Lambros, op. cit., pp. 169–72).

(2) On its title page, *Sprinkling Pilloried* employs the metaphor of a spider's web: the same metaphor is used by Argenti on the title page of his 1708 Notebook. This, although curious, is scarcely by itself conclusive.

(3) The Monastery of Kykko in Cyprus supervised the second editions both of the *Manual* and of *Sprinkling Pilloried.* But it does not follow that all the books edited at the Kykko Monastery were written by the same person.

[2] Lines 1682–91. For Christopher the Aetolian as the possible author of *Sprinkling Pilloried*, see T. H. Papadopoullos, op. cit., pp. 396–404.

[3] *Νέα Ἑλλάς*, p. 552.

not proven, fits the facts such as they are. It is easy to see how the book came in time to be attached to Argenti's name. Argenti was well known, Christopher comparatively obscure; and since it was remembered that Argenti had written on the Baptism question at Cyril's request, the anonymous *Sprinkling Pilloried* was understandably ascribed to him.

There is no reason to regret the dissociation of *Sprinkling Pilloried* from Argenti's name, since as a work of theology its value is negligible. A few instances of the author's normal methods of argument are of interest, as forming a vivid contrast with the polemics of Argenti. No reproach is too bad for the Latins: they have the Devil for their father, and their Church is an adulteress to Satan; their Baptism is not merely worthless but positively harmful, making those who receive it more filthy than before.[1] 'Just as God gave the holy font that He might thereby wipe away original sin and lead up to heaven those who have been born again by Baptism; so too Satan invented satanical sprinkling, saliva, and salt, that through these things he might hinder the wiping away of original sin, and lead down to hell those who have been sprinkled, spat upon, and salted.'[2] The Latin clergy shave—thus making clear to all that they do not possess the true priesthood—and they abstain from marriage 'that they may have the use of many mistresses'.[3]

But however worthless as theology, *Sprinkling Pilloried* is highly revealing as a picture of the way in which most Greeks thought and felt during the Turkish period.[4] The works of Eustratios Argenti, while not without limitations, were written by a man of marked intellectual ability, deeply learned in the Fathers of the Church, who had travelled and studied in the west. But there were not many such writers in the Greek world of the eighteenth century. The author of *Sprinkling Pilloried* is far more typical as a controversialist of the time—half-learned, lacking an academic training in the west, vehement but confused. There is a striking contrast between the two. It is with no small relief that one turns from the troubled pages of *Sprinkling Pilloried* to the more orderly and measured polemic of Argenti's *Manual*.[5]

[1] *Ῥαντισμοῦ Στηλήτευσις*, pp. 15, 67, 55.

[2] Ibid., p. 78.

[3] Ibid., pp. 137–8.

[4] As is rightly pointed out by T. H. Papadopoullos, op. cit., pp. 402, 438.

[5] In the Library at Zagora, Thessaly, there are two copies of *Sprinkling Pilloried* with critical annotations by Kallinikos IV, Cyril's successor and his chief opponent.

(*iv*) *The Sequel*

After 1755 a prospective convert could choose between two different ways of entering the Orthodox Church. He could knock at the Russian door: in that case he was assured that in view of his previous Baptism, a new Baptism at Orthodox hands was not required. Or he could travel a few hundred miles to the south: he was then told by the Patriarch of Constantinople that a new Baptism was absolutely necessary and could on no account be omitted. It is little wonder that westerners unfamiliar with the idea of economy should find this variation in practice disconcerting. Surely (they argued) if we are unbaptized, we cannot be received without Baptism; and if we are already baptized, it is a shocking thing that you should insist on baptizing us again. The Orthodox themselves were in general unaware of any discrepancy: Greeks and Russians each went their own way, taking little notice of one another. It is a curious fact that in all the literature of the Baptism Controversy there is scarcely a single reference to the Moscow Council of 1667. Even though, in view of the flexibility with which economy can be applied, the Greeks were under no obligation in 1755 to do what the Muscovites had done since 1667, yet the precedent of the previous century was surely not wholly irrelevant.

Two years after the Greek decision of 1755, the divergence between Moscow and Constantinople became still more marked, for in 1757 the Church of Russia adopted the principles of Moghila's *Trebnik* and no longer demanded that converts from Roman Catholicism should be chrismated.[1] At Moscow and Saint Petersburg a Roman Catholic was admitted after a simple profession of faith; at Constantinople and Jerusalem every sacrament which he had received was administered afresh.

In the *Pidalion*, compiled by Saint Nicodemus of the Holy

'This', writes Kallinikos in one copy, 'is the unscholarly book which threw the Church into confusion, brought persecution and exile upon the Synod, and put the teachers of the Church to flight. . . . This book caused great scandal, introducing division between father and son, between man and wife.' And in the other copy he says: 'If this book did not have the icon of the most Holy Mother of God of Kykko at the front, and at the end the theological chapters by Mark of Ephesus and Nicetas of Byzantium, it would deserve to be burnt and thrown into the sea, as blasphemous and heretical. . . . Flee from it, as from the dragon and from the spiritual serpent, lest hereafter you burn eternally in the fire of punishment.' (See C. Dyovouniotis in *Νέος Ἑλληνομνήμων*, vol. xii, Athens, 1915, pp. 216–17.)

[1] Jugie, *Theologia Dogmatica Christianorum Orientalium*, vol. iii, p. 116.

Mountain in the last years of the eighteenth century, the full rigour of the 1755 Definition is applied: 'Latin Baptism is baptism falsely so called, and for this reason it is acceptable neither on the principle of strictness, nor on that of economy.' The author recommends the *Manual concerning Baptism*: 'On the question of the three immersions, how necessary and indispensable they are, we say nothing. Whoever wishes may read—indeed, it is essential that he should read—the *Manual* of the most abundantly learned and wise Eustratios Argenti.' The *Pidalion* explains the past uses of economy in much the same way as Argenti. Formerly, when the Byzantine Empire was in the last stages of disintegration, the Orthodox dared not offend the Papacy and the powers of the west; but now that 'Divine Providence has set a guardian over us' (the Turk), there is no need to fear the Pope any longer. 'Economy, therefore, should be set aside and its place taken by strictness and the Apostolic Canons.' But in one respect, the *Pidalion* is slightly less outspoken than Argenti's *Manual*. For while it condemns the employment of economy in the present and is unenthusiastic about its use in the past, it does not actually say in so many words that economy towards Latin Baptism (i.e. Baptism without immersion) has always been, and must necessarily be, unlawful and unjustified.[1]

Yet not every Greek writer at this time is as stringent as Nicodemus. In a book first published in 1800 (the year in which the *Pidalion* appeared), in answer to a letter by a Jesuit, S. Vlasopoulos writes:

> And now I will defend the Greeks from the accusation which you shoot at them, to the effect that they believe Latin Baptism to be invalid. No, my dearest friend, I do not do you this wrong. You say in section 74 of your letter that 'some of the eastern clergy either from malice or from ignorance condemn the Baptism of the Italians as invalid'. But these few clergy do not by themselves constitute the Greek Church. Our Church has never dreamt of believing Latin Baptism to be invalid.[2]

[1] *Pidalion*, pp. 35–36. When he speaks of the Apostolic Canons, Nicodemus is thinking in particular of Canon 46: 'Any bishop or priest who accepts the baptism or sacrifice of heretics we order to be deposed; for what agreement has Christ with Belial? Or what part has the believer with the unbeliever? (2 Corinthians vi. 15)'

[2] *'Η ὑπεράσπισις τῆς Γραικικῆς 'Εκκλησίας*, p. 196. This work first appeared in Italian in 1800; the Greek translation, from which I quote here, was published in 1848.

In view of the decree of 1755, the last sentence seems disingenuous, to say the least. It is hard to believe that Vlasopoulos knew nothing whatever of Cyril's Definition.

On a notable occasion in 1846 the 1755 decree was followed strictly: when a Uniate Metropolitan in Syria, Macarius of Diyārbakr, applied with a large part of his flock for admission to the Orthodox Church, he and his people were all baptized. But two points in this incident should be noted. First, before the decision to baptize was taken, there was some discussion about the matter at Constantinople: the authorities did not at once apply the 1755 ruling as a matter of course. Secondly, it is possible that the decision was due not only to theological but to practical considerations: the authorities at Constantinople may have had grounds for doubting the good faith of Macarius, and perhaps wished to test his sincerity by making his entry to Orthodoxy as difficult as possible.

Five years after this an interesting test case arose. In 1851 a Fellow of Magdalen College, Oxford, and Deacon in the Church of England—William Palmer—applied to the Patriarch of Constantinople to be received into the Orthodox Church. Palmer had stayed several times in Russia and was a close friend of the Russian theologian Alexis Khomiakov. He was thus well aware that the Russians received converts without rebaptism, and was horrified at the inconsistency between them and the Greeks in this matter. He was not satisfied by an appeal to the principle of economy, which he dismissed as a species of ecclesiastical opportunism: he terms it 'connivance' and 'hypocritical dissimulation'.[1] He therefore submitted a lengthy 'Memorial' to the Ecumenical Patriarch, in which he pointed out that the Greek practice was comparatively recent—dating only from 1755—and also drew attention to the divergence existing between the Greeks and the Russians. In view of these facts he asked that if the Greeks insisted on rebaptizing him, he might be allowed to regard this second Baptism as *conditional*. (Evidently he was not willing to accept the Cyprianic principle of the absolute invalidity of heretical sacraments!) The Patriarch replied briefly and firmly:

[1] W. J. Birkbeck, *Russia and the English Church*, pp. 149, 179. Compare Palmer's pungent remarks on pp. 146–7.

There is only one Baptism. If the Russians allow any other, we know nothing of that, and do not recognize it. Our Church knows only one Baptism, and that without any detraction, addition or *change* whatever.[1]

Evidently the views of Eustratios Argenti still reigned supreme. Discouraged by this rebuff, in 1855 Palmer became a Roman Catholic; but in the Profession of Faith which he drew up at the time of his reception he made the somewhat surprising statement that in 'his own private judgement' he found himself unable to accept the teaching of the Roman Church 'not only on certain particular doctrines, *but even respecting the Definition of the Church*, on which they depend'![2]

But where Palmer drew back, other Anglicans advanced undeterred. In 1856 a member of the Church of England, Stephen Hatherly (or Hatherley), was received into Orthodoxy by rebaptism at the Greek church in London. He was subsequently ordained at Constantinople in 1871, returning to England where he started an English Orthodox mission.[3]

In 1870 a further instance of rebaptism occurred in England, during the visit of Alexander Lykourgos, Archbishop of Syros and Tinos. Lykourgos had a series of very cordial encounters with the Bishop of Ely, Mr. Gladstone, and other Anglicans, but he greatly astonished and distressed his English friends by rebaptizing and reordaining one James Chrystal, a priest of the Protestant Episcopal Church of America. Naturally he was pressed for some explanation of this act. George Williams, Fellow of King's College, Cambridge, has described how he and Lykourgos discussed the question at length:

My friend Mr. Beresford Hope and myself took the liberty of expressing to the Archbishop our deep regret at the view which he and his Church took of the invalidity of our Baptism; which he had himself countenanced by re-baptizing and re-ordaining a priest of the American branch of the Anglican Church. After long discussion, we were comforted to find that, while charging our form of Baptism,

[1] Palmer, *Dissertations*, p. 183. Oikonomos discusses the Palmer affair in *Τὰ σῳζόμενα ἐκκλησιαστικὰ συγγράμματα*, vol. i, pp. 492–515. Palmer does not appear to have read Argenti's *Manual*, but in *Dissertations*, pp. 163–77, he summarizes large parts of *Sprinkling Pilloried*, which he takes to be the work of Argenti.

[2] Birkbeck, *Russia and the English Church*, p. 180 (the italics are Palmer's own).

[3] See G. Florovsky, in R. Rouse and S. C. Neill, *A History of the Ecumenical Movement*, London, 1954, p. 206.

as now commonly administered by affusion, with such grave irregularity as to justify the iteration of the Sacrament, he still admitted its validity as conveying the Grace of Regeneration and the Gift of the Holy Spirit. This admission he was so good as to put in writing, at our earnest request, and for the general satisfaction of English Churchmen.[1]

But the Archbishop's 'Statement in vindication of the rebaptism of an Anglican priest' is not, perhaps, quite as explicit as George Williams implies, nor as comforting for 'English Churchmen':

> The Orthodox Eastern Church, holding it as a ruling and foremost principle, to preserve inviolate whatsoever she has received from the Holy Ecumenical Councils, suffers no change or alteration to be made, either in the doctrines (δόγμασιν) or in the very forms (τύποις) of the Holy Sacraments; consequently, since by the seventh Canon of the second Ecumenical Council it is enacted that every Baptism which is not performed by threefold immersion is invalid, whenever members of other Churches come to her communion, it is her practice to ask them whether they have received the perfect Baptism by threefold immersion; and if they profess that they have received such Baptism, she receives them simply by anointing them with the Holy Chrism, but if not, she baptizes them by threefold immersion. Alexander, Archbishop of Syros and Tinos, following this custom, baptized the American James Chrystal, coming to him of his own accord, and professing that he regarded the Baptism which he had received as null, and seeking consequently the perfect Baptism; but is it then just to select this simple act as evidence of lack of sympathy for the Anglican Church? The Eastern Church, since the time of her separation from the Roman, has given to no other of the heterodox Churches so many proofs of love as to the Anglican Church, nor has she ever doubted that she has in her the Spirit of Christ, and the Grace of Regeneration.[2]

I leave it to others to decide whether or not the practice of re-baptizing Anglican clergy indicates a certain 'lack of sympathy' for the Church of England. Precisely what status Lykourgos considered Anglican Baptism to possess is not very clear: if Anglicans have received 'the Grace of Regeneration', what need is there to baptize them again? But this much, at any rate,

[1] G. Williams, *A Collection of Documents*, p. 5.

[2] Ibid., pp. 27, 37; compare pp. 18–19. In the reference section of the Public Library, New York, there is a copy of the 1845 edition of Argenti's *Treatise against Unleavened Bread*, which once belonged to James Chrystal.

is evident: Eustratios Argenti would certainly have applauded the Archbishop's clear testimony concerning the necessity for threefold immersion.

But the Greeks were not absolutely consistent. Writing to Khomiakov in 1853, William Palmer mentions a recent instance at Athens in which economy was exercised towards a convert, who was received by Chrismation alone.[1] As the nineteenth century continued, such instances of economy became more frequent. In 1860, when a further group of Syrian Uniates followed Macarius of Diyārbakr into Orthodoxy, they were only chrismated. During 1879 and 1880 other cases occurred when converts—Roman Catholics of the western rite and Protestants—were received by Chrismation. Finally in 1888 the Patriarchate of Constantinople laid down as a general rule for the future that Baptism of converts should no longer be required: 'let economy be used'.[2] A similar declaration has since been made by the Church of Greece.[3]

Thus the situation today is once more very much as it was before 1755. Argenti's conclusions, although approved for more than a century by the Greek-speaking Orthodox world, have not gained permanent acceptance. His demands were too rigorous, the scope which he allowed to the principle of economy was too restricted. But while rejecting his conclusions, Orthodoxy has not therefore rejected all that he had to say. Today, just as much as in the 1750s, the Orthodox Church still regards threefold immersion as an integral part of the sacrament of Baptism, not to be omitted save in cases of genuine necessity; and Argenti's *Manual concerning Baptism* retains its value as a cogent and lucid exposition of her reasons for considering immersion so important.

Nor has the stricter and more rigorous position entirely disappeared. As recently as 1933 the Holy Synod of the Patriarchate of Antioch laid down that all converts to Orthodoxy received by clergy in its jurisdiction should be baptized, save in cases where a dispensation had been granted.[4] Thus while the application of economy is not excluded by this

[1] Birkbeck, op. cit., p. 149.

[2] M. G. Theotokas, *Νομολογία*, p. 371; compare pp. 368–70.

[3] Canonical Enactments of 29 October 1903 and 22 September 1932: Kotsonis, *Ἡ κανονικὴ ἄποψις*, pp. 124–6.

[4] See *Échos d'Orient*, vol. xxxiii, Paris, 1934, p. 99.

decision, it is not envisaged as a normal practice. And in more conservative circles in Greece today the Baptism of converts is considered necessary or at any rate highly desirable. Many Old Calendarists (*Palaioïmerologitai*) on the mainland of Greece insist that converts to Orthodoxy must be baptized; and the author of this book found a similar attitude among several monks on Mount Athos with whom he talked in 1961. 'Were you baptized when you became Orthodox?' they asked; and on hearing that he had been received not by Baptism but by Chrismation, they shook their heads sadly. 'I suppose it is all right to be received by Chrismation,' one monk conceded; 'but', he added fiercely, 'it is very much better to be baptized.' Yet if the Baptism of converts is still practised occasionally, it is now altogether exceptional.[1]

[1] In Greece during September 1963 two Roman Catholics were rebaptized on being received into Orthodoxy (see *Irénikon*, vol. xxxvi, Chevetogne, 1963, p. 537). One of these was received by the Old Calendarists, the other by the official (New Calendar) Church of Greece.

IV

THE LORD'S SUPPER

Remove not the ancient boundaries, which your fathers have set. PROVERBS xxii. 28.

Greeks and Romans, Indians and Ethiopians, Saint Photius the Great remarked, have different icons of Christ, each in their own image and fashion.[1] In the same way Orthodox—save in their more intolerant moments—have recognized it to be proper and fitting that the various parts of Christendom should follow varying ways of worship. But while not demanding that the Latin west should adopt the Byzantine Liturgy, they have felt that there are four points wherein the Latins have gone beyond what a legitimate diversity can tolerate. The Orthodox have not been willing to allow the use of unleavened bread, consecration otherwise than with an Epiclesis, the withholding of the Chalice from the laity, and the denial of communion to young children. To these four deviations Argenti devoted the most extended and elaborate of his works, *Treatise against Unleavened Bread.* The book arose, as did the *Manual concerning Baptism*, from a particular controversy; but whereas the *Manual* is little more than a pamphlet, the *Treatise*—over ten times as long—attempts a systematic and exhaustive treatment of its theme. It is probably the most thorough and detailed attack on the defects of the modern Roman eucharistic practice that any Orthodox controversialist has ever composed.

The *Treatise* is a work of polemic, and its author has little to say on matters where the two Churches agree; but it will be of value to consider first such general remarks as he makes concerning the Eucharist. His definition of a sacrament is the same here as in his book on Baptism: a sacrament is 'an action of the Catholic Church, ordained by God, in which through bodily and visible operations we are raised to the apprehension of things intelligible and spiritual'.[2] To illustrate this double

[1] *Ad Amphilochium*, Quaestio ccv (P. G. ci. 949D–951A).

[2] *Σύνταγμα κατὰ 'Αζύμων*, p. 172. Compare *'Εγχειρίδιον περὶ Βαπτίσματος*, pp. 28–29, quoted above, p. 91.

nature of a sacrament—outward and inward—he quotes Saint John Chrysostom: 'It is called a sacrament [or mystery, μυστήριον], because what we believe is not the same as what we see, but we see one thing and believe another. . . . When the Body of Christ is mentioned, I understand what is said in one sense, the unbeliever in another.'[1]

Argenti writes as follows of the presence of Christ's Body and Blood in the elements of bread and wine:

Instead of the flesh and blood of the Passover Lamb, the bread and wine of the Eucharist were delivered to us, transelemented (μεταστοιχειούμενα) through prayer and spiritual blessing into the Body and Blood of Our Lord Jesus Christ. Because of his deep love and his surpassing goodness, he was not satisfied to be present in his Church merely in a spiritual manner as God, but he was also pleased to be joined to her in a more bodily fashion through this sacrament, in order that being mingled and made one body with him, she may have a strong and sure comfort and consolation, and may not grow weary in awaiting him until he comes again in his glory. Thus the sacrament of the Eucharist is strictly and truly an antitype of the Lamb in the Jewish Law; but when compared with Christ it should rightly be called neither type nor antitype. For it is, and it is called and believed to be, the Body and Blood of the Lord himself.[2]

In this passage Argenti only uses the Patristic term 'transelementation' (*metastoicheiosis*), but elsewhere he frequently speaks of 'transubstantiation' (*metousiosis*). In his use of Latin terminology, however, he is more reserved than Dositheos and the Council of Jerusalem; for unlike them he nowhere employs the Scholastic distinction between 'substance' and 'accidents'. It is true that he does not explicitly find fault with this distinction, but this is doubtless because he was unwilling to attack openly what had been affirmed by an Orthodox Council.

But there is another Scholastic distinction which he does not hesitate to criticize—that between 'matter' and 'form' in the sacraments. To talk in such terms, so he argues, is to introduce 'naturalistic and Aristotelian explanations' into sacramental theology.[3] It is to apply the language of the Natural Sciences to the supernatural Mysteries of God:

[1] *Σύνταγμα κατὰ 'Αζύμων*, p. 172, quoting Chrysostom, *Hom. in I Cor.*, vii. 1 (P. G. lxi. 55–56).

[2] *Σύνταγμα κατὰ 'Αζύμων*, p. 2.

[3] Ibid., p. 100.

Nevertheless we are astonished that there can have been found men, professing theology and with a reputation for wisdom, who desire to explain the supernatural and divine sacraments as if they were natural things, seeking in them 'matter' and 'form', terms unknown and unheard of in the Christian theology of the Catholic Church.[1]

He also points out that while the distinction between form and matter may seem to work in the case of Baptism, Chrismation, the Eucharist, and Unction of the sick, it is impossible to apply it in any comparable way to the three remaining sacraments of Repentance, Ordination, and Marriage.[2]

In this connection, Argenti launches into a more general attack on Scholastic theology. Scholasticism is the source to which he believes most Latin errors must be traced:

More than a thousand years after the birth of Christ, there arose the heresy of the Scholastic Latin theologians, who wished to unite the philosophy of Aristotle with Christian theology. Nevertheless they did not imitate the holy teachers of the early Church, who made philosophy fit theology; but the Scholastics did the opposite, making the Gospel and the holy Christian faith fit the doctrines of the philosopher Aristotle. From this source there arose in the Latin Church so many heresies in the theology of the Holy Trinity, so many distortions of the words of the Gospels and the Apostles, so many violations of the Sacred Canons and the divine Councils, and finally so many corruptions and adulterations of the holy Sacraments.[3]

He goes on to call Thomas Aquinas 'the corrupter of theology'. He adds with regret that certain Orthodox in recent times, 'like young bullocks', have followed the Latin Scholastics. 'There is no advantage', he adds drily, 'in mentioning their names here.' Probably he is thinking of such writers as Nicholas Bulgaris, Peter of Moghila, and perhaps even Dositheos.

Thus in assessing the theological divergences between Orthodoxy and Rome, Argenti attributes cardinal importance to the rise of Scholasticism in the west during the Middle Ages. The same point of view is found in many other Orthodox writers. 'Those who subject the dogmas of the faith to chains of syllogistic reasoning', wrote the Byzantine theologian Joseph Bryennios (early fifteenth century), 'strip of its divine glory the

[1] *Σύνταγμα κατὰ Ἀζύμων*, p. 99. [2] Ibid., p. 172. [3] Ibid., pp. 171–2.

very faith that they strive to defend. They force us to believe no longer in God but in man. Aristotle and his philosophy have nothing in common with the truths revealed by Christ.'[1] When the western speakers at Florence kept appealing to Aristotle, a delegate from the Church of Georgia exclaimed impatiently, 'What about Aristotle, Aristotle? A fig for your fine Aristotle!'[2] Attacking the 'dialectic' of the west, Symeon of Thessalonica protests:

> You are a disciple not of the Fathers but of the pagan Greeks. If I wished, I too could produce syllogisms to answer your sophistic reasonings—and better syllogisms than yours at that. But such methods of argument I reject, and take my proofs from the Fathers and their writings. You will answer me with Aristotle or Plato or one of your modern teachers; but to oppose you I will invoke the fishermen of Galilee, with their simple preaching and their true wisdom which to you seems foolishness.[3]

As a result of the Scholastic method, so Nektarios, Patriarch of Jerusalem, maintains, the west has largely lost the idea of theology as something mystical and apophatic:

> You have expelled, so it seems to us, the mystical element from theology. . . . In your theology there is nothing that lies outside speech or beyond the scope of inquiry, nothing wrapped round with silence and guarded by piety: everything is discussed. . . . There is no cleft in the rock to confine you when you confront the spectacle on which none may gaze; there is no hand of the Lord to cover you when you contemplate His glory (Exodus xxxiii. 22–23).[4]

Such are a few among the criticisms which Orthodox make of Scholastic theology.

Argenti, then, uses the term transubstantiation without subscribing to the full Scholastic theory which lies behind it. He agrees here with the attitude adopted by the Russian Church during the nineteenth century. In 1838 the Holy Synod issued a Russian version of the Acts of the Council of Jerusalem, in

[1] Quoted in *Dictionnaire de théologie catholique*, vol. ii, Paris, 1903, col. 1159.

[2] J. Gill, *The Council of Florence*, p. 227.

[3] *Adversus omnes haereses*, 29 (P. G. clv. 140BC). The passages from Bryennios and Symeon are both quoted by M.-J. le Guillou, *Mission et Unité*, vol. ii, pp. 35–36; see p. 277, note 55 for similar protests in the west against an excessive reliance on secular philosophy.

[4] *Πρὸς τὰς προσκομισθείσας θέσεις*, p. 195.

which the word transubstantiation (*presushtchlestvlenie*) was retained, but the statements concerning substance and accidents were carefully adapted, so that all use of this technical distinction was eliminated.[1] In the following year a *Longer Catechism*, composed by Metropolitan Philaret of Moscow, was put out with the approval and authority of the Holy Synod, in which the following passage occurred:

Question: How are we to understand the word *transubstantiation*?

Answer:... The word transubstantiation is not to be taken to define the manner in which the bread and wine are changed into the Body and Blood of the Lord; for this none can understand but God; but only this much is signified, that the bread truly, really, and substantially becomes the very true Body of the Lord, and the wine the very Blood of the Lord.[2]

Here, although the adverb 'substantially' occurs, the technical distinction between substance and accidents is deliberately avoided. The *Longer Catechism* continues with a quotation from Saint John of Damascus:

If you inquire how this happens, it is enough for you to learn that it is through the Holy Spirit.... We know nothing more than this, that the word of God is true, active, and omnipotent, but in its manner of operation unsearchable.[3]

Argenti would have found nothing objectionable in the guarded language of the *Longer Catechism*. In view of the extensive discussion concerning the acceptance of transubstantiation by the Council of Jerusalem in 1672, it is not without interest to have seen how a Greek theologian approached the matter in the following century.

(*i*) *Azymes*

The first controversial point discussed in the *Treatise* is the Latin use of 'azymes' or unleavened bread in the Eucharist, a subject to which Argenti devotes the earliest of the three sections

[1] See A. Riley, *Birkbeck and the Russian Church*, p. 355, where the original text of the Acts and the Russian version of 1838 are printed in parallel columns.

[2] R. W. Blackmore, *The Doctrine of the Russian Church*, p. 92. Compare the remarks of Metropolitan Philaret in A. C. Headlam, *The Teaching of the Russian Church*, London, 1897, pp. 8–9.

[3] *De Fid. Orth.*, IV. xiii. 7 (P. G. xciv. 1145A).

in his book.[1] When Leo, Archbishop of Ochrid, first broached this question in his letter to John of Trani at the end of 1052, he could scarcely have predicted the mass of controversial literature which it was to provoke in the centuries to follow. From the time of Cerularius the use of azymes has remained one of the standard accusations made by the east against the Roman Church, and a Patriarch of Antioch in the early twelfth century went so far as to call it the chief cause of the schism.[2] But while it has been emphasized by Orthodox, most Roman Catholic writers on the other hand have striven to minimize the significance of the dispute, calling it a matter of indifference—*adiaphoron*—and even a 'frivolous question' or 'mesquinerie liturgique'.[3] Anselm of Canterbury expressed the normal Latin view when he wrote: 'Both equally are bread. For leavened and unleavened bread do not differ substantially, as some think.'[4] The Council of Florence regarded the difference as a liturgical variation involving no matter of doctrine, and therefore declared that both kinds of bread can with equal propriety be used in the Eucharist. Orthodox, however, have not suffered the question to be set aside so lightly. Little if any of what Argenti has to say on the subject is entirely new. A vast array of arguments—many of them ingenious rather than edifying—had already been put forward in the course of the controversy, particularly during the eleventh century, so that Argenti's task was primarily one of selection and arrangement.

In the Byzantine period the azymes dispute centred in great part around the question of symbolism. The west in the Middle Ages took as its starting point the words of Saint Paul: 'Christ, our Passover, has been sacrificed; let us therefore keep the feast not with the old leaven, the leaven of malice and wickedness, but with the unleavened bread (or "azymes") of sincerity and

[1] *Σύνταγμα κατὰ ᾿Αζύμων*, pp. 5–90.

[2] John IV Oxita, *De Azymis*, 2 (Leib, p. 113): 'The chief and primary cause of the division between them and us is the matter of azymes. . . . The matter of azymes involves in summary form the whole question of true piety.' But Theophylact of Bulgaria, writing a few years earlier, adopts a far more tolerant position, setting azymes aside as a difference of no great importance (see Palmer, *Dissertations*, pp. 25–31).

[3] For these expressions, see Jugie, *Theologia Dogmatica Christianorum Orientalium*, vol. i, p. 344; E. Amann, in Fliche and Martin, *Histoire de l'Église*, vol. vii, Paris, 1940, p. 141.

[4] *De azymo et fermentato*, 1 (P.L. clviii. 541D).

truth' (1 Corinthians v. 7–8). Western writers accordingly regarded leaven as a symbol of uncleanness and azymes as a symbol of purity.[1] Therefore, since Christ's body is pure and was conceived without sin, it is appropriate that the bread which becomes his Body in the Mass should be unleavened.

The Byzantines approached the matter differently. When they thought of leaven and its symbolism, they had in mind not so much the incarnation of Christ as his death and resurrection. Leaven, they argued, is a symbol of life: leavened bread is alive, unleavened bread is lifeless and without soul. But the bread of the Eucharist is the Bread of Life, enlivened by the Holy Spirit; in communion we receive not the dead but the risen and ever living Christ. Therefore it is appropriate that the bread of the Eucharist should be leavened.[2] Some Greek writers pressed this line of argument to fanciful extremes: since leaven symbolizes life and soul, those who celebrate the Eucharist with unleavened bread deny Christ a soul, and so are guilty of the Apollinarian heresy!

Thus the two sides saw different, but equally legitimate, meanings in the same symbol. So long as the dispute is carried on at this level, it is scarcely possible to speak of one party as right and the other wrong; the controversy does not really admit of any solution. But besides the question of symbolism there is the question of historical fact, and it is this which Argenti chooses to discuss in his *Treatise against Unleavened Bread.* He makes virtually no use of symbolical arguments, and one cannot but feel that he was wise in this.

He divides his subject into two main headings:

(1) As a matter of historical fact, what kind of bread did Christ use when instituting the Eucharist at the Last Supper?

(2) As a matter of historical fact, what kind of bread did the early Church use for the celebration of the Eucharist?[3]

The first question involves another: was the Last Supper a Passover Meal? Previous Orthodox theologians had differed in their answers. Theophylact of Bulgaria, at the end of the eleventh century, maintained that Christ first ate the Jewish

[1] See Peter Damian, *Liber qui appellatur Gratissimus*, 19 (P.L. cxlv. 129B).

[2] See D. N. Egender, 'La Rupture de 1054', *Irénikon*, vol. xxvii, Chevetogne, 1954, pp. 146–7.

[3] *Σύνταγμα κατὰ 'Αζύμων*, p. 6.

Passover in the ordinary way, and then instituted the Eucharist with the bread that lay before him—unleavened bread;[1] but no Orthodox writer after Theophylact upheld this view. They argued either that Christ first celebrated the Jewish Passover as the Law enjoined (i.e. with azymes), and then—revoking the Old Law—celebrated his New Passover with leavened bread;[2] or that the Last Supper was not a Passover Meal at all, but was held on the day before the Passover, on the evening of 13 Nisan, when ordinary bread was still in normal use. This last alternative was preferred by the great majority of Byzantine writers from Nicetas Stethatos and Peter of Antioch onwards, and it is the view which Argenti himself adopts.[3]

He appeals above all to the clear and undoubted testimony of Saint John's Gospel, which dates the Last Supper to the day before the Jewish Passover, 13 Nisan (xiii. 1; xviii. 28; xix. 14).[4] He is not willing to admit any discrepancy between John and the other three Evangelists, but he argues that if rightly understood the Synoptic narratives are consistent with John's dating. The Greek phrase τῇ πρώτῃ τῶν ἀζύμων (Matthew xxvi. 17) is indecisive; it may mean 'on the first day of the feast of unleavened bread', but it can also be translated 'on the day *before* the feast of unleavened bread'. The second rendering, he urges, is no personal or arbitrary interpretation, since John Chrysostom, Theophylact, and others have understood the passage in this way. Matthew's ambiguous words must, therefore, be interpreted in the light of John's unambiguous evidence.[5] When Luke writes 'then came the day of unleavened bread' (xxii. 7), 'came' is used in the sense 'was near at hand': for this looser use

[1] *De iis quorum Latini incusantur*, 8 (P.G. cxxvi. 233BC).

[2] For example, see Gennadios Scholarios, *De sanctis ingressibus*, in Jugie, *Theologia Dogmatica Christianorum Orientalium*, vol. iii, p. 237.

[3] Certain Orthodox writers further complicate the question by supposing, either (1) that in the year of Christ's crucifixion the Jews *postponed* the celebration of the Passover to the evening of 15 Nisan, while Christ celebrated it at the usual time, on the evening of 14 Nisan; or else (2) that Christ, when celebrating the Passover at the Last Supper, *anticipated* the normal time by a whole day or by a few hours. For (1), see the *Confession* of Kritopoulos (Karmiris, *Μνημεῖα*, vol. ii, pp. 533–4); for (2), see Symeon of Thessalonica, *De sacra liturgia*, 91 (P.G. clv. 272B). Argenti passes over both these theories, perhaps because he could find no evidence for them in the Bible.

[4] *Σύνταγμα κατὰ Ἀζύμων*, pp. 7–8, 14.

[5] Ibid., pp. 72–74. According to some modern commentators there is a similar ambiguity in the equivalent Aramaic phrase.

of the word, compare the Greek of Matthew xxvi. 45 with that of Mark xiv. 41. In any case, 13 Nisan was the day of preparation (ἑτοιμασία) for the Passover, so that in a general sense it could naturally be said of the feast that it had 'come'.[1] Preparations for the Passover began, indeed, as early as the tenth day of the month (Exodus xii. 3), four days before the Passover itself; hence no difficulty is raised by the statement that the disciples 'prepared the Passover' (Matthew xxvi. 19, etc.), for it does not follow that they actually ate it.[2] Christ's words, 'with desire I have desired to eat this Passover' (Luke xxii. 15), refer not to the Passover of the Law but to the New Passover which he is about to institute: that is his reason for saying not simply 'the Passover' but '*this* Passover'.[3] Argenti concludes, therefore, that there is nothing in the Synoptic Gospels which flatly and unambiguously contradicts the Johannine dating.

When we turn to consider the details of the meal described by the four Evangelists, Argenti continues, we find that it bears not one of the outward marks of a Passover meal. Nowhere in the accounts of the Last Supper is there any reference to 'unleavened bread' (ἄζυμα), but only to 'bread' (ἄρτος), without further qualification. The Passover was eaten standing, but it is explicitly stated that Christ and his disciples sat down. The Passover Lamb was eaten dry, without sauce or gravy, while the disciples are said to have dipped in the dish. A 'sop' is mentioned: can this have been made of unleavened bread? The Mosaic Law strictly forbade anyone to go out of doors on the night of the Passover, but both the Jews and Christ with his disciples moved freely during the night of the Last Supper, and when Judas went out during the meal none of the disciples expressed surprise.[4] There is no mention of a lamb and bitter herbs, nor of staff, sandals, and girded loins, nor of blood upon lintel and doorposts; 'and to put it briefly, no trace, sign, recollection, or circumstantial evidence of the Passover is to be found there; from which we conclude that it was not a Passover meal, but was the Mystical Supper eaten with leavened bread.'[5]

[1] *Σύνταγμα κατὰ Ἀζύμων*, pp. 74–76.
[2] Ibid., pp. 26–27.
[3] Ibid., pp. 24–25, 79.
[4] Ibid., pp. 9–12.
[5] Ibid., pp. 27–28. Compare M.-J. Lagrange, *Évangile selon Saint Marc*, Paris, 1947, p. 357: 'Si la cène de Marc surtout se lisait isolée de son contexte, personne ne songerait à en faire un repas pascal.'

The Gospels also imply that the day of the Crucifixion was an ordinary working day.[1]

Argenti adds two further arguments. First, it is agreed by all Christendom that the descent of the Holy Spirit at the Feast of Pentecost occurred on a Sunday. Reckoning backwards on this basis, it will be found that the Passover night must have fallen not upon Thursday evening but upon Friday evening; therefore the Last Supper, which was eaten on Thursday, cannot have been the Passover meal.[2] Secondly, Christ is a priest after the order not of Aaron but of Melchizedek; but azymes belong to the Aaronic priesthood, while Melchizedek is said in Genesis to have offered not *azyma* (azymes) but *artos* (bread).[3]

It is a sound Orthodox principle to treat the Fathers as the authoritative interpreters of Holy Scripture, and to the Fathers therefore Argenti appeals, submitting a lengthy 'Harmony'.[4] He argues that they are overwhelmingly in support of the dating which he has suggested:

> The holy Fathers are agreed in teaching that Christ was sacrificed on the Cross on the actual day and hour when the Passover of the Law was sacrificed, so that according to the holy Fathers Christ instituted the Lord's Supper *before* the beginning of the period of unleavened bread.[5]

Among the Fathers there is only one notable exception—John Chrysostom—who, while sometimes agreeing with the general view, at other times speaks as if he considered the Last Supper to be a Passover Meal. Argenti says that since Chrysostom writes 'in an ambiguous, careless, and contradictory manner', we cannot be certain what he really thought about the Last Supper. In any case, his testimony alone does not entitle us to set aside the evidence of so many other Fathers.[6]

In answer, then, to the first of his two questions Argenti replies that the Last Supper was held not on the evening of the Passover, but on the previous evening; and since it was not a

[1] Argenti, op. cit., pp. 8–9.

[2] Ibid., pp. 19–22. Argenti bases the principles of his calculation on texts from Philo and Josephus.

[3] Ibid., pp. 47–49.

[4] Ibid., pp. 34–45.

[5] Ibid., p. 34.

[6] Ibid., pp. 62–72. The main passages in Chrysostom around which the discussion has centred are *De Prod. Judae Hom.* i. 4 and ii. 4 (P. G. xlix. 379, 388).

Passover meal, Christ used ordinary bread at the institution of the Eucharist.

In answer to the second question—what kind of bread did the early Church use at the Eucharist?—Argenti first points out that even if Christ had used unleavened bread at the Last Supper, it would not follow that the Church must do the same. We who enjoy the liberty of the sons of God are not subject to the Law as Christ himself was. He was circumcised and as a rule observed the Jewish Sabbath, but these ordinances do not apply to his followers; why then should they use the azymes of the Jewish Passover? On the contrary, the Church would have been justified in substituting leavened for unleavened bread, if only for the reason that Christians ought not to agree with Jews![1] But in fact there was no such substitution, since Christ, as we have seen, himself used leavened bread at the Last Supper.

There is in fact indirect evidence that the Apostolic Church used leavened bread at the Eucharist (so Argenti continues). The Lord's Supper was celebrated continually, and not merely on the days of unleavened bread. Saint Paul (1 Corinthians x, xi) says nothing of unleavened bread, but implies rather that the Eucharist formed part of an ordinary meal; and with his strong views upon freedom from the Jewish Law, it is unlikely that he would impose Jewish azymes upon his Gentile converts. The debate at the Apostolic Council (Acts xv) upon the relation of Christians to the Law of Moses would have been a suitable occasion on which to promulgate rules about unleavened bread, had any such rules existed.[2] Outside the New Testament, two early practices are found which suggest that ordinary bread was used: first, members of the congregation used themselves to bring to church the bread which the priests offered in the Holy Sacrifice; secondly, any bread left over from the service, and not consecrated, was distributed to the faithful who took it to their own homes and ate it there. In both cases, the implication is that the bread was such as they ordinarily employed for food, and not 'those thin, round wafers whose pieces, if left over from the service, do not serve to strengthen man's heart, nor are they of any use as food, but only for sealing letters'.[3]

[1] Argenti, op. cit., pp. 46–47, 80. The same argument is used by Theophylact (P.G. cxxvi. 234C) and by Symeon of Thessalonica (P.G. clv. 272D–273A).

[2] Argenti, op. cit., p. 33.

[3] Ibid., p. 45.

Search how we will through the first ten centuries of Christian history, we will find no evidence of unleavened bread in the Eucharist:

> Truly one might wonder how it is that in the whole of divine Scripture, in all the Councils, ecumenical and local, orthodox and heretical, in all the holy Fathers, in all the historians, there nowhere appears any mention of unleavened bread or use of the word in connection with the Lord's Supper. So far as I have been able to examine the matter (and I have examined many things), I have found no trace of unleavened bread in any writer, save only in the case of the heretical Ebionites, of whom Saint Epiphanius writes that they kept Jewish customs and celebrated the sacraments with unleavened bread, as Judaizers. Elsewhere I have found no mention of unleavened bread among Christians.[1]

> None of the holy Fathers, eastern or western, ever said, or wrote, or imagined anything about unleavened bread, nor did any of them use it in the Holy Eucharist; but on the contrary, most of them speak of common and ordinary bread. But if the Papists object, let them produce their evidence and be justified.
>
> The Eastern Church from the time of Christ and the Apostles used leavened bread, as she does today; and she will continue to celebrate this all-holy sacrament with leavened bread until the consummation of the age.
>
> The Western Church in the time of her orthodoxy also offered leavened bread at the holy altar, since the western Fathers are found to be in agreement with the eastern on this point. . . . The most holy Photius, writing to Pope Nicholas and enumerating in detail the differences between the Liturgies, says nothing about azymes; from which we learn that in the time of Photius the Great, the use of azymes had not yet arisen among the Latins.[2]

Not only the Orthodox, but the Copts—'strict guardians of antiquity'—the Ethiopians, the Syrian Maronites, the Chaldaean Nestorians, and the Jacobites all employ leavened bread. Even the Protestants, albeit innovators and 'revolutionaries' in other respects, have restored its use.

If the Western Church once used ordinary bread, at what date must the introduction of azymes be placed? Rejecting the view upheld by some Greek writers that they were introduced at

[1] Ibid., pp. 33–34; see Epiphanius, *Haeres.*, XXX. xvi. 1 (ed. Holl, p. 353).

[2] Ibid., p. 60.

Rome as early as the second or fourth century, Argenti maintains that they were first brought into the Church by Leo IX in the middle of the eleventh century.[1] Papist azymes, like the unleavened cakes of the Jews, at first retained the outward appearance of bread, and it was only after the Council of Florence that the papery wafers of the present Roman use became general.[2] Argenti's date for the introduction of azymes is certainly too late, if he means that unleavened bread was not employed at all in the western Eucharist before 1050, since Rabanus Maurus provides testimony to its use, at any rate in some places, during the ninth century.[3] There is, however, a sense in which Argenti is justified, since Leo IX was the first Pope to give explicit approval to the use of azymes.[4]

Argenti adds, by way of appendix, that the Latins in celebrating with azymes have lost a proper fraction in their Liturgy. They no longer possess the symbol of the one loaf divided among many, representing the oneness of Christ's members in his Mystical Body. 'Why do you not take bread which strengthens man's heart,' he protests to the Papists, 'that you too may partake not from many but from the one loaf, as the Catholic Church did and still does, and as Christ and the Apostles did; that you may become one body with your Head—not the Pope but Christ—and with the members of Christ, the Orthodox?'[5]

In answer, then, to his second question Argenti states that the use of unleavened bread was universal in the Christian Eucharist until the eleventh century (the only exception being the Armenians, who introduced azymes around A.D. 600, in opposition to the Orthodox).[6] In the bread of the Eucharist, as in the administration of Baptism, the Latins are seen to be innovators, without reverence for the tradition of antiquity. We can now see why Argenti and other Orthodox regard the question of leavened bread *versus* azymes as more than a harmless diversity of ecclesiastical custom. They believed that the practice of using

[1] Argenti, op. cit., pp. 49–51, 57–60. [2] Ibid., pp. 85–86.

[3] *Inst. Cler.*, I. 31 (P.L. cvii. 318D–319B). Certain texts in Bede, Alcuin, and Paschasius Radbertus are often cited as evidence for the use of unleavened bread in the Eucharist, but the meaning of the passages in question is very much open to dispute, and Bede's words in particular seem to prove nothing to the point. See R. M. Woolley, *The Bread of the Eucharist*, pp. 15–16, 18–19.

[4] P.L. cxliii. 747C, 775B.

[5] Argenti, op. cit., p. 296. [6] So Argenti, op. cit., p. 61.

leavened bread in the Eucharist could be traced back to the time of the Apostles and justified from Scriptural texts; they therefore condemned the abandonment of this usage as a betrayal of Apostolic institutions and of Our Lord's own will. In the words of another Greek, writing a generation after Argenti's death, 'The use of azymes, opposed as it is to the ordinance of God, is a serious innovation which has caused scandal and schism. Why have you abandoned the ancient tradition, when he who holds fast to it can never go wrong?'[1]

(ii) The Epiclesis

The second and longest of the three sections[2] in the *Treatise against Unleavened Bread* is devoted to the consecration in the Eucharist. Are the bread and wine consecrated solely by the recitation of Christ's words, *This is my body*, *This is my blood*, as Roman Catholics believe; or is it necessary to add an Epiclesis or prayer for the sending of the Holy Spirit, as in the Liturgies of the Eastern Church? This question did not clearly emerge in controversy between the two Churches until the fourteenth and fifteenth centuries, when the classic statement of the Orthodox position was set forth by Nicholas Cabasilas and Symeon of Thessalonica. Roman Catholics, while placing azymes among the 'matters of indifference', agree with Orthodox in attaching importance to the dispute over the Epiclesis: Uniate clergy are permitted to use leavened bread when celebrating the Byzantine Liturgy, but they must 'intend' to consecrate not by the Epiclesis but by the 'Words of Institution'.

The second section of Argenti's book is divided, as the first, into two questions: (1) How did Our Lord consecrate the bread of the Eucharist and the chalice at the Last Supper? (2) How should the priests of the Church perform the consecration?

In answer to the first question, Argenti replies that it is quite clear that at the Last Supper Christ consecrated the bread and wine 'by thanksgiving, blessing, and invocation (*epiclesis*)'; the so-called 'Words of Institution' are not words of consecration, but of explanation and administration. In support of this, Argenti submits a simple analysis of the sequence of events at the Last Supper. Christ

[1] S. Vlasopoulos, *'Η ὑπεράσπισις τῆς Γραικικῆς 'Εκκλησίας*, pp. 135–6.
[2] *Σύνταγμα κατὰ 'Αζύμων*, pp. 91–250.

(1) took bread;
(2) gave thanks and blessed;
(3) broke;
(4) gave to his disciples, saying, 'Take, eat. . . .'

To make any sense of this narrative, we must put the consecration at stage (2): for where else can the consecration be placed, if not at that point? When Christ broke the bread, it was already his body; thus the consecration must come before the fraction (stage (3)). If we say that the blessing was not consecratory, we render it entirely pointless: for what other purpose can Christ have had when he blessed the bread, save that of consecrating it? But the words, *This is my body*, *This is my blood*, occur only at stage (4), when Christ was distributing what he had *already* blessed and consecrated; and so these words cannot be words of consecration.

'Hence we conclude', Argenti comments, 'that it was the blessing of Our Lord which consecrated and transubstantiated the bread into the Body of Christ.' As for the 'Words of Institution',

> Those words were spoken after the blessing and after the breaking of bread; therefore they were spoken not in order to bless nor to consecrate, but to explain the sacrament to the Apostles. . . . Through those words Christ teaches the Apostles what he has done in giving thanks.[1]

When Christ distributed the sacrament to the Apostles, he gave them something which still looked like bread and wine; and so he said 'This is my body', 'This is my blood',

> not in order to consecrate, but only to define and make clear the sacrament hidden under the appearances of bread and wine; and so we call those words sacramental (μυστηριώδη), because they make clear the meaning of the sacrament.[2]

We should note the exact form which Christ's words took:

> Christ did not say, *Let this be*, or *become*, or *be made my body*, or *This becomes my body*, but he said *This is*; hence it is clear that the bread and wine had already become his Body through the blessing, and therefore he said rightly and correctly, *This is*, and not *Let this be made my body*.[3]

[1] *Σύνταγμα κατὰ Ἀζύμων*, pp. 92, 93. [2] Ibid., p. 95. [3] Ibid., pp. 93–94.

Argenti also points out that the Roman Canon reads, 'Take, eat, *for* this is my body'; and in the same way Matthew xxvi. 28 has, 'Drink of it, all of you, *for* this is my blood'. What is the purpose of the connecting link *for*, save to indicate that the words which follow are intended as an explanation why the Apostles should eat and drink?

In an Appendix[1] Argenti brings evidence to show that the three terms 'blessing' (*εὐλογία*), 'thanksgiving' (*εὐχαριστία*), and 'invocation' (*ἐπίκλησις*) are to be taken as synonymous. A Christian does not bless a thing directly and in his own name, but invokes the name of God; if asked for a blessing he replies, not 'I bless you', but 'May God bless you'. And when praying for the blessing of God and invoking His Name, it is natural to make mention of what He has done in the past and to give Him thanks for all His marvellous works. In the Eucharist, therefore, it makes no difference whether the central action be called blessing, thanksgiving, or invocation (*epiclesis*), since these three terms are no more than different ways of describing the same thing.

In another appendix[2] Argenti makes his customary appeal to the Fathers, in proof that his interpretation of the sequence of events at the Last Supper is no mere personal opinion, but has the support of Tradition:

> We do not interpret Holy Scripture according to our own notions, as is the custom of heretics, but according to the united opinion of the Orthodox Fathers and the Catholic Church, even as the Orthodox are bound to believe.[3]

Argenti then turns to his second and more complicated question: the practice of the Church. He first gives his general answer:

> Christian priests ought to consecrate the bread and wine of the Lord's Supper by means of thanksgiving, blessing, and invocation, and not by means of the words *This is my body*. As well as the blessing, they also use these words. But they should use them not in order to consecrate thereby, but to show that they intend to accomplish what Christ did; and also to explain to the partakers what is being given to them, just as Christ also explained this to the Apostles.[4]

[1] Ibid., pp. 117–29.
[2] Ibid., pp. 130–41.
[3] Ibid., p. 130.
[4] Ibid., p. 142.

In support of this contention Argenti submits two general considerations, and then brings forward the historical evidence. He points out first that Christ said *Do this*, thereby commanding his disciples to copy his actions rather than to repeat his words; Christian priests ought therefore obediently to imitate Christ, and to do as he himself did. Since Christ consecrated, not through the words *This is my body*, but through blessing, thanksgiving, or Epiclesis, the priests of the Church should likewise consecrate by Epiclesis.[1] Apart from Christ's command to do as he did, we possess in the second place the parallel of the remaining six sacraments. Although all of them are mentioned in the New Testament, yet in every case the Church believes that it is by certain prayers and invocations—and not by reading the relevant texts in Scripture—that the sacrament is effected. We do not baptize by reading the verse, 'Go therefore and make disciples of all nations'; Chrismation (confirmation) is not administered by reading the eighth chapter of Acts, nor are sins absolved in the sacrament of Repentance by saying, 'Receive the Holy Spirit; whosoever sins you forgive, they are forgiven' (John xx. 22–23). As with other sacraments, so with the Eucharist: the consecration is effected by a prayer, not by reading the narrative of the Last Supper or repeating the words of Christ.[2]

There is another general argument in regard to the Epiclesis which Orthodox writers often employ. While not actually used in *Treatise against Unleavened Bread*, it is found in an unpublished tract, possibly by Argenti, which is contained in manuscript 5 of the Kecskemét Library.[3] The argument in question raises the issue how far the priest at the Eucharist is to be considered as speaking *in persona Christi*. According to Latin sacramental theology the priest at the consecration represents Christ and acts in his stead: he effects the consecration by pronouncing the words of Christ in the first person, just as if he were Our Lord himself. But at the climax of the Byzantine Liturgy—and, indeed, of the Roman Liturgy rightly understood—the priest does not speak *in persona Christi* but *prays to God* to effect the consecration. He is not Christ's vicar, but a suppliant before God. As the tract in the Kecskemét manuscript puts it:

[1] *Σύνταγμα κατὰ ᾿Αζύμων*, p. 142. [2] Ibid., pp. 166–7, 174–80.
[3] On this manuscript, see above, pp. 58-59.

Thus the Pope of Old Rome is a transgressor of the law, for when celebrating this sacrament he is not satisfied simply with being the Vicar of Christ (i.e. instead of Christ[1]), but with impious presumption he assigns to himself the whole of Christ's authority; for he claims to consecrate those papery azymes of his in virtue of his own power, saying in the first person, *This is my body*. . . . But we Orthodox, recognizing our own helplessness (sinners that we are), do not trust at all in our own power; but with earnest prayers and fervent supplications we beseech the Heavenly Father to send down His All-Holy Spirit, that *He* may accomplish that divine and ineffable change.[2]

But Argenti bases his case not so much upon general considerations of this kind, as upon the testimony of Tradition. As in his first section upon azymes, he prefers specific historical evidence to more abstract and speculative arguments. He draws up a lengthy *catena* of Patristic quotations, indicating the belief and practice of the early Church concerning the consecration of the Eucharist.[3] He begins with the three Liturgies of James, Mark, and Clement, which he assumes to be truly primitive, the work of the saints whose names they bear. Each of these Liturgies clearly intends to consecrate by Epiclesis. The same view of consecration is implied in the writings of Dionysius the Areopagite, which Argenti of course takes to be authentic.[4] In the second century Justin Martyr and Irenaeus, in the third century Clement of Alexandria and Origen, although they do not specify the exact content of the Eucharistic prayer as they knew it, yet use language which applies most naturally to con-

[1] A play on words: 'instead of Christ' (ἀντὶ Χριστοῦ) i.e. Antichrist.

[2] Kecskemét Library, Ms. 5, ff. 125r–125v. Compare the remarks of a contemporary Russian theologian, Father Bobrinskoy: 'Selon la théologie latine, les paroles du Christ sont prononcées par le prêtre *in persona Christi*, en raison de ce que le prêtre représente le Christ, est son vicaire. Une telle définition du ministère sacerdotal est inacceptable pour des orthodoxes, car le président de l'assemblée eucharistique ne consacre pas seul, *ex sese*, devant la congrégation présente mais passive; l'Eucharistie est liturgique, c'est-à-dire qu'elle est l'action commune de toute l'assemblée au nom de laquelle et avec laquelle le ministre agit. Celui-ci ne peut donc être vicaire ou représentant du Christ. C'est l'assemblée qui dans sa totalité incarne l'église locale, dans toute sa plénitude et catholicité, c'est-à-dire le Corps du Christ ou l'Epouse du Christ; c'est l'assemblée dans son ensemble, hiérarchie et fidèles, qui s'unit au Christ par le descente du Saint-Esprit dans la communion eucharistique.' (B. Bobrinskoy, 'Le Saint-Esprit dans la Liturgie', *Studia Liturgica*, vol. i, Rotterdam, 1962, pp. 55–56.)

[3] Σύνταγμα κατὰ Ἀζύμων, pp. 143–66.

[4] *De Eccl. Hier.*, III. 12, VII. 10 (P.G. iii. 441C–444B, 565C).

secration by an invocation or Epiclesis of some kind.[1] From the next century he cites the unambiguous testimony of Cyril of Jerusalem; other writers from the same period, such as Basil the Great, Gregory of Nyssa, Ephrem of Syria, and Optatus, either allude explicitly to an Epiclesis for the sending of the Holy Spirit, or at any rate imply that the consecration is not effected solely by the words *This is my body*.[2] Among later authorities he cites Cyril of Alexandria, Augustine of Hippo, Nilus of Ancyra, Theodoret of Cyrrhus, Fulgentius of Ruspe, John of Damascus, the sixth session of the seventh Ecumenical Council, and Nicephorus of Constantinople. Even the Popes of Rome, Gregory the Great and Nicholas I, are found to favour the Orthodox rather than the modern Roman teaching.[3]

But among this cloud of witnesses Argenti is confronted by two whose statements raise difficulties and require a more detailed scrutiny: John Chrysostom[4] and Ambrose of Milan.[5] A passage in Chrysostom's *Homily upon the Treachery of Judas* has been quoted by many Roman writers, as teaching that the consecrating power lies in the words *This is my body* recited afresh at each celebration of the Eucharist: '*This is my body*, Christ says; and this saying transforms (*metarrhythmizei*) the elements.'[6] To this Argenti gives a threefold answer:

(1) There are numerous other passages in Chrysostom—above all, the Anaphora of his Liturgy—which teach that consecration is effected through the priest's prayer for the descent of the Holy Spirit; and in estimating Chrysostom's true mind

[1] Justin, *Apology*, I. 65, 66 (P.G. vi. 428A–429A); Irenaeus, *Adv. Haer.*, I. xiii. 2, IV. xviii. 4 (P.G. vii. 580A, 1027AB); Clement, *Paedag.*, II. 2 (ed. Stählin, p. 168); Origen, *Contra Celsum*, VIII. 33 (ed. Koetschau, p. 249), and *Comm. in Matt.*, XV. 11 (ed. Klostermann, p. 57).

[2] Cyril of Jerusalem, *Catechetical Orations*, XIX. 7, XXI. 3, XXXIII. 7, 19 (P.G. xxxiii. 1072AB, 1089C–1092A, 1113C–1116A, 1124B); Basil, the Anaphora of his Liturgy, and *De Spiritu sancto*, xxvii (66); Gregory of Nyssa, *Orat. Catech.*, 37 (P.G. xlv. 96D–97A) (this passage, so Argenti argues, has been misinterpreted by the Latins); also Gregory of Nyssa, *Hom. de Bapt. Christi* (P.G. xlvi. 581C) and *In laud. fratr. Basilii* (P.G. xlvi. 805C); Ephrem of Syria, *On the Priesthood* and *On the most holy sacraments* (*Opera Omnia*, ed. J. Assemani, vol. iii, Rome, 1746, pp. 2, 609); Optatus, *De schism. Donat.*, VI. 11 (P.L. xi. 1065A).

[3] Gregory, *Epistles*, Book IX, indict. ii. 12 (P.L. lxxvii. 957A); Paul Warnefrid, *Vita S. Greg.*, 23 (P.L. lxxv. 53B); Nicholas, *Ep.* iv (P.L. cxix. 778D).

[4] *Σύνταγμα κατὰ 'Αζύμων*, pp. 155–8, 227–41.

[5] Ibid., p. 159.

[6] *De Prod. Judae Hom.* i. 6 (P.G. xlix. 380).

we must rely, not upon 'a single ambiguous saying', but upon the evidence of his works as a whole.[1]

(2) But the text in the *Homily upon the Treachery of Judas*, if correctly understood, gives no support to the Latin view. When Chrysostom writes that Christ's saying 'transforms the elements', he is to be interrupted as meaning 'shows forth the elements as transformed': *metarrhythmizei* signifies *metarrhythmisthenta deiknysi*. For the disciples thought of the bread and wine at the Last Supper as ordinary bread and wine until Christ said *This is my body*. It was only then that they realized what the bread and wine had become, and therefore *from the disciples' point of view* these words indeed 'transformed the elements'.[2]

This explanation is surely somewhat far-fetched. But there is another—very much more probable—interpretation of Chrysostom's words which Argenti might have used. In the sentence immediately following that which the Latins quote, Chrysostom proceeds to compare Christ's words *This is my Body* with the words used by God at creation, *Be fruitful and multiply*. But, as several Orthodox writers before Argenti's time—for example Nicholas Cabasilas and Saint Mark of Ephesus—had observed, this declaration of God in Genesis requires a certain human co-operation to bring it into action; so too Christ's words call for action on our part—namely, the Epiclesis which the priest recites—in order that they may take effect today. Chrysostom, so far from saying that the consecrating power resides in the 'Words of Institution' *recited at each celebration of the Eucharist*, asserts something very different by his parallel with the words of creation. Just as God's declaration at creation, made once for all, enables living things to increase on the face of the earth, so Our Lord's declaration, *also made once for all*, gives the priest power to consecrate by the Epiclesis at the Eucharist.[3]

(3) But even if the Roman Catholics were correct in their interpretation of this particular text in Chrysostom, one saying

[1] *Σύνταγμα κατὰ Ἀζύμων*, pp. 155–8, quoting Chrysostom, *Hom. in Ioann.* xlv. 2 (P.G. lix. 253); *Hom. in I Cor.* xxiv. 1, 5 (P.G. lxi. 199, 204); *Hom. in II Cor.* xx. 3 (P.G. lxi. 540); *Hom. in Ep. ad Hebr.* viii. 1 (P.G. lxiii. 111); *De beato Philogonio*, vi. 4 (P.G. xlviii. 753); *De coemet. appel.*, 3 (P.G. xlix. 397–8); *De sancto Pentecoste Hom.*, I. 4 (P.G. l. 459); *De Sacerdotio*, iii. 4, vi. 4 (P.G. xlviii. 642, 681); etc.

[2] *Σύνταγμα κατὰ Ἀζύμων*, pp. 239–41.

[3] Nicholas Cabasilas, *Interpretation of the Divine Liturgy*, 29 (P.G. cl. 429AB); Mark of Ephesus, *Libellus de Consecratione*, 5 (Patrologia Orientalis, xvii. 430–1). Compare E. G. C. F. Atchley, *On the Epiclesis of the Eucharistic Liturgy*, p. 68.

would not settle the whole dispute: 'whether Chrysostom's words be taken thus or differently, the general truth is not impaired by a single statement of one teacher.'[1] We must apply here what was earlier said concerning Chrysostom and the date of the Last Supper: when so many authorities plainly support the opposite opinion, is an obscure sentence from the *Homily upon the Treachery of Judas* to be considered decisive? Holy Scripture and the Seven Ecumenical Councils alone are infallible; but the Fathers fell at times into error—Saint Augustine, for example, wrote on the Procession of the Holy Spirit in unguarded and misleading language—and so they must always be read critically, 'with a little salt'. All heresies start by seizing upon some small saying, *lexidion ti*, in the Scriptures or the Fathers, and pressing this to the exclusion of all else; it is the mark of the true Catholic to base himself not upon isolated texts, but on the general consensus of authorities. Argenti emphasizes the linguistic connection, obvious in Greek, between 'catholic' and general or universal, and between 'heretic' and one who picks and chooses: 'heresy bears the same relation to Catholicity as the part to the whole.'[2]

The same considerations apply to Ambrose of Milan as to John Chrysostom: whatever this one Father says, his opinion alone cannot settle the question. Roman Catholics have made much of the passage in *De Sacramentis*, which attributes the consecratory power in the Eucharist to the *sermo Christi*, the word or declaration of Christ, as repeated by the priest.[3] Argenti questions whether Ambrose is in fact the author of *De Sacramentis*, or at any rate of the fourth book, and he brings forward other passages from Ambrose which speak of consecration by a 'blessing', not merely by the recitation of the words of Christ at the Last Supper.[4] He adds that in any case the reference in *De Sacramentis* to the *sermo Christi* must be under-

[1] *Σύνταγμα κατὰ Ἀζύμων*, p. 241.

[2] Ibid., p. 229; compare Pascal, *Pensées*, 861 (862). In admitting the possibility of disagreement among the Fathers, Argenti is more realistic than Mitrophanis Kritopoulos, who says in his *Confession*: 'You will never find two of the holy Fathers in disagreement with one another'! (Karmiris, *Μνημεῖα*, vol. ii, p. 560.) So also Gabriel Severus: 'The Fathers do not disagree concerning anything, but over every point they are all in agreement' (*Ἔκθεσις*, Part 2, p. 55).

[3] *De Sacr.*, IV. iv. 14 (P.L. xvi. 440A).

[4] See, for example, *De Mysteriis*, ix. 50 (P.L. xvi. 405C).

stood as signifying not merely the words *This is my body*, but 'all the sayings and narratives of the Gospel', since these are recalled as a whole in the Anamnesis. He might have added that when the author of *De Sacramentis* goes on to cite in detail the words by which the consecration is effected, he includes the Anamnesis and a prayer for acceptance as well as, and after, the narrative of the Last Supper.[1]

The Patristic evidence, therefore, as interpreted by Argenti, supports the conclusion that the Eucharistic consecration is effected, not by the recitation of the narrative of the Last Supper, but by an Epiclesis or invocation for the descent of the Holy Spirit. Taking into account the testimony of Scripture, of the ancient Liturgies, and of the Fathers, he summarizes the central action of the Eucharist in seven items:

Christian priests, when celebrating the holy sacrament of the Lord's Supper, ought:

First, to take true bread and ordinary wine mixed with water.

Secondly, then to glorify and sing praise to God; and to give Him thanks for the good things and the benefits which He has conferred on the race of men.

Thirdly, to commemorate the incarnation of God the Word, his conception, birth, and baptism, his teaching and miracles, his betrayal, passion, crucifixion, and burial, his resurrection and ascension; since he said, *Do this in remembrance of me.*

Fourthly. But above all they ought to commemorate that night on which, when about to go to his voluntary Passion, he celebrated the Mystical Supper; when he took bread and wine, and having given thanks and blessed, he gave to his disciples and Apostles, saying, *Take, eat, this is my body*; and *Drink of this, all of you, for this is my blood.* This narrative, I say, the priests ought to relate and to present in words, together with these two sayings of the Lord, not in order to consecrate thereby, but in order thereby to show that they intend to perform the very thing which Christ himself did; and that they intend to perform it in remembrance of him.

Fifthly. And after this they ought to pray and with earnest supplications to call upon (*epikaleisthai*) God, that He may send down the All-Holy Spirit, and may consecrate and transubstantiate the bread, into the Body; and the wine, into the Blood of the Lord; and this invocation (*epiklesis*) the Church calls the 'blessing'.

Sixthly. And after the consecration follows the breaking of the

[1] *De Sacr.*, IV. v. 21–22 (P.L. xvi. 443A–444A).

bread (for Christ broke the bread at this point); and the breaking of the bread is now called by the Church the 'division of the bread'.

Seventhly. And last of all the priest distributes the sacrament to the communicants, at the same time explaining the meaning of what is given to them, telling them that this is the Body and Blood of Our Lord and God and Saviour Jesus Christ; even as Christ also did the same, saying to his disciples, *This is my body and my blood.* Therefore these words of the Lord properly and truly have their place at the distribution of the sacrament and not in the consecration, since Christ himself spoke them when giving the sacrament to his disciples.[1]

In his treatment of the Eucharistic Epiclesis Argenti displays certain limitations natural to his time and circumstances. It was inevitable that he should foreshorten the historical development of the Liturgy, and that he should treat as Apostolic or primitive documents which are today no longer regarded as such. Had the results of modern research been at his disposal, he would doubtless have been more cautious in his use of certain texts. It is, however, unlikely that his main conclusion would have been different.

Two criticisms in particular may be made of Argenti's discussion. First, he subdivides the one Eucharistic act too rigidly into separate parts, contrasting one part with another and stating a bald alternative between them: the consecration is effected *either* by the Epiclesis *or* by the words *This is my body*; and if it be effected by an Epiclesis, then the 'Words of Institution' are merely narrative and explanatory, and are devoid of consecrating power. But is not this to take too restricted a view of the *status quaestionis*? The Eucharistic Anaphora is to be conceived as a unity. Within this unity are distinguished the three cardinal elements (1) of thanksgiving (culminating in the commemoration of Christ's redemptive work, and making mention of the Last Supper); (2) of offering or oblation; and (3) of invocation or Epiclesis. These are preceded by an initial dialogue and followed by a concluding doxology. Yet since these three elements form a single action, no one of them can be considered in isolation from the other two, but all three are in their several ways necessary for the performance of the consecration.

In illustration of this essential unity, we may appeal to the

[1] Σύνταγμα κατὰ Ἀζύμων, pp. 168–9.

words of an Anglican theologian of the eighteenth century, John Johnson, an older contemporary of Argenti:

> The Subordinate or Mediate Cause [of the consecration] is, 1. The Reciting the Words of Institution. 2. The Oblation of the Symbols. 3. The Prayer of Invocation. All these three did, in the Ancient Liturgies, immediately follow each other, in the order that I have mentioned them; and each of them was believed to contribute toward the Consecration of the Elements into the Body and Blood.... And it is very evident to anyone that looks into the Ancient Liturgies, that the Consecration begins by the Priest's pronouncing the Words of Institution, is continued by the solemn Act of Oblation, and finished by the Invocation of the Holy Ghost. The Church of *Rome* attributes the consecration wholly to the Words of Institution; the *Greek* Church, wholly to the Prayer of Invocation; but I conceive the Ancients did not attribute the Consecration to any one of these Actions, in such a manner as to exclude the other.[1]

Johnson is perhaps justified in his charge against the Greeks of his day; but if in practice the Orthodox have at times tended to emphasize the Invocation to the exclusion of the other two 'Actions', there is no reason why they should do so. A somewhat more flexible attitude is found in Philaret's *Longer Catechism* of 1839, which—although it says nothing of the second of Johnson's three elements—yet links the Words of Institution and the Epiclesis closely together:

> *Question.* What is the most essential act in this part of the Liturgy?
> *Answer.* The utterance of the words which Jesus Christ spake in instituting the Sacrament; *Take, eat, this is my body*; *Drink ye all of it for this is my blood, of the New Testament*; Mat. xxvi, 26, 27, 28; And after this the invocation of the Holy Ghost, and the blessing the gifts, that is, the bread and wine, which have been offered.
> *Question.* Why is this so essential?
> *Answer.* Because at the moment of this act, the bread and wine are changed, or transubstantiated, into the very Body of Christ, and into the very Blood of Christ.[2]

With this may be compared the remark by Isidore of Kiev at the Council of Florence, that the words of Christ recited in the

[1] *The Unbloody Sacrifice*, London, 1714, quoted by W. Jardine Grisbrooke, *Anglican Liturgies of the Seventeenth and Eighteenth Centuries*, Alcuin Club Collections No. XL, London, 1958, pp. 81–82.

[2] Blackmore, *The Doctrine of the Russian Church*, pp. 91–92.

Liturgy are as the seed, but there is need of further prayers for this seed to produce its fruit.[1]

But if Argenti poses a false alternative and makes too rigid a division between the different parts of the consecratory prayer, this does not affect his main thesis against the Church of Rome: that the recitation of the words, *This is my body*, *This is my blood*, does not *by itself* complete the consecration. These words must be followed by an Epiclesis; therefore, if we are to speak of a 'moment of consecration' (as in some sense we are compelled to do), this moment cannot be placed before the conclusion of the Epiclesis.

The second criticism which may be urged against Argenti is that he has too limited a conception of what in fact constitutes an Epiclesis. It is for him invariably a prayer of the exact form found in the Liturgies of Saint Basil the Great and Saint John Chrysostom; and he takes no account of the fact that the word *epiclesis* can be used in at least four distinct ways, some vague and some precise,[2] so that the term 'invocation' may not possess so definite a meaning for a Father of the second century as it does for a Byzantine writer of the ninth. As a result, he does not consider the possibility that the essential components of the Eucharistic Epiclesis might be embodied in prayers which vary widely in their outward appearance.

This point has an important application to the Roman Canon. Although Argenti knew and used the work of Nicholas Cabasilas, he nowhere mentions Cabasilas' suggestion that the prayer *Supplices te rogamus* is to be understood as an Epiclesis.[3] To Cabasilas it makes no fundamental difference, in the context of the Eucharistic consecration, whether the Epiclesis be descendant or ascendant: whether we ask for the Holy Spirit to come down upon the gifts, as in the Byzantine Liturgies, or for the 'Angel' to carry the offering up to the Heavenly Altar, as in the Roman Canon. The Byzantine Liturgies are simple and direct in their language, the Roman 'embodies its meaning in

[1] Gill, *The Council of Florence*, p. 281.

[2] See F. Cabrol, 'Epiclèse', *Dictionnaire d'archéologie chrétienne et de liturgie*, vol. v, Paris, 1922, cols. 143–4.

[3] Cabasilas, *Interpretation of the Divine Liturgy*, 30 (P.G. cl. 433C–437B). Symeon of Thessalonica also considers that the Roman Canon contains an Epiclesis (*De sacro templo*, 88: P.G. clv. 740B). His language is obscure, but he seems to place it before the narrative of the Institution, in the *Quam oblationem*.

symbolic forms',[1] but both the Greek Epiclesis and the *Supplices te* occur at the same place in the structure of the service, and each alike is a prayer to God for His intervention in the Mystery. But while Cabasilas is willing to consider the text of the Roman Liturgy more orthodox than its modern exponents, Argenti is less tolerant. He says merely that the Roman Mass once contained an Epiclesis (by which he means an Epiclesis of the developed Byzantine type), but this has since been excised, and the second part of the Roman Canon corrupted.[2] It may be that he is right about the elimination of an Epiclesis from the Roman Canon; yet is he not, perhaps, a little harsh on the western Liturgy in its present form?

(*iii*) *The Use of the Sacrament*

The third and concluding part[3] of the *Treatise against Unleavened Bread* is devoted to the 'use' of the sacrament, by which Argenti means the manner in which it is to be given and received. Before turning to the two main questions at issue here between the Churches—the refusal of the Chalice to the laity, and infant communion—he gives a general description of the Liturgy, with special reference to the worship of the early Church. He displays a considerable measure of liturgical common sense, and he avoids the spurious symbolism into which so many writers, both eastern and western, have fallen. He recognizes that defects and corruptions have crept into Orthodox worship, and he singles out for special mention the

[1] Louis Duchesne, *Christian Worship*, 5th edition, London, 1919, p. 181.

[2] *Σύνταγμα κατὰ 'Αζύμων*, pp. 162, 165, 196–200. On this question of an Epiclesis in the Roman Canon, see Atchley, *On the Epiclesis of the Eucharistic Liturgy*, pp. 187–189, 191–2; M. de la Taille, *The Mystery of Faith*, London, 1941–50, vol. i, pp. 215–234, and vol. ii, pp. 139–85; M. de la Taille, 'Letter to a Theologian on the Angel of Sacrifice and the Sacrifice in Heaven', in *The Mystery of Faith and Human Opinion contrasted and defined*, London, 1930, pp. 59–79; J. Barbel, *Christos Angelos*, Bonn, 1941; Bishop Alexis van der Mensbrugghe, *La Liturgie orthodoxe de rit occidental*, Paris, 1948, pp. 80–93; and by the same author, 'L'Expositio Missae Gallicanae est-elle de Saint Germain de Paris?', in *Messager de l'Exarchat du Patriarche russe en Europe occidentale*, No. 32, Paris, 1959, pp. 217–49. For the opposite point of view, see Dom Bernard Botte, 'L'ange du sacrifice', in *Cours et conferences des semaines liturgiques*, VII, Louvain, 1929, pp. 209–21; and 'L'ange du sacrifice et l'épiclèse de la messe romaine au moyen age', in *Recherches de Théologie ancienne et médiévale*, vol. i, Louvain, 1929, pp. 285–308.

I am very grateful to Mr. W. Jardine Grisbrooke, who kindly supplied me with the greater part of these references.

[3] *Σύνταγμα κατὰ 'Αζύμων*, pp. 251–372.

way in which the Psalms are either omitted entirely or read with irreligious haste, whereas 'two hours are spent in singing one *troparion* or one *Alleluia*'. 'Things have been put the wrong way round,' he complains. 'The main task is treated as something incidental, and what is incidental is treated by fools as the main task.'[1]

Yet he believes that Orthodox worship, for all its defects, is far less in need of purification and reform than the worship of the west. It is evident that his sense of reverence had been deeply affronted by what he saw of Roman Catholicism during his travels. He describes, for instance, a service which he attended at Leghorn in his youth. Although the city had 'almost as many churches as ordinary houses', one of the Religious Orders thought it necessary to set up a tent in the harbour square, for use as a chapel. Here they celebrated Mass 'in the presence of many Hebrews, Turks, English, and Flemish; some of whom secretly, and others without any concealment, made insulting comments, blasphemed, spat, and jeered; while others said to one another, "Let us go to see the comedy in the Papists' tent." But it is in a way only appropriate that after corrupting and curtailing the sacrament, the Papists should also make of it a game, a comedy, and a mockery to the Gentiles.'[2]

Above all he charges the Roman Catholics with having lost in their public worship the communal sense which the Orthodox, despite many shortcomings, have retained. If a man wishes to pray by himself, let him do so by all means—in his own home; when he goes to services in church, let him share in the Church's worship:

> What then are we to say of the Papist laity, who always take books of prayers when they go to church, and each reads his own book in private and says his own private prayers, while the priest is celebrating? I answer that the laity deserve no condemnation for this, since they have a plausible excuse: for they see their priest celebrating and observe some of his gestures during the service, but they hear not a word of what is said, since he mutters alone by himself; . . . and so each of the laity is forced to say his private prayers. He is *forced*, I say; for what else can the poor Papist layman do, except find some way of not remaining without prayer? But in the Catholic Church,

[1] *Σύνταγμα κατὰ 'Αζύμων*, p. 271. [2] Ibid., p. 261.

where the prayers and Holy Scriptures and lections are read in a loud voice and clearly, none can neglect what is said publicly, and pray or read by himself, without being guilty of sin.[1]

Passing on to more particular matters, Argenti attacks the Latin refusal of the Chalice to the laity on three grounds: first, it is in open disobedience to Christ's explicit command; secondly, it is an innovation; thirdly, it overthrows the symbolism of the sacrament. First, Christ said, 'Unless you eat the flesh of the Son of Man *and drink his blood*, you have no life in you' (John vi. 53), and he commanded his disciples, 'Drink of it, *all of you*' (Matthew xxvi. 27). It is impossible to reconcile the present Roman practice with these words of Our Lord. Nor, secondly, is their present practice consistent with the testimony of the ancient Fathers and the observances of the early Church, for the early Church gave communion to the laity under both kinds. And in the third place, the Eucharist requires both bread and wine in order to show forth the death of Christ and the shedding of his blood: therefore, if Christ's people are to participate fully in the Mystery they must be given communion under both kinds. Here, as elsewhere, Argenti insists upon the nature of a sacrament as a representative sign, involving a correspondence between outward action and inner meaning; sacraments effect what they symbolize, but they must also symbolize what they effect.[2]

The excuses which the Latins make in their defence, Argenti maintains, are pitiably inadequate. First, they point out that in emergencies the Orthodox permit communion under one kind; but this is irrelevant, since what is allowed in exceptional circumstances is not thereby justified as a general practice.[3] They argue in the second place that Christ is fully present in either species alone (the doctrine of *concomitance*); but this again is nothing to the point, since the question in dispute is not the Eucharistic presence, but the manner in which the sacrament is to be received. Christ is fully *present* in each element separately, but his Body and Blood are not fully *represented* separately in each: 'the Body of Christ remains complete in bread alone and in wine alone; but the sacrament only remains complete in the

[1] Ibid., pp. 279–80. By the 'Catholic Church' Argenti means of course the *Orthodox* Catholic Church of the East.

[2] Ibid., pp. 304–7, 323–4.

[3] Ibid., pp. 328–9.

bread and wine together.'[1] Therefore, 'whosoever without necessity refuses to drink from the Cup of Christ, receives the sacrament incomplete and commits grave sacrilege.'[2]

In denying communion to young children the Roman Church has acted once more in defiance of Christ's command, and is once more guilty of arbitrary innovation against the universal practice of the ancient Church, western as well as eastern. 'They have driven away from the holy table and from the Mystical Supper of the Lord, those very children whom Christ took in his arms and blessed, and concerning whom he gave commandment that they should be suffered to come to him': yet the rebuke which shamed the Apostles has proved of no avail against the Papists. Christ's injunction in the Gospel of John, 'Unless you eat the flesh of the Son of Man . . .', was not limited to any class or age, but applies to all alike.[3] The Papists cannot deny that they once gave communion to small children, as the east, whether Orthodox or heterodox, has continued to do.[4]

To justify their innovation the Latins urge that a young child cannot 'discern the Lord's Body' nor 'examine himself', as Saint Paul requires (1 Corinthians xi. 28, 29). But in this passage Paul was concerned with those who communicated unworthily; since little children have not attained the age of moral responsibility, they cannot partake unworthily and so the exhortation to self-examination does not apply to them. Furthermore, if this argument against infant communion were to be accepted, the same objection could be made equally against infant Baptism. Babies cannot distinguish the waters of Baptism from ordinary washings: are we therefore to withold from them the benefits of baptismal regeneration? If the Eucharist requires repentance and faith, the same is also true of Baptism; and if the faith of parents or the community avails for children at their Baptism, how much more ought the parents' 'discernment' to avail for children, once baptized, as they receive the Eucharist.[5]

[1] *Σύνταγμα κατὰ ᾿Αζύμων*, pp. 322–4. [2] Ibid., p. 305.

[3] Ibid., p. 348. Some Orthodox writers seem to maintain, on the basis of this text, that children who receive Baptism but not communion are denied salvation: see, for example, Symeon of Thessalonica, *De sacramentis*, 69 (P.G. clv. 236C). But Argenti explicitly rejects this gruesome argument: *Σύνταγμα κατὰ ᾿Αζύμων*, p. 366.

[4] Argenti, op. cit., pp. 354–61. Infant communion survived in the west until well on in the Middle Ages; in parts of South America the practice persisted until the beginning of the twentieth century.

[5] Ibid., pp. 352–4.

In short, the arguments against infant communion apply equally to infant Baptism, and if admitted in the one case they must be admitted in the other. As the early Church realized, there can be no good reason to separate the three sacraments of Baptism, Chrismation, and communion. As Argenti remarks elsewhere, 'Who would not lament the misfortune of Latin children!'[1]

He adds a few cursory remarks upon the Latin doctrines of Intention (σκοπός), which he calls 'heretical and blasphemous'. To ensure a valid sacrament, he says, two things are required: (1) a validly ordained minister, of proper canonical status; (2) the correct performance of the rite. The celebrant's 'intention' is sufficiently indicated by his recitation of the required words and his execution of the required outward actions; to insist also on some inward intention or assent is to render it for ever uncertain whether a sacrament has been validly celebrated, for who, save God, can be sure precisely what is going on in the celebrant's mind?[2]

Such are the defects of the modern Roman rite as seen by an Orthodox writer of the eighteenth century. Taken singly, some of the points in Argenti's indictment may appear of minor importance, but it is his belief that in their cumulative effect they produce a serious distortion of the whole nature of the sacrament. 'The Latins talk about the Eucharist, but in practice they are diametrically opposed to the Eucharist of Christ, the Apostles, and the Holy Fathers.'[3] So he writes at the beginning of the *Treatise*; and on its final page he concludes:

> Therefore in many and various ways they have altered, corrupted, curtailed, despised, and with innovations from all manner of heresies distorted this most holy sacrament; they accept it in bare name alone, but in practice and in fact they utterly repudiate it.[4]

The reference to *innovations* is of particular importance. Again and again in the course of his *Treatise* Argenti has used the same argument: it is an appeal to Tradition, to the Early Fathers, to the practice of the primitive Church, eastern and western. Appealing for the deletion of the *Filioque* from the Creed, Saint Mark of Ephesus had said: 'This Symbol, this

[1] Ἐγχειρίδιον περὶ Βαπτίσματος, p. 41; compare pp. 36–41.
[2] Σύνταγμα κατὰ Ἀζύμων, pp. 367–9. [3] Ibid., p. 4. [4] Ibid., p. 372.

noble heritage of our Fathers, we demand back from you. Restore it then as you received it.'[1] Argenti said the same to the Latins concerning the sacraments of Baptism and the Eucharist: restore them again as they were once. *Remove not the ancient boundaries, which your fathers have set.* Such is the real onus of the charges made against the Latins: the weight of Tradition is against them, nor can they give any good reason for thus wantonly departing from the ancient practice of the universal Church. Seen in this light, matters such as unleavened bread and the denial of the Chalice to the laity acquire a significance which they may not at first sight appear to possess.

[1] Gill, *The Council of Florence*, p. 163.

V

THE FIRE OF PURGATORY

How unsearchable are His judgements, and His ways past finding out! ROMANS xi. 33.

(*i*) *Argenti's Predecessors*

When Bessarion, Archbishop of Nicaea, was asked by Emperor John VIII Palaeologus to expound the Greek view upon purgatory to the Council of Florence, he begged to be excused, protesting that he knew not what to say.[1] His reluctance is understandable. The Greek Fathers, when they reflect on the life after death, look primarily to the Last Day: they speak of such things as the Final Judgement, the resurrection of the body, the transfiguration of the whole material creation, but concerning the state of souls between death and resurrection they have for the most part little to say. Western theology, on the other hand, is far more explicit about the condition of mankind in this intermediate stage. Over two things all Orthodox are agreed: that the members of the Church on earth have a duty to pray for those who have gone before, and that the faithful departed undoubtedly benefit from these prayers. But what is the exact status of these departed souls for whom we pray? In what way do our prayers help them? Here Orthodoxy tends to be very much more reserved than Rome, generally preferring a reverent agnosticism to detailed formulations about the next world. God's judgements are unsearchable, and His ways past finding out.

But when brought into close contact with the west and its more explicit theology on the subject, Orthodox have found it difficult to adhere strictly to a position of reserve and reticence. Under western pressure they have at various times committed themselves to more specific statements. This was what happened at Florence, when the Latins kept urging the Greeks to define more exactly their attitude to the doctrine of purgatory. It also happened in the seventeenth century: confronted by the conflicting views of Rome and the Reformers concerning the

[1] Gill, *The Council of Florence*, p. 118.

state of the departed, Orthodox theologians attempted to determine more precisely the position of their own Church in relation to western controversies.

It cannot be said, however, that they were conspicuously successful in the attempt, for they disagree violently among themselves. Some writers dissent sharply from the Roman Catholic view, others—although they are not always willing to admit the fact—approximate fairly closely to it. They leave the whole subject in a state of great confusion. Thus it is not altogether surprising to find that of all the works of Argenti the *Short Treatise against the Purgatorial Fire of the Papists* is the most obscure in its reasoning and the most indecisive in its conclusions. In his books on Baptism and the Eucharist the main thread of argument is abundantly plain, and each point in the discussion falls clearly into place; but in his essay on purgatory the sequence of thought is far harder to follow. For this we must blame Argenti's predecessors rather than Argenti himself. They are confused, and he has inherited some of their confusion.

To understand where Argenti stands, it will be necessary to consider in some detail the state of the question before he came to treat it. Over three matters in particular the Greeks of the seventeenth century seem to disagree:

(1) Is there a *Particular Judgement*, such as Roman theology affirms? This is denied by some, but maintained by others.

(2) During the period between death and judgement, are souls assigned by God to *three* different places—heaven, hell, and an intermediate place equivalent to (though not necessarily identical with) the purgatory of Roman theology? Or are there only *two* places, heaven and hell? Here again there is some confusion. Orthodox authors as a rule state that there are two places alone—heaven and hell—but at the same time divide the departed into three classes: the saints, the damned, and those who for the time being are in an intermediate condition. But if we distinguish three classes of departed souls, is this not tantamount to affirming (as the Latins do) the existence of three places?

(3) Do the souls in this intermediate condition (if any such souls there be) undergo *expiatory suffering*, thus 'rendering satisfaction' for sins committed in this life? And if they suffer, is this suffering effected through the agency of *fire*? Once more there

is considerable obscurity among eastern writers. Most Orthodox repudiate the idea of purgatorial fire; but some who deny purging by fire, still admit the idea of expiatory suffering after death. Others, again, deny that there can be any expiation after death. Many who inveigh against purgatorial fire do not seem to be clear in their own minds what they are attacking: is it simply the idea of purging by fire, or is it rather the possibility of expiatory suffering in *any* form, or perhaps the existence of a third place as such?

Orthodox writers of the seventeenth century evidently left many things in need of further clarification, and a Greek theologian in the next century might well be in some perplexity as to whom he should follow, since the authorities disagreed so strongly among themselves. Let us look more carefully at the three topics mentioned above.

(1) *The Particular Judgement.* Rome and Orthodoxy agree, of course, in affirming that at the Last Day Christ will come again in power and great glory to judge the living and the dead. But in addition to this General Judgement at the end of the world, is there also a Particular Judgement immediately after the death of each person, at which his or her eternal destiny is decided? Rome teaches that there is such a Particular Judgement (while this is not, perhaps, formally *de fide* in the Roman Catholic Church, it is certainly *sententia fidei proxima*). After death departed souls are judged forthwith, and go either to heaven or to hell or to purgatory—the saints to enjoy their full reward, the damned to receive their full punishment, the souls in purgatory to undergo a period of expiatory suffering and purification before they are completely admitted to the vision of God.

Orthodox teaching is far less clear. Some—for example, Methodios III, Patriarch of Constantinople (1668–71)[1]—deny altogether that there is a Particular Judgement. From this denial, it follows logically that until the General Judgement at the Last Day there is no distinction in status among departed souls; and this is certainly a conclusion which a number of Orthodox have drawn. Aaron Hill writes of the Greeks whom he met:

> They rigorously dissent from the Opinion of the *Roman Catholicks*, in relation to the *Existence* of a Purgatory; maintaining, most of them

[1] See Jugie, *Theologia Dogmatica Christianorum Orientalium*, vol. iv, p. 20.

at least, *that the departed Souls of Mortal Men are sensible of neither Joy nor Torment till the Day of Judgement.*[1]

But other Orthodox authorities—for instance, the *Orthodox Confession* of Peter of Moghila, both in its original and in its revised form[2]—definitely affirm the existence of a Particular Judgement. Others, again, neither employ nor repudiate the term 'Particular Judgement', but leave the matter undecided. In practice, however, most members of this third group assume some distinction in status among the departed before the Last Judgement, and so logically they must admit the *fact* of a Particular Judgement, even though they refrain from using the technical term.

But the difference between those who affirm and those who deny a Particular Judgement, is not quite as great as might at first appear. For those who affirm a Particular Judgement, while naturally believing that souls before the Last Day are in some degree 'sensible of joy and torment', would yet add that no one has so far received his *full* reward. The righteous and the wicked, although already in different conditions, enjoy only a foretaste of the blessedness or torment which will eventually be theirs: they are only in a relative and provisional heaven, a relative and provisional hell. Until the resurrection of the body and the Final Judgement, all alike are in a state of waiting and expectation. The Mother of God, of course, is an exception here, for in her case (as in that of Enoch and Elias, and perhaps others) the resurrection of the body has been anticipated.

Thus on one point almost all Orthodox seem agreed in dissenting from the Roman Catholic view: the saints, so Orthodox believe, do not at once enter upon their perfect blessedness, nor are the wicked received at once into the fullness of their torment. This constitutes the fourth of the 'Five Differences' of Florence.[3] As the revised version of Moghila's *Orthodox Confession* puts it:

Before the Final Judgement neither the just nor sinners receive the full reward for their works; nevertheless they are not all in one and the same state, nor are they all sent to the same place. . . . The souls of the just, though they are in heaven, have not received their full

[1] *A Full and Just Account*, p. 184.

[2] Part i, question 61: εἶναι λοιπὸν μερικὸν κριτήριον (Karmiris, *Μνημεῖα*, vol. ii, p. 621).

[3] See above, p. 63.

crown before the Final Judgement, nor do the souls of the damned suffer their full punishment; it is only after the Last Judgement that their souls, reunited with their bodies, will receive in full the crown of glory or the punishment due to them.[1]

In so far as the *Orthodox Confession* assigns souls to different places before the Last Day, it affirms what certain Orthodox (for example, those with whom Aaron Hill talked) would deny. But practically all Orthodox of the seventeenth and eighteenth centuries would agree with it when it states that neither just nor wicked receive their reward in full before the resurrection of the body.

Writing to the Eastern Patriarchs in 1716, the Nonjurors said:

> None do immediately ascend into the heaven of heavens, but do remain until the resurrection in certain inferior mansions, appropriated to them, waiting in hope for the revelation of that day, and joining in the prayers and praises of the militant Church upon earth, offer'd up in faith.[2]

In their reply of 1718 the Greek Patriarchs made no objection to this statement.[3]

(2) *Three Places or Two?* Here, so it seems at a first glance, there is no doubt whatever about the Orthodox position. Peter of Moghila, in the original draft of his *Orthodox Confession*, maintained that there is a third place for departed souls, apart from heaven and hell; but he stands alone. Other Orthodox writers speak only of two places, heaven and hell; and most of them go out of their way specifically to deny the existence of purgatory. 'Between Abraham's bosom and the torments of hades,' writes Meletios Pigas, Patriarch of Alexandria from 1592 to 1601, 'we are taught that there is a kind of chaos, but no purgatory.'[4] And Meletios Syrigos, in the revised version of Moghila's Confession, is most definite on this point:

> *Question.* Perhaps men die who are midway between the saved and the damned?
>
> *Answer.* There are no men in this position. . . .
>
> *Question.* What should we believe about the fire of purgatory?

[1] Part i, questions 61, 68 (Karmiris, *Μνημεῖα*, vol. ii, pp. 621, 624). In the original version Moghila upheld the normal Roman teaching that the saints enter at once upon their full blessedness.

[2] Williams, *The Orthodox Church of the East in the Eighteenth Century*, pp. 8–9.

[3] Karmiris, *Μνημεῖα*, vol. ii, p. 806; Williams, op. cit., p. 46.

[4] *Διάλογος 'Ορθόδοξος Χριστιανός*, p. 31.

Answer. This fire is not mentioned anywhere in Scripture, nor does Scripture say anywhere that there is a temporary punishment which purifies souls after death. Indeed, it was for this very reason that the opinion of Origen was condemned by the Church at the second Council of Constantinople.[1]

The doctrine of purgatory, writes the Synod of Constantinople in its Encyclical Letter of 1838 (a document remarkable chiefly for the extreme violence of its language) is 'an evil and new-fangled invention, something altogether contrary to the Gospels and opposed to God'.[2]

So far all seems clear. But on closer inspection we can discern certain complications in the Orthodox position. Let us take as an example a passage in Elias Miniati's celebrated book, *The Rock of Offence*, first published in 1718 and many times reprinted.[3] 'Holy Scripture', he writes, 'speaks of two places (τόποι), namely a place of rest and a place of everlasting punishment; but we are told nothing of a third place. Nevertheless we acknowledge three different states (καταστάσεις) of souls.'[4] The first state consists in the just who die in the grace of God; the second in the wicked who are guilty of mortal sins and who die unrepentant. 'The third state of souls consists in those who after sinning have repented, but because of an untimely death, or else through negligence and laziness, they have failed to perform their "canon" here in this life; and so, since they have not satisfied divine justice here, it is necessary for them to satisfy it in the next world.'[5]

Three *states*, but not three *places*: such is the position upheld by Miniati, as well as by many other Orthodox including Argenti himself, as we shall see shortly. Miniati's treatment of the subject (in which certain 'Latinisms' are perhaps present) may be compared with that by a Russian writer of the present century, Archpriest Sergius Bulgakov:

The Orthodox Church recognizes two states in the world beyond the tomb: on the one hand, the beatitude of Paradise; on the other,

[1] Part i, questions 64, 66 (Karmiris, *Μνημεῖα*, vol. ii, pp. 621–3). Origen was condemned for teaching that the torments of hell are not eternal.

[2] Karmiris, op. cit., vol. ii, p. 900.

[3] *Πέτρα Σκανδάλου*, first edition, Leipzig, 1718; I have used the Athens edition of 1863. A Latin translation was published in London in 1762, under the title *Lapis Offendiculi*.

[4] *Πέτρα Σκανδάλου*, p. 127.

[5] Ibid., p. 130.

a state of suffering. The Orthodox Church does not know Purgatory as a special *place* or state. There are not sufficient Biblical or dogmatic foundations for asserting the existence of a third place of this nature. Nevertheless, the possibility of a *state* of purification is undeniable—an idea common to both Orthodoxy and Catholicism. . . . What is fundamentally important is not the distinction between hell and Purgatory as two different places where souls live; it is more their distinction as different *states*.[1]

But, it may be objected, is this not a quibble? It is meaningless to affirm three states beyond the grave, and then to deny three places; for when applied to the life after death the two terms *topos* (place) and *katastasis* (state) amount to the same thing. To speak at all of 'places' in the next world is to think in terms of analogy, for spatial concepts cannot be applied literally to it. Heaven is not a geographical area up in the sky, nor is hell a geographical area under the ground, but both are states, the one of beatitude and the other of everlasting suffering. If, then, Orthodox theologians are willing to allow a third state for departed souls, in addition to the states of blessedness and unending torment, they are by implication admitting the existence of a third place besides heaven and hell. Perhaps they understand this third place differently from the Romans, and for this reason prefer not to call it by the name 'purgatory'. But that is not the point in question at the present moment, for we are here concerned not with the character of this third place, but with the possibility of its existence.

Let us look more closely at the arguments of those who affirm three states but only two places, taking as a typical example the *Ekthesis* of Gabriel Severus, Metropolitan of Philadelphia (1541–1616),[2] which is closely followed by many later Orthodox authorities, and in particular by the Council of Constantinople in 1722.[3] Over the question of purgatory, writes Severus, we agree in part with the Roman Catholics, and in part we differ from them. We agree with them that the dead are benefited through the prayers and alms of the living; we differ from them in that we deny the existence of a 'third place'. Scripture speaks of heaven and hell, but says nothing of purgatory. Gabriel continues:

[1] *The Orthodox Church*, pp. 208–9 (italics in the original).

[2] *Ἔκθεσις*, Part 2, pp. 46–53.

[3] See Karmiris, *Μνημεῖα*, vol. ii, pp. 822–59, and in particular pp. 851–5.

We believe, however, that these two places—both that of the just and that of the sinful—contain many different 'mansions' or dwelling places (μοναί), even as the Truth Himself says: 'In my Father's house are many mansions' (John xiv. 2). Note that he speaks of only one house, but of many mansions, thus indicating that there is only one place, although there are many mansions in it.[1]

Thus, so Gabriel argues, there is one 'place of punishment'—hell—and there is one 'place of light and brightness'—paradise. But within this one place of punishment are many different 'mansions', each with its particular type of suffering, adapted to the nature of the sin to be punished. Now some of these 'mansions' are places of *eternal* punishment, from which there is no release; thither are sent the utterly wicked and unrepentant, who have no hope. But there are other 'mansions' where less wicked souls are sent, there to remain for a time only and not for ever. Here they endure not an everlasting but a 'partial' chastisement, 'according to the measure of their sins'. Accordingly the fire in hell may be termed, from one point of view, an everlasting fire, for its flames will never be extinguished; but it is at the same time a 'transitory' (πρόσκαιρος) fire, for some of the souls who are cast into it remain there only for a limited period:

The fire is termed temporary, not in virtue of its nature, but because of those souls who are delivered from it; yet on account of those souls who are punished there eternally, it is termed eternal.[2]

These 'mansions' of temporary punishment Severus refuses to call by the title 'purgatory' (καθαρτήριον), but he terms them τόποι ἱκανοποιοί, 'places that make reparation or satisfaction', which (so one would think) amounts to much the same thing.

Thus, according to Severus, it is possible for those who at the moment of their death are consigned to hell, to be liberated thence before the Day of Judgement:

Christ, when he descended into hell, opened it and freed his ancestors and all the just men who were there. It must be realised that since that time hell has not yet been closed, but up to the present it still remains open.[3]

It is precisely on this account that the Church prays for the departed:

[1] Ἔκθεσις, Part 2, p. 49. [2] Ibid., p. 51. [3] Ibid., p. 52.

Since hell is still open and God in His infinite compassion is ready to show mercy, souls not only receive alleviation and comfort as a result of the prayers offered to God on their behalf, but also a complete release and deliverance from punishment.[1]

After the Last Judgement the gates of hell are presumably closed, and there is no further possibility of release.

Such are the views of Severus upon the state of the departed. Between him and Latin theologians there is certainly a difference of terminology, but it is difficult to discover any fundamental contradiction in thought. The Latins speak of three places, heaven, hell, and purgatory; Severus denies that there is any third place, but he divides hell into two parts, the one a place of eternal torment, the other a place of temporary punishment. As Leo Allatius not unjustly observes, 'Rem fatetur Philadelphiensis, et nomen refugit.'[2] Once we have admitted the existence of a class of departed souls who undergo temporary punishment, it matters very little whether we put these souls in an upper division of hell, in a lower division of paradise, or in a third and separate 'place' intermediate between the two.

Father Richard Simon comments to this effect, and points out that the Greek way of speaking, whereby what the Latins call purgatory is treated as a subdivision of hell, can also be found in some of the prayers in the Roman rite:

The *Latins* . . . commonly establish a Place of Purgatory, and a Fire which torments Souls. But the *Greeks* deny both, though they acknowledge a certain State of Purgatory; and therefore they pray to God for the Dead. . . . There is this difference, nevertheless, betwixt the *Greeks* and the *Latins*, as to their praying for the Dead, that the latter have explained themselves more fully; whereas the former, and all the other Orientals, have continued in more General Terms. The *Latins*, however, in their Prayers for the Dead at Mass, retain the Ancient form, which agrees pretty well with what the *Greeks* believe of Hell, Purgatory and Paradise. This is the manner of praying for the Dead in the Mass of the *Latins*. *Domine Jesu Christe, libera animas omnium fidelium defunctorum de paenis inferni et de profundo lacu: libera eas de ore Leonis, ne absorbeat eas Tartarus, ne cadant in obscurum*, &c. These words seem to confirm the Opinion of the *Greeks* and other Christians of the East, for they suppose but one Place, which is Hell, where the Souls are detained as in a dark Prison, and

[1] Ibid., p. 53.

[2] *De perpetua in dogmate de Purgatorio consensione*, p. 219.

they pray that the Souls may pass from that obscure Place, to a Place of Light and Rest, which is Paradise: and this exactly agrees with the Prayer that the Priest says at the Mass which is called *in die obitus*.

. . . When they pray that God would deliver Souls out of Hell, that is to be understood of the State of Purgatory; I mean, that in that obscure Prison which they call Hell, there are two sorts of Souls; one sort whose Sins are not so enormous as to be condemned for them to Eternal Punishment there; and another who are really condemned to Hell, there to abide for ever. Of these last it may be said, that *in inferno nulla est redemptio*; whereas in respect of the first sort of Souls, it may be said, that *in inferno est redemptio*.[1]

Thus between the Greeks who affirm two places after death and the Latins who affirm three, there is not necessarily any basic disagreement. One cannot but feel that Orthodox theologians have sometimes been over-anxious to discover differences between themselves and Rome.

(3) *Expiation and Fire*. But granted that most Greeks—at any rate by implication—acknowledge the existence of a third or intermediate place for departed souls, how far do they envisage this third place in the same terms as the Latins? For many Greek writers, as for the Latins, it is a place of suffering: but (i) do they consider the suffering to be expiatory? and (ii) if so, in what form is the suffering inflicted—by fire or by some other means?

Over the question of expiatory suffering after death, there is a genuine conflict of opinion among Orthodox of the seventeenth and eighteenth centuries. Some agree here with the Roman Catholics and definitely accept the doctrine of expiation after death. Three examples may be taken: Gabriel Severus; the Council of Jerusalem in 1672; and Elias Miniati. Severus, as we have already seen, when describing his 'mansions' of temporary punishment, calls them places of reparation or satisfaction (τόποι ἱκανοποιοί), a title which surely indicates the expiatory character of the sufferings which souls there undergo. It is not very clear why, having gone so far as this, he stops short of the term 'purgatory'.

Turning next to the *Confession* of Dositheos, accepted by the Council of Jerusalem, we find that Dositheos, like Severus,

[1] *The Critical History*, pp. 18–20.

avoids the word 'purgatory', but he too gives what is in all essentials the Roman Catholic teaching: 'catholice omnino sonat', as Martin Jugie observes.[1] Those, writes Dositheos in his eighteenth chapter, who have received forgiveness for mortal sins, but who have not had time to bring forth fruits of repentance and so perform satisfaction (*ἱκανοποίησις*) in this life, descend to hell and there undergo a temporary punishment or penalty (*ποινή*) for their past offences. They possess the sure and certain knowledge that they will be released before the Last Day, but the exact time of their release is known to God alone.[2] Here Dositheos adopts the normal Latin distinction between sin (*ἁμαρτία*) and temporal punishment (*ποινή*): the former (if mortal) can be effaced by repentance alone, and only in this life; the latter can be undergone either in this world or in the next. Like Severus, Dositheos divides hell into two parts—the one a place of eternal torment for the utterly wicked, the other (like the Roman purgatory) a place of temporary punishment for those who will eventually be received into heaven.

Much the same position is upheld by Miniati in a passage which we have already cited.[3] If a man has sinned and afterwards repents, then (according to Miniati) divine justice requires that he render satisfaction by performing his 'canon'; and those who for some reason have failed to do this before death, must satisfy divine justice by suffering for a time in the world to come. This is indistinguishable from the Roman teaching, as expounded at Lyons (1274), and reaffirmed at Florence (1439): 'If men die in true repentance and charity before they have rendered satisfaction for their sins and omissions by worthy fruits of repentance, their souls are purged after death by purgatorial or purifying punishments.'[4] 'The temporal punishments for sins', writes a contemporary Roman Catholic theologian, 'are atoned for in Purgatory by the so-called suffering of atonement (*satispassio*), that is, by the willing bearing of the expiatory punishments imposed by God.'[5]

But there are other Orthodox in this period who altogether rejected the Roman teaching. Once more three examples may

[1] *Theologia Dogmatica Christianorum Orientalium*, vol. iii, p. 360.

[2] *Confession*, Decree xviii (Karmiris, *Μνημεῖα*, vol. ii, p. 764, note 10).

[3] See above, p. 144, quoting *Πέτρα Σκανδάλου*, p. 130.

[4] Denziger, *Enchiridion*, section 464; compare section 693.

[5] Ludwig Ott, *Fundamentals of Catholic Dogma*, Cork, 1957, p. 485.

be given: Meletios Pigas; the Council of Jassy in 1642; and Dositheos in later life. Pigas calls in question the basic assumptions underlying the Latin teaching, and in particular rejects the whole idea of man 'rendering satisfaction' to divine justice. Once sin has been forgiven by God, no further stain of guilt remains: God's forgiveness is complete, and so there is no need for expiation, atonement, or satisfaction on man's part either in this life or after death. 'Fruits of repentance' are not to be considered as an act of reparation nor as a recompense for sin, required by divine justice, but are simply indications of the sincerity of a man's repentance, springing voluntarily from his contrite heart. Therefore if a man dies penitent before he has time to display these fruits of repentance, God does not exact expiation from him in the world to come, but grants him a full purification, in virtue of Christ's merits and his most precious Blood.[1]

The same anti-expiationist view is found in the revised *Orthodox Confession*, as adopted at Jassy. In the original, Peter of Moghila followed the standard Roman teaching, but this was one of the passages which Meletios Syrigos changed. It sometimes happens (so the revised version states) that the souls of sinners are released from hell, yet this release is not secured through any penance or satisfaction which the departed themselves render, but is brought about by the prayers which the living offer on their behalf:

> After death the soul cannot perform any work whereby it may procure release from the bonds of hell. Its release is effected solely by the Holy Liturgies, the prayers, and the alms of the living. . . . The Church has good reason to offer the Bloodless Sacrifice on behalf of departed souls and to send up prayers to God for the forgiveness of their sins. But the departed do not purify themselves by the suffering which they undergo.[2]

Even Dositheos, who in his *Confession* inclined to the Roman view, was in later life converted to Pigas' way of thinking. In his *Manual refuting the Madness of the Calvinists*, published in 1690, he openly admits that he was mistaken in his earlier opinions. There are no καθαρτικαὶ τιμωρίαι, no expiatory or purifi-

[1] Jugie, *Theologia Dogmatica Christianorum Orientalium*, vol. iv, pp. 143–7.

[2] Part i, questions 64, 66 (Karmiris, *Μνημεῖα*, vol. ii, pp. 622–3).

catory punishments, after death. Souls are sometimes released from hell, but this release is effected through the offering of the Liturgy, through the prayers, almsgiving, and good works of the living; it is not the result of any act of reparation rendered by the souls themselves. Dositheos, following Saint Mark of Ephesus,[1] argues that small or 'venial' (ἀθανάσιμα) sins, for which a man has not repented before he dies, are freely forgiven by God in His mercy. As for mortal sins, if a man has sincerely repented, then God forgives him and he will be admitted to heaven, even though he has no time to bring forth fruits of repentance before his death. No valid separation can be made between ἁμαρτία and ποινή, between guilt and temporal punishment: if the first is forgiven, then the second also is remitted, and so there can be no question of a penalty or 'satisfaction' which still remains to be paid after death. In thus rejecting any idea of satisfaction after death (together with the distinction between guilt and temporal punishment), Dositheos definitely repudiates the position which he adopted in the eighteenth section of his *Confession*.[2]

It is evident that we are confronted here with a serious discrepancy among Orthodox theologians of the seventeenth century. Both those who supported the Roman doctrine of expiatory suffering after death and those who rejected it could claim weighty support. The *Confession* of Dositheos, in which the doctrine was upheld, had been formally ratified by the Council of Jerusalem, the most important of the seventeenth-century councils; and in the answer which the Eastern Patriarchs sent to the Nonjurors in 1723, the *Confession* was treated as an authoritative exposition of the Orthodox faith. (Admittedly Dositheos had later changed his mind; but it was his earlier, and not his later, view which possessed conciliar ratification and which was sent to the Nonjurors.) On the other hand, the revised version of Moghila's *Orthodox Confession*, in which the doctrine was rejected, had been approved by the Council of Jassy in 1642 and officially endorsed by the four Eastern Patriarchs in the following year. To whom was Argenti to turn,

[1] *Patrologia Orientalis*, xv. 76.

[2] Ἐγχειρίδιον ἐλέγχον τὴν Καλβινικὴν φρενοβλάβειαν, pp. 81–86; Karmiris, *Μνημεῖα*, vol. ii, pp. 765–8. (Karmiris prints the original version of the *Confession*, as ratified by the Council of Jerusalem, in a footnote; in his main text he gives the later version, as emended by Dositheos in the *Manual* of 1690.)

when he came to write his *Short Treatise against the Purgatorial Fire of the Papists*?

Closely related to this question of expiation is the further problem of fire. If the dead suffer—whether by way of expiation or not—does this suffering take the form of fire? Elias Miniati leaves the question entirely open:

> But in what way are they punished? By fire, for example, or by water? This we do not know; for we find no answer to this question either in the Holy Scriptures or in the holy Fathers, for these speak of one fire only—the unquenchable fire of everlasting punishment.[1]

But the great majority of Orthodox writers take up a far more intransigent position, denying altogether the possibility of a temporary punishment by fire. In their letter of 1718 to the Nonjurors, the Eastern Patriarchs term the fire of purgatory 'a fiction and a doting Fable, invented for lucre and to deceive the simple.'[2] Even the most Latin of the Latinizers, Peter of Moghila, while maintaining in the original version of his *Orthodox Confession* the existence of a third place apart from heaven and hell, yet denies that there is suffering by fire in this third place.

There are, however, three matters in this connection which are calculated to cause confusion. First, most Orthodox writers seem to attach an altogether inordinate importance to this question of purgatorial fire, turning it into a major issue in their controversy with Rome. Apart from Miniati[3] (and perhaps a few others) the Greeks overlook the fact that the Church of Rome, while making belief in purgatory *de fide*, has never put out any dogmatic statement concerning purgatorial *fire*. The Councils of Lyons, Florence, and Trent state *that* the departed suffer in purgatory, but they do not state *how* they suffer. The belief that this suffering takes the form of fire, so Cardinal Bellarmine held, is no more than 'probabilissima opinio'. (Others, such as Allatius and Arcudius, are more emphatic and claim that it is 'sententia *certissima*'.)[4] It is surely a mistake on

[1] *Πέτρα Σκανδάλου*, p. 130.

[2] Karmiris, *Μνημεῖα*, vol. ii, p. 807; Williams, *The Orthodox Church of the East in the Eighteenth Century*, p. 47.

[3] Op. cit., p. 130.

[4] Allatius, *De perpetua in dogmate de Purgatorio consensione*, p. 158; P. Arcudius, *Utrum detur Purgatorium et an illud sit per ignem*, pp. 14–15.

the Orthodox part to make a major issue out of something which Rome has never formally defined.

In the second instance, when Orthodox controversialists start arguing against Purgatorial fire, it often seems that they are uncertain in their own minds precisely what they are trying to attack. Their arguments, while ostensibly directed against temporary suffering by fire, have in many cases a more extensive scope; they fail to distinguish between the question of fire, on the one hand, and the far wider questions of expiatory suffering after death and the existence of a third place as such, on the other. Inevitably this gives rise to confusion: for obviously it is possible to assert the existence of a third place and to maintain that souls render satisfaction and expiation by suffering there, without necessarily holding at the same time that these sufferings take the form of fire.

Thirdly, many of those Greeks who deny the existence of purgatorial fire yet maintain (as we have seen) that the departed are in some cases sent for a limited period to be chastised in the fire of hell. Thus while rejecting the fire of purgatory as such, they then readmit the idea of temporary punishment by fire in a slightly different form. Not unreasonably Allatius comments:

> You say that there is a fire in hell, which by burning tortures and purges souls; and yet you deny purgatorial fire. But it makes little difference whether the place where this fire produces its effect be termed hell or purgatory, so long as we agree that there is a fire, and that it punishes and purges.[1]

Once more, one cannot but suspect an unconscious desire on the part of some Orthodox to exaggerate their differences with Rome.

But not all Greeks admit a temporary suffering by fire, for there are some who maintain that before the Last Judgement there is no fire in hell (nor in any third place, if such a place there be). Only after the resurrection, when man's soul has been reunited to his body, can he undergo punishment by fire: souls, being immaterial, cannot be burnt. This view was put forward by Greeks at Florence,[2] and it was also adopted by Dositheos in his *Manual refuting the Madness of the Calvinists*.[3] Clearly on this

[1] *De perpetua in dogmate de Purgatorio consensione*, p. 219.

[2] Gill, *The Council of Florence*, pp. 123–4.

[3] *'Εγχειρίδιον*, p. 82; Karmiris, *Μνημεῖα*, vol. ii, p. 767.

theory there can be no question of temporary chastisement by fire in *any* form, whether in hell or in purgatory.

When so many points of disagreement and confusion existed among his predecessors, it is easy to understand why Argenti himself should sometimes be uncertain in his discussion of purgatory.

(*ii*) *Argenti's Short Treatise*

The *Short Treatise against the Purgatorial Fire of the Papists* falls into three parts. The body of the work (as the title indicates) is devoted to an attack upon the doctrine of purgatorial fire (pp. 17–43); this is followed by some remarks of more general application (pp. 43–51); finally there is a short explanation why the Church prays for the dead (pp. 51–54).

In the first part Argenti develops the usual Greek argument against the fire of purgatory: lack of evidence. Belief in purgatorial fire, he urges, can claim no support from Scripture, and has nowhere been affirmed unambiguously and as a dogma (δογματικῶς) by any of the Fathers. Following John Chrysostom, he interprets 1 Corinthians iii. 13–15 as referring to the Last Judgement and the fire of hell.[1] Among the Fathers to whom the Latins appeal, Augustine is hopelessly obscure, and nothing certain can be deduced from what he says; furthermore he intended to express no more than a private opinion.[2] The texts quoted from Gregory the Great may well be spurious, and if authentic, have been misunderstood. When Gregory of Nyssa uses the term *kathartirion*, he does not mean by the word what the modern Roman Church reads into it, and we have only to look carefully at what he really says to be convinced that, so far from supporting the Roman doctrine, he is in direct opposition to it. As for Origen, his teaching on the after-life is certainly not that of the Papists, and in any case he was condemned as a heretic by the fifth Ecumenical Council.[3] It is to be regretted that in his discussion Argenti does not distinguish more clearly between the general question of the existence of a third place as such, and the subsidiary issue of purging by fire: his arguments

[1] *Συνταγμάτιον κατὰ τοῦ Παπιστικοῦ καθαρτηρίου πυρός* (henceforward abbreviated as *Συνταγμάτιον*), pp. 19–25, quoting Chrysostom, P.G. lxi. 75–79.

[2] *Συνταγμάτιον*, p. 35; compare *Σύνταγμα κατὰ 'Αζύμων*, p. 283.

[3] *Συνταγμάτιον*, pp. 27–37. Argenti appeals in particular to Gregory of Nyssa, P.G. xlvi. 428AB, drawing attention to the words *οὔτε τιμωμένων οὔτε κολαζομένων*.

would have been more effective, had he decided more exactly what he was trying to disprove. This, as has been noted, is a defect common to many Greek writers of the period.

Where does Argenti stand in relation to the three topics treated above—the Particular Judgement, the existence of a third place, and the possibility of expiatory suffering after death? About the Particular Judgement he says nothing explicit, neither using the term nor attacking it. He assumes, however, that in the life after death the souls of the departed, even before the resurrection, will be divided into different classes and assigned to different places; and so by implication he allows some kind of judgement immediately after death.[1] Naturally he accepts the normal Orthodox view that the departed enter upon the fullness of their blessedness or torment, not immediately after death, but only after their resurrection at the Last Day.[2]

Concerning the existence of a third place, he follows the view normal among Orthodox at this time: three *states* after death, but only two *places*. On one page he asserts bluntly that the Catholic Church knows of two places only, heaven and hell; there is no third place or 'temporary punishment' in the life to come.[3] But elsewhere he qualifies this, admitting a third class of departed souls, intermediate between the just in heaven and the wicked in hell. He appeals to Saint Gregory of Nyssa, who wrote:

> As it seems to me, the souls of men will be divided into three classes in the life which we await. . . . The first is the order of the just, who deserve praise; the second, of those who are neither honoured nor punished; the third, of those who are being punished for their sins.[4]

Commenting on Saint Gregory's words, Argenti argues that while they clearly indicate the existence of a third or middle state of departed souls, yet this middle state is not at all the same as the Latin purgatory; for the souls there do not undergo suffering, but are 'neither honoured *nor punished*':

> In the Liturgy, the Church makes mention of three orders: (1) the living, (2) the saints, (3) those who have fallen asleep in faith. The living fall outside the scope of our present discussion; and for the saints the Church does not intercede, but she makes mention of them

[1] Συνταγμάτιον, pp. 33–34, quoted below, at the foot of this page.
[2] Συνταγμάτιον, p. 51, quoted below, p. 157, items 2, 3, and 4.
[3] Ibid., p. 44. [4] P.G. xlvi. 428AB.

when giving thanks to God. She intercedes, then, for those who are simply called 'faithful'. But Saint Gregory teaches that in the life to come, men are divided into three groups: (1) the saints, (2) those in the middle (μέσοι), (3) those who are being punished. Now for the saints and those being punished the Church does not pray; therefore she prays for those in the middle.

But concerning those in this middle state, Saint Gregory writes that they are *neither honoured nor punished.* Therefore, the order of 'faithful', for whom the Church prays, is not being punished, that is, they are not undergoing torments and retributive chastisement.[1]

It is difficult to see how Argenti, having gone as far as this, can logically avoid admitting the existence of a third place; and perhaps it is only his fear and suspicion of things Roman which prevents him from doing so. For if there is no third place, where does Argenti think that the souls in this middle state are to be found? To this he gives no answer, and it is not easy to imagine what answer he could in fact give. He cannot say, as Severus does, that they are in an upper division of hell; for if they were in hell, they would be suffering punishment. He cannot say that they are in the lower 'mansions' of heaven, for in that case they would be to some extent in a position of honour. Surely his middle state of souls implies a middle place between heaven and hell? Here Argenti, like other Greek theologians of this period, does not seem to have worked out clearly the implications of his position. Had he done so, he might have arrived at different conclusions—conclusions not necessarily identical with the Roman teaching, but at any rate less directly opposed to it.

On the third topic—expiatory suffering after death—Argenti's position will already be plain to some extent. As we have seen, he definitely rejects the idea of 'retributive chastisement' in the life to come, and holds that the souls in the middle state do not suffer. He adopts the views of Pigas and of Dositheos in later life; of the two schools of thought current in seventeenth-century Orthodoxy—the expiationist and the anti-expiationist—he chooses without hesitation the one more hostile to Rome. There can be no question, so he argues, of the faithful departed 'rendering satisfaction' or 'making reparation' after death for their sins. First, so far as venial sins are concerned, if a man has not repented of them before he dies, then at the moment of

[1] Συνταγμάτιον, pp. 33–34; compare Σύνταγμα κατὰ Ἀζύμων, p. 283.

death God in His great mercy freely forgives these small failings. (Here Argenti follows Mark of Ephesus and Dositheos' *Manual.*) Nor, in the second place, is a man required to make expiation after death for the mortal sins of which he has repented. It is not we by our own sufferings but Christ the Lamb of God who takes away the sin of the world. It is Christ who, by suffering on the Cross, has 'purged our sins' (Hebrews i. 3) and who by his precious Blood 'cleanses us from all sin' (1 John i. 7). Since Christ is the only satisfaction, expiation, and purgation for the sins of the faithful, when once we have repented, no further act of reparation on our part is either necessary or possible. To affirm otherwise is to imply that Christ was crucified in vain.[1]

Like Calvin, who called purgatory 'exitiale commentum quod Christi crucem evacuat',[2] Argenti believes that the Roman teaching undermines the fullness of Our Lord's redeeming sacrifice:

> The Catholic Church believes and teaches that after death and before the general resurrection the souls of those who have fallen asleep in faith are assisted by the prayers of the Church, through the satisfaction made by Christ, and through his Cross and Death—through this alone, and through nothing else. . . . We differ from the Papists not only over the question of fire, but we also deny all other expiatory punishment and torment. That is to say, we do not believe that those who have fallen asleep in the hope of everlasting life, and have died in repentance, are punished or chastened in expiation of their sins over which they have repented; but God in His divine loving-kindness appropriates to them the expiation wrought by Christ, the Church praying for this.[3]

But why pray for the faithful departed, since they have been freely forgiven, and suffer no torment or punishment in the middle state? Argenti gives a series of reasons why we must offer prayers on behalf of the dead:

> 1. To show that their souls are alive, and have not passed into non-existence as the irrational beasts.
> 2. In confirmation of the general resurrection.
> 3. In confirmation of the Last Judgement.
> 4. To confirm that each of them has not yet received his reward (as the holy Fathers teach).

[1] *Συνταγμάτιον*, pp. 44–47. [2] *Institutes*, III. v. 6.
[3] *Συνταγμάτιον*, pp. 47–48; compare pp.25–27.

5. To remind us that they are our members, and that we ought to commemorate them.

6. To help them. 'For sacrifices and almsgiving help some, effecting for them a complete remission; while for those who have been condemned, they perhaps make the punishment more tolerable' (Augustine, *Enchiridion*, chapter 109).

7. To comfort and console their relatives who are still alive. . . .

8. In accordance with teaching of the greatest antiquity, handed down to us from the Fathers, that we should pray for those who have fallen asleep and commemorate them. . . .

9. Because we are under an obligation to pray for one another. The Calvinolutherans are thus misanthropists and haters of their brethren, for after burying their kinsfolk they then refuse to make any further mention of them.[1]

Several different arguments can be distinguished here. There is the usual appeal to antiquity (reason 8), and to the fact that such prayers console surviving relatives (reason 7). In addition to these Argenti adduces three other considerations which lead closer to the heart of the problem. First, he brings forward the usual Orthodox vision of the whole Church—whether on earth or in the world to come—as a single family, intimately linked together. Death changes location, but cannot sever the bond of love. We pray for others when they are alive; when they die, do they cease to exist, that we should cease to pray for them (reasons 1, 5, 9)? Secondly, we pray for the faithful departed because they are still in a state of expectation, awaiting the Final Judgement at the Last Day and the resurrection of the body. Since they are in an intermediate stage and have still to complete their course, having 'not yet received their reward' (that is, their full and final reward), we must continue to pray on their behalf (reasons 2, 3, 4). Thirdly, Argenti follows Saint Augustine in suggesting that such prayers secure remission (ἄφεσις) for some souls, and lighten the torments of others (reason 6). Here Argenti follows Severus, Dositheos, and others, in teaching that the gates of hell stand open until the day of the Last Judgement, so that souls can occasionally be released from there. This is not, however, an idea to which he gives any great prominence, since nowhere else in the *Short Treatise* does he mention

[1] *Συνταγμάτιον*, pp. 51–52. The reference to Augustine's *Enchiridion* should actually be chapter 110 (P.L. xl. 283D–284A). Argenti translates the Latin somewhat freely.

such a possibility. Indeed, as we have seen, he definitely states that we do not pray for those in hell; but here he seems to admit such a practice.

It is interesting to compare Argenti's *Short Treatise* with the discussion of the same topic in the *Dogmatic Theology* of a leading Greek theologian at the start of the present century, Christos Androutsos. The two are substantially in agreement. Androutsos, like Argenti, will have nothing to do with the term 'purgatory' or with the idea of purging by fire. Like Argenti, although less explicitly, he divides the departed into three classes or states, but denies the existence of a third place. He holds that souls are occasionally released from hell, but adds that the sufferings which these souls undergo for a time in the infernal regions must not be regarded as an act of reparation or 'satisfaction' for their sins: 'there is no room in the Orthodox system for expiatory punishments.' The act of repentance by itself secures a full and perfect remission of sins. 'Works of repentance' and penances imposed by a confessor are not to be considered as expiatory; therefore, if a man dies repentant, but without having performed these 'works', he is not required to render satisfaction in the next world. Repentance is a second Baptism; and so he who repents becomes by that very act a sharer in eternal life, to the same extent as do the newly baptized. If a man dies immediately after Baptism, he is received into heaven; and so if a man dies truly penitent, he is received into heaven likewise.

What of prayers for the departed? These, Androutsos affirms in harmony with Argenti, express the abiding fellowship and communion between the living and the dead. For the rest, 'these prayers must be defined negatively within the limits in which the early Church determined them, excluding all theological speculation as to the manner or character of the assistance which they afford to the departed.' Here Androutsos displays the characteristic Orthodox reticence and reserve. There are gaps in our knowledge, he says, which we must frankly recognize and accept; it is no use trying to gloss over our ignorance by making 'unnecessary distinctions', which are merely 'the efforts of human curiosity' and 'serve no religious ends'.[1]

[1] Androutsos, *Δογματική*, pp. 432–6; compare Gavin, *Some Aspects of Contemporary Greek Orthodox Thought*, p. 414. For a more recent statement by a Greek theologian, presenting much the same point of view, see J. N. Karmiris, *Σύνοψις τῆς δογματικῆς διδασκαλίας τῆς Ὀρθοδόξου Καθολικῆς Ἐκκλησίας*, pp. 108–9, especially p. 108, note 6.

Argenti's tract—remaining, as it did, unpublished until 1939—has naturally exercised no direct influence upon later Greek theologians; but it does in fact reflect the way in which Orthodox thought on this subject has tended to develop. In contemporary Orthodoxy there are few if any who would uphold the more Romanist teaching of Dositheos' *Confession* and Miniati's *Rock of Offence*, with their acceptance of 'satisfaction' and expiatory suffering after death.

Argenti affirms what every Orthodox is bound to believe: that we have a duty to pray for the faithful departed. From this he draws the natural conclusion that in some sense the dead are divided into three groups: the saints, the wicked, and those in the middle state. It is for this third group that the Church prays, in the certain knowledge that her prayer helps them. Exactly how it helps, he does not attempt to say; but he definitely rejects any suggestion that the souls in the middle state suffer expiatory punishment, for this would be inconsistent with the full forgiveness secured through Christ's atoning sacrifice.

VI

THE PAPAL CLAIMS

And his brethren said to him, Shalt thou indeed reign over us? GENESIS xxxviii. 8.

During the seventeenth and eighteenth centuries the number of Greek tracts upon the Papacy is legion. If the Procession of the Holy Spirit formed the chief topic in polemics between east and west before the fall of Constantinople, the Orthodox in the Turkish period came to place greater emphasis upon the Papal Claims, considering these the fundamental point at issue. 'The notorious question of Papal supremacy is the cause of the schism between the Churches,' wrote Maximos the Peloponnesian;[1] 'at the present time,' said Elias Miniati, 'this is the great wall of partition which separates the Churches.'[2] Miniati's book was entitled, in allusion to Saint Peter's name, *The Rock of Offence*: and such indeed the Papal Claims had proved to the Orthodox world.

Argenti's contribution to the subject is comparatively modest. He devoted to the Papacy the three short treatises preserved in manuscript at the Zaviras Library, Budapest; as we have seen, only the first of these has ever been published, and that not in the original Greek but in Arabic.[3] The opening treatise bears the superscription: *Concerning the False Infallibility of the Pope of Rome; that is, a Brief Demonstration against the Pope of Old Rome, in which it is clearly and plainly shown that it is possible for the Pope of Rome to become a heretic, and that many have actually become heretics, and that the Catholic Church teaches how it is possible for the Pope of Rome to become a heretic: which is also confirmed by the analogy of the faith.* As the title indicates, the work is concerned not with the primacy of the Pope, on which most Greek polemicists concentrated, but with his infallibility.

Argenti does not confuse infallibility with impeccability, a common error among Orthodox writers.[4] He is careful to state

[1] Ἐγχειρίδιον κατὰ τοῦ σχίσματος τῶν Παπιστῶν, p. 4.

[2] Πέτρα Σκανδάλου, p. 77.

[3] See above, p. 49.

[4] Such a confusion is made easier by the fact that the same Greek word, ἁμαρτάνειν, means both 'to make a mistake' and 'to sin'.

at the outset that his theme is not the moral failings of the Popes:

> Nevertheless it is not our purpose here to reproach the Papists for the lawless and guilty actions of the Popes, nor for their schisms and anti-popes, nor for their simony, nor for their arbitrary and ungodly deeds. For these things are known to all, and the Papists themselves do not dare to deny them; and he who wishes can learn about them from ecclesiastical history. But above all we know that we ourselves and our own members are accused of much the same things.[1]

This last admission displays a generosity all too rare in the controversy of the time. On the whole Argenti keeps this promise to avoid the moral corruptions of the Popes, although he later has something to say in passing about Pope Joan, of whose historical existence he is firmly persuaded.[2]

After his opening remarks Argenti proceeds to enumerate some of the Popes who have fallen into heresy;[3] this list, he says, is no more than a selection, since the number of heretical Popes is so great that to mention them all would take far too long, and prove a waste of time and paper; in any case 'it is not our intention to trouble the souls of the departed, whatever the manner in which they died'.[4] Among his thirteen examples he includes Pope Liberius, who in 358 subscribed to Arianism, and Vigilius, who for a time opposed the fifth Ecumenical Council (553), although eventually he acknowledged his error; but some of Argenti's other instances are of more questionable historical accuracy. At the end of this list he turns to his main topic,[5] the case of Honorius I, who reigned from 625 to 638 and who was anathematized for heresy by three Ecumenical Councils, the sixth, the seventh, and the eighth. The last of these, the anti-Photian Synod of 869–70, is (as Argenti points out) without authority for the Orthodox; he includes it in his argument because Roman Catholics reckon it as ecumenical. This threefold condemnation, he continues, was accepted without demur by the Popes of the time. This, so he rightly perceives, is a most important point: the condemnation of Honorius was not only a conciliar but a *Papal* condemnation. Argenti carefully cites detailed evidence for the condemnation of Honorius—a

[1] Zaviras Library, Budapest, Ms. 32, p. 1.
[2] Ibid., pp. 5–9.
[3] Ibid., pp. 2–9.
[4] Ibid., pp. 1–2.
[5] Ibid., pp. 9–40.

task which today would be largely unnecessary, since Roman Catholics now openly admit the facts: but in Argenti's time they often suppressed the documentary evidence, or dismissed it as a forgery.

How, Argenti asks, do the Papists attempt to explain away these inconvenient facts? They take up two different lines of defence, arguing either that Honorius' words were misunderstood by the Councils, and are not heretical if correctly interpreted; or else that his words are heretical, but are not embodied in any formal pronouncement, so that he was condemned not as Pope but as a private individual.[1] Those who follow the first line of defence appeal to Saint Maximos the Confessor, who sought to exonerate Honorius from the charge of Monothelitism. To this Argenti retorts that the unsupported opinion of one Father can carry no weight against the united decision of three General Councils. Maximos wrote before the sixth Council met, but had he lived to learn of its pronouncements, he would undoubtedly have submitted his private judgement to superior authority.[2] Nor is the second alternative tenable. Honorius' letter to Patriarch Sergius of Constantinople is clearly intended as the formal and considered verdict of the Pope of Rome; and when the Councils condemned Honorius, they clearly intended to condemn him as Pope.

Developing this point, Argenti brings forward three considerations. He first compares the position of Sergius and Honorius in the seventh century with that of Cyril of Alexandria and Pope Celestine in the fifth: the cases are exactly parallel,

[1] The same two lines of argument are to be found in more recent Roman Catholic writers. In the later editions of Bishop Hefele's *Conciliengeschichte* (i.e. the editions published after 1870), it is stated that Honorius intended to teach the whole Church *ex cathedra*, but that what he wrote was not heretical, if properly understood. Abbot John Chapman, on the other hand, regarded the teaching of Honorius as heretical, but denied that it was given *ex cathedra* (*The Condemnation of Pope Honorius*, London, 1907, pp. 16–17, 110, 114).

In justice to the memory of Bishop Hefele it should, however, be noted that the view of Honorius which he maintained at the time of the first Vatican Council differs considerably from the treatment of Honorius to be found in the later editions of the *Conciliengeschichte*. At the 1870 Council Hefele, like Eustratios Argenti, held that Honorius taught heresy in a formal statement of faith. A leading opponent of the proposed definition of Papal infallibility, Hefele's principal ground of objection was precisely the case of Pope Honorius. (See C. Butler, *The Vatican Council*, vol. ii, London, 1930, pp. 32, 35, 115–16; also Hefele's own speech before the Council, in Mansi, *Amplissima Collectio Conciliorum*, vol. lii, cols. 80–84.)

[2] Budapest Ms., pp. 22–24.

save that the latter were praised for their orthodoxy, the former condemned for their heresy. Sergius wrote to Honorius as to a Pope and Honorius as Pope made formal reply, just as Cyril wrote to Celestine as to a Pope and Celestine replied as such. Therefore, the third General Council praised Celestine as Pope, and the sixth General Council condemned Honorius as Pope.[1] Argenti continues:

> Secondly, we have been taught and we believe that Christ is endowed with two natures, the one passible and the other impassible; but that his vicar also has two natures, the one fallible and the other infallible—this we have only recently been taught, yet for all that we have never yet accepted it nor do we believe it.
>
> Thirdly, the first four Ecumenical Councils did not anathematize the priestly or episcopal dignity of Arius, Macedonius, Nestorius, or Eutyches, but they simply anathematized Arius, Macedonius, Nestorius, and Eutyches; and in the same way the sixth anathematized Honorius.[2]

If the members of the sixth, seventh, and eighth Councils had believed the doctrine of Papal Infallibility, it is inconceivable that they would have condemned Honorius in such unqualified terms, without guarding against possible misunderstanding by framing a statement of infallibility which would exclude his lapse:

> So many holy Fathers, eastern and western, in three Ecumenical Councils, listened to and voted in support of an anathema against the Bishop of Rome, and none of them opened his mouth to oppose such audacity. None of them answered and said, 'How can the Pope of Rome either be misled or mislead others in the dogmas of the faith?' None of them stood up and said, 'What are you about to do, brethren, in anathematizing the Head of the Catholic Church and the Vicar of Christ?'[3]

We are faced, Argenti concludes, with a choice between the belief of the General Councils and the teaching of the modern Roman Church. Either the Councils were wrong in condemning Honorius as a heretic, or else the modern Roman Church is wrong in maintaining, contrary to the decision of the Councils, that the Pope cannot err in formal pronouncements upon matters of faith. The General Councils stand opposed to the Pope: both cannot be right. If we have any reverence for the authority of General Councils, then we must reject the modern

[1] Budapest Ms., pp. 31–33. [2] Ibid., pp. 33–34. [3] Ibid., pp. 34–35.

Roman teaching on Papal Infallibility as 'heretical and blasphemous'.[1]

Had Argenti been writing after the Vatican Council of 1870, he would no doubt have formulated his discussion of Papal Infallibility in more specific terms, but it is unlikely that his arguments would have been very different. Obviously it is possible so to interpret the Vatican definition of infallibility that almost any Papal pronouncement of the past falls outside its scope. Argenti, we may suspect, would gladly have left such distinctions and qualifications to Roman theorists: for him it was enough to know that Popes can err and have erred in matters of the faith; that a Pope was condemned for heresy by the Ecumenical Councils; and that the Papacy accepted this condemnation and proclaimed it without any reservations.

In the second of his three treatises, Argenti turns from Honorius to another crucial era in Papal history: the early fifteenth century. This second part, which bears the title *The Acts and History of the Council of Constance*,[2] is not an original work. It consists in a Greek translation of the more important acts of the Council, together with an account of the historical background, based on Roman Catholic writers. He begins by describing the 'Babylonian Confusion'[3] of the Western Church in the later Middle Ages, with its schisms and its rival Popes; he mentions the attempted solution at Pisa (1409); he then analyses the course of events at Constance itself (1414–18), quoting in full the major decisions taken at the fourth, fifth, sixth, and seventh sessions of the Council. The reason for his interest in Constance is manifest. In his tract on Honorius he had ended with the choice between Pope and General Council; here at Constance was a gathering of western bishops, endowed —at any rate in its own eyes—with ecumenical authority, which unambiguously affirmed the superiority of Council to Pope. What is more, the Fathers of Constance carried their theory into effect: in stripping Pope John XXIII of office, they deposed and subjected to censure a Pope *whom they themselves recognized.*[4]

[1] Ibid., p. 35. [2] Ibid., p. 44.

[3] Argenti uses this phrase in *Σύνταγμα κατὰ 'Αζύμων*, p. 317.

[4] 'C'était la première fois que dans l'Église on déposait un pape *reconnu* de ceux que le déposaient' (*Dictionnaire de théologie catholique*, vol. iii, Paris, 1907, col. 1208).

But though recognized by the 'Ecumenical' Council of Constance, Pope John XXIII has since been demoted. His exact status remained, however, an open

Whatever else the Council of Constance proves, it shows that the developed doctrine of the Papacy was not generally accepted in the west at the start of the fifteenth century.[1]

The third treatise follows, *A Manual concerning the Latin Pope and Antichrist. In which it is shown from the words and testimony of Holy Scripture and of the orthodox Fathers that the Pope of Old Rome is he who is pre-eminently called the Antichrist.*[2] There is a subtitle, *Outline of Antichrist according to the Old and New Testament.*[3] The manuscript is incomplete and only about a third of the work has survived; this fragment, however, is sufficient to indicate Argenti's views on the subject, and it affords us little occasion to regret the disappearance of the rest. Relying upon the well-worn texts in Daniel, 2 Thessalonians, and Revelation, he argues that Antichrist is not to be interpreted as the Devil, but as a man. This man will establish himself in the Christian Church, setting up his throne in a city of seven hills, just as the Scarlet Woman in Revelation sits upon a beast with seven heads. Antichrist will spring not from outside but from within the Church—an apostate or heretic of some kind—and 'he will claim to be the representative of Christ, i.e. to be instead of Christ (ἀντὶ Χριστοῦ), which is called in Latin, *vicarius* of Christ'. The number 666 is explained as representing the name Λατεῖνος (*sic*) or 'Latin'.[4]

The later parts of the treatise are missing, but there can already be little doubt where the argument will lead. Apart from the Patristic quotations, which are as plentiful here as in Argenti's other books, there is little to distinguish his treatment of the subject from the innumerable anti-Papist compositions once so popular in Protestant circles, and still to be found in the ecclesiastical underworld. But although his approach is

question among Roman Catholics until very recently. In the *Dictionnaire de théologie catholique*, for example—a standard and authoritative Catholic work of reference —he is described as 'Pope', not 'anti-Pope' (vol. viii, Paris, 1924, col. 641). But with the accession of a new Pope John XXIII in 1958, the situation has now been clarified.

[1] Much of the material on Constance which Argenti here collected, he used in Σύνταγμα κατὰ Ἀζύμων, pp. 313–20.

[2] Budapest Ms., p. 79.

[3] Ibid., p. 81.

[4] The same interpretation of the name Λατεῖνος occurs in a work by Gabriel Severus, preserved in manuscript at the Monastery of Saint Catherine, Mount Sinai (V. Gardthausen, *Catalogus codicum graecorum Sinaiticorum*, Oxford, 1886, p. 233).

strangely familiar to western ears, there is nothing to prove that he is in fact borrowing from Protestant sources.

A Manual concerning the Latin Pope and Antichrist indicates the bitterness of Argenti's feeling against the Church of Rome, but it must not be thought that the identification of the Pope with Antichrist formed an important element in his thought. Elsewhere in his writings he only refers once to 'our short treatise on the marks of Antichrist',[1] and apart from the present work he scarcely if ever explicitly identifies the Pope with Antichrist. And lest it be considered surprising that a man of Argenti's intelligence and learning should descend to arguments of this character, it may be remembered that the future Cardinal Newman in his early years firmly believed the Bishop of Rome to be Antichrist, a conviction whose effects he only shook off by slow degrees and with great difficulty, as he himself relates.[2]

If the greater part of Argenti's three pieces on the Papacy are devoted to comparatively technical points, there is one passage which indicates his general attitude on the subject:

> The Papists wish to strip and to divest the Bride of Christ, the Catholic Church, of the gifts and the pledge of the Holy Spirit, wherewith she was adorned by her Bridegroom, Jesus Christ, and in their place they would endow her with one poor and puny man, whom they revere as an idol. For they say that without the authority of the Pope of Rome the Catholic Church has no power or strength. They deprive the Church of inerrancy and infallibility, and give it to the Pope. According to the Papist view, it follows from this that when the Pope is deceived, the whole Church is necessarily deceived as well. If this were true, it would mean that the gates of hell have prevailed against the Church; for it has already been clearly and plainly demonstrated that it is possible for the Pope of Rome to be deceived and to become a heretic, and that he has in fact been deceived many times. Nevertheless, the Catholic Church, aided by the Spirit of her Bridegroom, has ever continued to crush the head of the dragon. . . .[3]

It is the familiar complaint of Orthodoxy against Rome: Roman Catholics assign to a single bishop the infallibility which

[1] *Σύνταγμα κατὰ Ἀζύμων*, p. 347.

[2] *History of my Religious Opinions*, London, 1865, p. 7.

[3] Budapest Ms., p. 41. Compare L. E. Mesoloras, *Συμβολικὴ τῆς Ὀρθοδόξου Ἀνατολικῆς Ἐκκλησίας*, vol. ii, Athens, 1893, p. 22: the Roman Catholics 'have deified a mortal man, assigning to him the attributes which belong to God alone and to the Universal Church under the guidance of the Holy Spirit'.

properly belongs neither to him alone nor yet to the hierarchy in general, but only to the Body of Christ as a whole.

Argenti, however, is careful to add that the Popes of the past occupied a high position in Christendom, a position which their successors could occupy again, if they would abate their excessive claims and return to the true Catholic Church which they have deserted:

The orthodox and catholic Popes of Rome are praised, honoured, and seated in the first place and in the first rank among those who preside over the Church. They are called the successors of Peter, catholic teachers, fathers of fathers, ecumenical patriarchs, ecumenical popes, exarchs of the councils, canons of the faith, columns and pillars of orthodoxy, heads of the Church, apostolical popes, judges of the bishops, supreme pontiffs, greatest pontiffs, guides of the truth, bishops of the Catholic Church, exponents of the Gospel. They are named chief, most blessed, most holy, best, lords, and masters. Other names and titles of honour may rightly be given to them; and these and similar titles of honour and praises are heaped upon their writings and their throne.

But as soon as these same Popes begin to wander beyond the walls and frontiers of orthodoxy, peace, and brotherly love; as soon as they also lay claim to a tyrannical monarchy and to an arbitrary position in the Councils, such as that which Dioscorus assumed; when they desire to be exalted over their brethren, and when they attempt to place their throne above the clouds of heaven: then, I say, they are despised, they are set at naught, rebuked, excommunicated, deposed, condemned, persecuted, and anathematized.[1]

Since it was not Argenti's custom to flatter the Roman See idly, we may assume that when he speaks of it in respectful language he means what he says. He is willing to call an orthodox Pope the successor of Peter and even the head of the Church, while the phrase 'judges of the bishops' suggests some degree of general appellate jurisdiction, such as the Sardican Canons, for example, had allowed. Thus far will Argenti go, but no further. The Pope is first among the bishops, but he is only *primus inter pares*. He enjoys a primacy of honour or rank, but not a supremacy of power or rule; an appellate jurisdiction, but not coercive or supreme ordinary jurisdiction. To call his throne the greatest in Christendom is not to endow him with functions different *in nature* from those exercised by his colleagues.

[1] Budapest Ms., pp. 42–43.

Argenti's position is that of Nilus Cabasilas, four hundred years before: 'As long as the Pope observes due order and remains in the truth, he preserves the first place which belongs to him by right; he is the head of the Church and supreme pontiff, the successor of Peter and of all the Apostles; all must obey him and treat him with complete respect. But if he departs from the truth and refuses to return to it, he deserves condemnation.'[1] It was because the Popes of Rome had 'departed from the truth' or, as Argenti put it, 'wandered beyond the walls and frontiers of orthodoxy', that the Eastern Patriarchs had been obliged to sever communion with them; nor could communion be restored until the errant Popes ceased from their wanderings. As Alexis Khomiakov put it: 'We are unchanged; we are still the same as we were in the eighth century. . . . Oh that you could only consent to be again what you were at that time, when we were joined by unity of faith and communion of spiritual love and prayer!'[2]

[1] *Περὶ τῆς τοῦ Πάππα ἀρχῆς* (P.G. cxlix. 728D–729A). Nilus Cabasilas is the uncle of his better known namesake, Nicholas.

[2] From a letter to William Palmer (Birkbeck, *Russia and the English Church*, pp. 36–37).

CONCLUSION

To determine more exactly the place of Eustratios Argenti, it will be instructive to compare him with four men: with Cyril Lukaris (1572–1638) and Dositheos (1641–1707), and with Eugenios Bulgaris (1716–1806) and Saint Nicodemus of the Holy Mountain (1748–1809). The first and second of these, standing at opposite extremes, dominate the Greek religious scene during the seventeenth century; the remaining two, likewise at opposite extremes, overshadow it at the end of the eighteenth.

How, then, does Argenti stand in regard to Cyril and Dositheos? What is his relation to the two theological 'schools'—the semi-Protestant and the Latinizing—which arose under western influence in the Orthodox Church of the seventeenth century? Argenti had studied in the west, and it is only to be expected that marks of his western training should be apparent in what he wrote. Western influence is sometimes evident, for example, in his style and method of argument, in his tendency to classify and subdivide his subject with a certain Scholastic rigidity. (Yet this is surely no great fault, if it contributes to clarity of thought!) It is evident also in his choice of authorities from whom to quote. For while he is thoroughly at home among the earlier Greek Fathers, citing them copiously, on the whole the authors whom he invokes are those to whom western theologians also appealed. Although he sometimes uses later Byzantine writers, in particular Nicholas Cabasilas and Symeon of Thessalonica, he does not seem to be familiar with the works of Saint Isaac the Syrian, Saint Symeon the New Theologian, or Saint Gregory Palamas. Here can be seen a limitation that is in part the result of his western academic background.

But although Argenti has been influenced by the west, this influence is far less profound than in the cases of Lukaris and Dositheos. He cannot be placed either in the Protestantizing group or among the Latinizers. Unlike Lukaris, he is firmly convinced of the objective reality of Christ's presence in the Eucharistic elements and he is willing to speak of 'transubstantiation'; but unlike Dositheos, he avoids the technical distinction between 'substance' and 'accidents'. Unlike Lukaris, he believes in seven sacraments, not two; but unlike Latinizing Orthodox such as Nicholas Bulgaris, he rejects the distinction between 'matter' and 'form' in the sacraments, as also the Latin elaboration of the doctrine of Intention. While Lukaris teaches that souls after death 'depart immediately either to Christ or to condemnation',[1] Argenti admits a 'middle state'; but unlike Dositheos in the *Confession*, he denies the possibility of expiatory suffering after death. Thus despite certain western characteristics in his work, Argenti stands apart from both the westernizing 'schools' of seventeenth century Orthodoxy.

During the last years of Argenti's life, however, there had begun to emerge in the Greek world a new westernizing movement, of which Eugenios Bulgaris may be taken as the leading exponent. The west to which Bulgaris looked for inspiration was not that of the Middle Ages and the Counter-Reformation, nor yet that of Luther and Calvin; it was rather the west of the Enlightenment and the Encyclopedists, with its rationalism, its secular philosophy, and its science. In sharp contrast to Bulgaris and the occidentalists stand the leaders of the Hesychast renaissance at the end of the eighteenth century, most notably the editor of the *Pidalion* and the *Philokalia*, Saint Nicodemus of the Holy Mountain.

Argenti has little in common with Bulgaris. Both studied in North Italy, and it goes without saying that both wrote against the Church of Rome; but there the similarity ends. Eugenios was a monk, a deacon for most of his life, eventually a bishop; Eustratios was married and a layman. The monk, however, was the more worldly of the two. Bulgaris spent his later years in the courts of Frederick II at Berlin and Catherine II at Saint Petersburg—an environment which would scarcely have suited Argenti. Bulgaris, as head of the Athonite School and subsequently as professor at the Patriarchal Academy of Constantinople, had introduced modern western philosophy and science into his teaching, a step for which he was sharply attacked and swiftly expelled; Argenti, while he certainly profited from his studies in Europe, never gave his critics occasion to suspect him as a westernizing innovator. Argenti concentrated upon a single

[1] Karmiris, *Μνημεῖα*, vol. ii, p. 568.

theme; for Bulgaris anti-Latin polemic was but one among many interests. He wrote on logic and mathematics as well as on theology; he translated a book by Voltaire into modern Greek; he produced a rendering of the works of Virgil in Homeric hexameters. Argenti, even if he had the ability, certainly lacked the inclination to follow Bulgaris in such achievements. The multifarious activities of Bulgaris have given him an importance in the history of modern Greece which Argenti naturally does not possess. But as a theologian Argenti is superior: his writings in the field are more substantial and his views more trustworthy.

Argenti is far closer to Nicodemus and his circle. True, Nicodemus was concerned above all with mystical theology and the Prayer of the Heart, subjects on which Argenti does not touch. Nicodemus is primarily (though not exclusively) a spiritual and devotional author, Argenti a dogmatic theologian and a writer of controversy. But both in their different ways are traditionalists, denouncing western innovations, appealing for loyalty to the ancient paths; and as such both stand opposed to Bulgaris.

But while Nicodemus went back to the roots, to the spiritual foundations of the eastern monastic tradition, Eustratios Argenti was more superficial. Like most polemical writers, he was more concerned negatively to rebut the arguments of his opponents than in a positive way to carry the whole question to a deeper level. From first to last Argenti was a controversialist; and while recognizing that the circumstances of his time made a negative and belligerent attitude natural, not to say inevitable, yet we cannot be blind to the unfortunate effects which follow from an exclusive absorption in polemics.

What effects do we mean? In his study of Christian reunion, *Mission et Unité*, Father le Guillou describes the leading features which works of controversy have usually tended to display in polemic alike between Orthodox and Catholics, and between Catholics and Protestants. It is not an alluring portrait. In these works of controversy, he writes, the utmost emphasis is placed upon every possible point of disagreement. Opposition is developed and justified for its own sake. Both sides try to discover as many 'heresies' as they can in the other (witness the huge 'lists of errors' compiled by Greeks and Latins: for example the list by Caucus, Latin Archbishop of Corfu, with its thirty-one indictments).[1] Only a few writers make any effort to verify what they say about the other side, while most are content simply to copy their predecessors. There is little or no sense of proportion. Save in rare instances, no attempt is made to distinguish essential matters of theology from trivial and insignificant divergences; every difference—whether doctrinal, liturgical, or simply a matter of varying local customs—tends to be regarded as equally important. Most controversialists view their task in terms of a *disputatio* or dialectical joust, in which the aim is not to understand an adversary, but to force him into self-contradiction and absurdity, and so to triumph over him. Little or no effort is made to enter into the experience of the other side, looking at its tradition from within and seeking to grasp its distinctive starting point and way of thinking. Theological polemic is carried on in a vacuum, no account being taken of the pressure which other factors—language, culture, social environment, politics—exert upon the formulation of doctrine.[2]

Such is the picture which le Guillou paints. How far does it apply to Argenti? Like most controversialists, he is too much concerned with contrasts and opposition, too much animated by the spirit of the *disputatio* or dialectical joust. He stresses superficial points of disagreement when, had he looked deeper, he might have discovered common ground: see, for example, his criticism of the Roman Canon for lacking an Epiclesis, or his treatment of the question of purgatory. Like most controversialists, he treats theology too much in a vacuum, making no allowance, for example, for the non-theological factors in the west which may have led to changes in the manner of administering the sacraments. Like most controversialists, he often lacks a sense of proportion, failing to discriminate between the fundamental and the secondary. Orthodox of today, without rejecting his arguments concerning azymes and immersion, would yet feel that he attaches too great an importance to these questions.

Yet not all of le Guillou's strictures apply to Argenti. It cannot be said that he makes no effort to verify his points. He had travelled and lived in the west, and he knew the Roman

[1] See above, p. 67.

[2] M.-J. le Guillou, *Mission et Unité*, vol. ii, pp. 43–54.

Catholic Church at first hand; he was widely read in Latin theology, modern as well as ancient. What he says about western Christendom, although written without sympathy, is usually well informed and accurate in matters of fact. He avoids the wild and unfounded charges made by many of his contemporaries, just as he refrains almost entirely from their virulence and abuse. Argenti's restraint will be evident to any who sets side by side his *Manual concerning Baptism* and the anonymous *Sprinkling Pilloried.*

Le Guillou, while he has many severe things to say about the controversial *genre*, yet does not condemn it entirely. 'Works of controversy', he says, 'despite their unattractive character, remind us forcibly that the confrontation between different Christian traditions must take place on the level of truth, and never on that of doctrinal compromise. . . . Those who engage in such controversies are anxious to remain faithful to the tradition of truth in the Church.'[1]

A respect for truth, a refusal of all doctrinal compromise, a deep loyalty to the Tradition of his Church: these good qualities are indeed apparent in Argenti's work. And they are accompanied by other virtues. His style is clear, he argues in a simple and straightforward way. In contrast with many Greek writers, he is sober and literal in his use of Holy Scripture—perhaps at times almost too literal. He is generally content with the plain meaning of the Bible, not ransacking it for recondite allegories and figurative arguments. He displays that deep knowledge and love of the Fathers which is characteristic of modern Orthodox theology at its best. His books are full of Patristic quotations, and if at times he uses the Fathers too much as a quarry for 'proof texts', yet on other occasions he cites not isolated sentences but whole passages, which he attempts to place and interpret in their proper context.

A traditionalist and an admirer of the Fathers, Argenti did not strive after originality. As he puts it in the preface to his greatest work, the *Treatise against Unleavened Bread:*

> You who come across this book, whoever you may be, do not expect from us subtle and ingenious speculations, or elegant tricks of style, for we know nothing of such things. Note, rather, the truth

[1] *Mission et Unité*, vol. ii, pp. 95–96.

that lies behind our words, and become a disciple of the saints who received and taught these doctrines. For in this book we have not put forward some personal theory peculiar to ourselves, but we have gathered together in a single work the teaching of the inspired Fathers concerning the Eucharist. And if we have also added any ideas of our own, these in all humility we submit to the judgement of the Catholic Church.[1]

Such was the spirit in which Eustratios Argenti undertook his work as a theologian. He did not seek to innovate: he wrote as the inheritor and guardian of Tradition—a Tradition which he had not invented but received. At a time of doubt and weakness in his Church, he sought to strengthen his fellow Orthodox, reminding them of the authentic Orthodox Tradition, presenting with fresh force and new thoroughness the ancient truths entrusted to him.

[1] *Σύνταγμα κατὰ 'Αζύμων*, p. 4.

APPENDIX

A LIST OF THE WRITINGS OF EUSTRATIOS ARGENTI

I. PUBLISHED WORKS

(All references in the text of this book are to the pages of the first edition, in cases where there is more than one.)

(*i*) *Manual concerning Baptism* (*see pp.* 61–62):

(a) First edition: *'Εγχειρίδιον περὶ βαπτίσματος καλούμενον χειραγωγία πλανωμένων. Συντεθὲν παρὰ τοῦ ἰατροφιλοσόφου κυρίου Εὐστρατίου ἀργέντου χίου, θείῳ ζείλῳ κινηθέντος, τρανῶς ἐν αὐτῷ ἀποδεῖξαι, ὅτι ἀδύνατον ἄλλως πως ἐκτελεῖσθαι τὸ θεόθεν τοῖς ἀποστόλοις δοθὲν βάπτισμα, εἰ μὴ ἐν τρισὶ ταῖς καταδύσεσιν ὡς παρ' ἐκείνων δογματικῶς ἡ ἁγία τοῦ χριστοῦ καθολική, ἀποστολική, καὶ ἀνατολικὴ ὀρθόδοξος ἐκκλησία διεδέξατο, καὶ μέχρι τοῦ νῦν ποιεῖ. Ἤδη δὲ τύποις ἐκδοθὲν δι' ἀδείας τοῦ παναγιωτάτου οἰκουμενικοῦ πατριάρχου κυρίου κυρίου Κυρίλλου. 'Εν Κωνσταντινουπόλει. Τῷ ,αψνς' σωτηρίῳ ἔτει, μαρτίου α'.*

(b) Second edition: *Ἄνθος τῆς Εὐσεβείας· ἤτοι Συνταγμάτιον, περὶ ἀναβαπτισμοῦ. Διῃρημένον εἰς λβ' Κεφάλαια. Συντεθὲν παρὰ τοῦ 'Εξοχωτάτου 'Ιατροφιλοσόφου Εὐστρατίου 'Αργέντου· καὶ Τυπωθὲν Πρῶτον, 'Εν Κωνσταντινουπόλει. Προτροπῇ, τοῦ Παναγιωτάτου Οἰκουμενικοῦ Πατριάρχου Κυρίου, Κυρίου Κυρίλλου. Τἀνῦν δὲ τὸ Δεύτερον, Τύποις ἐκδοθὲν, διὰ δαπάνης τοῦ Εὐγενεστάτου Ἄρχοντος, Κυρίου Σκαρλάτου τοῦ Μαυροκοδράτου, Κωνσταντίνου τοῦ ἐκ Χίου. Κινηθέντος ἐκ Θείου ζήλου, πρὸς ὠφέλειαν τῶν Χριστιανῶν· καὶ ἀφιερωθὲν τῇ 'Ιερᾷ Μονῇ τοῦ Κύκκου, τῆς κατὰ τὴν Κύπρον. 'Επιμελείᾳ τοῦ Τιμιωτάτου Κυροῦ Νικολάου 'Ιωάννου, ἐξ 'Αγράφου, ἐκ Χωρίου Ζελενίτζας. 'Εν Λιψίᾳ τῆς Σαξωνίας,* 1757. *παρὰ 'Ιωάννῃ Γόττλοπ 'Εμμανουὲλ Πρέϊτκοπφ.*

(*ii*) *Treatise against Unleavened Bread* (*see pp.* 56–57):

(a) First edition: *Σύνταγμα κατὰ 'Αζύμων εἰς τρία διαιρεθὲν τμήματα. Ὧν τὸ μὲν πρῶτον ἐστὶ, περὶ ὕλης τοῦ Μυστηρίου, τῆς 'Αγίας Εὐχαριστίας. Τὸ δὲ δεύτερον, περὶ ἁγιασμοῦ τοῦ Μυστηρίου. Τὸ δὲ τρίτον, περὶ χρήσεως τοῦ Μυστηρίου. Συντεθὲν παρὰ τοῦ φιλοσοφοτάτου, καὶ ἐν 'Ιατροῖς 'Αρίστου Μακαρίτου 'Ευστρατίου τοὐπίκλην 'Αργέντη τοῦ Χίου. Καὶ πρῶτον μὲν εἰς ἀραβικὴν ἑρμηνεύθη γλῶσσαν καὶ εἰς τύπον ἐδόθη. παρὰ τοῦ Μακαριωτάτου Πατριάρχου 'Αντιοχείας Κυρίου Κυρίου Σιλβέστρου. Νῦν δὲ Δι' ἐξόδων συμπατριωτῶν τινῶν φίλων καὶ συζηλωτῶν τοῦ Μακαρίτου 'Ευστρατίου, τῇ ἰδίᾳ φράσει ἐτυπώθη. ἀκριβῶς τε καὶ ἐπιμελῶς διορθωθὲν παρὰ τοῦ ἐν 'Ιερομονάχοις Κυρίου Γεδεὼν 'Αγιοταφίτου τοῦ Κυπρίου. 'Εν Λιψίᾳ τῆς Σαξωνίας. Παρὰ 'Ιωάννῃ Γόττλοπ 'Εμμανουὴλ Βρέϊτκοπφ. ,αψξ'.*

(b) Second edition: Nauplia, 1845.

(*iii*) *The letter from Egypt, April 1751 (see p. 52):*
Κατάστασις τῆς τῶν 'Αλεξανδρέων ἐκκλησίας ἐν τῷ ιή αἰῶνι, in K. A. Uspenski, *The Patriarchate of Alexandria*, vol. i, Saint Petersburg, 1898, pp. 340–7. Reprinted in P. P. Argenti, *'Ιστορία τοῦ Χιακοῦ οἴκου 'Αργέντη*, Athens, 1922, pp. 307–14.

(*iv*) *Short Treatise against the Purgatorial Fire of the Papists (see p. 57):*
Συνταγμάτιον κατὰ τοῦ Παπιστικοῦ καθαρτηρίου πυρός, edited with an introduction by M. Constantinides, Athens, 1939.

II. WORKS IN MANUSCRIPT

A. *Definitely by Argenti*

(*i*) *The notebook of 1708 (see pp. 44–45):*
Εὐστρατίου 'Αργέντη ἔξοδα καὶ πόνημα 1708 *κατὰ μῆνα Αὔγουστον.* Choremis Library, Chios.

(*ii*) *The Budapest manuscript (see p. 49):*
(a) p. 1: *Εὐστρατίου 'Αργέντου, χίου περὶ τῆς Ψευδοῦς ἀψευδείας τοῦ πάπα ῥώμης. Τουτέστι, Σύντομος ἀπόδειξις, κατὰ τοῦ πάπα τῆς παλαιᾶς ῥώμης, ἐν ᾗ τρανῶς καὶ λαμπρῶς ἀποδείκνυται ὅτι ὁ πάπας τῆς ῥώμης ἠμπορεῖ νὰ γίνῃ αἱρετικός, καὶ ὅτι πολλοὶ ἀληθῶς ἔγιναν αἱρετικοί, καὶ ὅτι ἡ καθολικὴ ἐκκλησία διδάσκει πῶς ὁ πάπας τῆς ῥώμης ἠμπορεῖ νὰ γίνῃ αἱρετικός, τὸ ὁποῖον βεβαιοῖ καὶ ἡ ἀναλογία τῆς πίστεως.*

(b) p. 44: *Τὰ πρακτικά, καὶ ἡ 'Ιστορία τῆς ἐν Κωνσταντίᾳ Συνόδου ταύτης.*

(c) p. 79: *Περὶ τοῦ λατινικοῦ πάπα καὶ τοῦ ἀντιχρίστου ἐγχειρίδιον. 'Εν ᾧ λόγοις, καὶ μαρτυρίαις τῆς θείας γραφῆς καὶ τῶν ὀρθοδόξων πατέρων, ἀποδείκνυται ὅτι ὁ πάπας τῆς παλαιᾶς ῥώμης ἐστὶν ὁ κατ' ἐξοχὴν λεγόμενος ἀντίχριστος.*
(Subtitle, p. 81: *'Ιχνογραφία τοῦ ἀντιχρίστου. Κατὰ τὴν παλαιὰν καὶ νέαν διαθήκην.*)
Library of the Institute of Modern Greek, Budapest University (Zaviras collection), Ms. 32.

B. *Of uncertain authorship*

(*i*) *The medical manuscript* (*see* *p.* 47):
(a) f. 1r: *Ἰατροσόφιον πάνυ ὠφεῖον ὑπὸ πολλῶν σοφῶν καὶ διδασκάλων διαφόρων ὑποθέσεων καὶ πολλὰ καλῶν εἰσὶ ταῦτα.*
(b) f. 118r: *Ἀντιδοτάριον ἐξηγημένον ἀπὸ τὴν ἰταλικὴν γλῶσσαν εἰς τὴν τῶν γραικῶν: παρὰ νικολάου ἱερόπαιδος τοῦ τὴν ἰατρικὴν ἀσκοῦντος ἐκ πολλῶν ἰατρῶν ἀντίδοτες.*
Library of Dr. P. P. Argenti, London.

(*ii*) *The Kecskemét manuscript* (*see* *pp.* 58–59):
f. 131r: *Κατάλογος τῶν βιβλίων τῆς βιβλιοθήκης τοῦ ἁγιωτάτου θρόνου τῆς ἀλεξανδρείας, κατὰ ἀλφάβητον.*
Library of the Greek Community, Kecskemét, Hungary, Ms. 5 (see I. Hajnóczy, *A Kecskeméti Görögség Története*, p. 40).

(*iii*) *Further material on Purgatory*:
A. K. Demetrakopoulos, *Προσθῆκαι καὶ διορθώσεις εἰς τὴν Νεοελληνικὴν Φιλολογίαν Κωνσταντίνου Σάθα*, p. 82, attributes to Eustratios Argenti a composition with the following title: *Περὶ τῆς ἐσχάτης ἀνταποδόσεως ἐκλογαί, καί τινα περὶ τοῦ παπικοῦ καθαρτηρίου πυρός.* This further material on Purgatory, as Demetrakopoulos points out, is to be found in the same manuscript as Argenti's *Short Treatise against the Purgatorial Fire of the Papists*, viz., Jerusalem, Patr. Bibl. 386 (see A. Papadopoulos-Kerameus, *Ἱεροσολυμιτικὴ Βιβλιοθήκη*, vol. i, Saint Petersburg, 1891, p. 400). But whereas the manuscript explicitly ascribes the *Short Treatise* to Argenti, it contains nothing to indicate that the *Eklogai* are also his work.

C. *Not Traced*

Greek historians and bibliographers of the late eighteenth and the nineteenth centuries attribute to Eustratios Argenti various other writings which it has not proved possible to trace:

(*i*) *Three historical works*
(a) *Ἡ σειρὰ τῶν τῆς Ἀλεξανδρείας πατριαρχῶν.*
(b) *Ἐπιτομὴ χρονολογικὴ περὶ τῶν μαρτυρησάντων ἁγίων ἀνδρῶν.*
(c) *Ἐπιτομὴ χρονολογικὴ ἀπὸ Χριστοῦ γεννήσεως μέχρι τοῦ παρόντος χρόνου.*
These are mentioned by G. Zaviras, *Νέα Ἑλλάς*, p. 302 (see above, pp. 57–58).

(*ii*) *Περὶ τοῦ κυριακοῦ δείπνου.*

This is occasionally listed by bibliographers as a separate work, but it is clearly none other than the *Treatise against Unleavened Bread*, designated by the title which Argenti himself originally assigned to it (see pp. 56–57).

(*iii*) *Περὶ ἀναβαπτισμοῦ.*

This is listed as separate work by K. N. Sathas, *Νεοελληνικὴ Φιλολογία*, p. 470, but it is almost certainly to be identified with the *Manual concerning Baptism*, the second edition of which bears the subtitle *Συνταγμάτιον περὶ ἀναβαπτισμοῦ.*

(*iv*) *Κατὰ Λατίνων.*
Περὶ τῶν πέντε διαφορῶν.

These two items appear in a number of lists, but in no case do the bibliographers who mention them display any personal knowledge of existing copies. They seem to derive their information from an obscure sentence in G. Vendotis, *Προσθήκη τῆς Ἐκκλησιαστικῆς Ἱστορίας Μελετίου*, p. 222, who writes: *Ἐυστράτιος Ἀργέντης Χῖος Ἰατροφιλόσοφος, συνέγραψε κατὰ Λατίνων, καὶ εἰς τὰς πέντε διαφοράς.*

Now it is possible that Vendotis means to give the actual titles of two books by Argenti; but it seems much more probable that, so far from supplying specific titles, he intends no more than to state in general terms that Argenti wrote against the Latins, on the points of difference between the Churches. Vendotis is in that case referring, not to any fresh writings otherwise unknown, but to the extant anti-Latin works with which we are already familiar, such as the *Treatise against Unleavened Bread* and the *Manual concerning Baptism.*

BIBLIOGRAPHY

ALLATIUS, LEO, *De Ecclesiae Occidentalis atque Orientalis Perpetua Consensione*, Cologne, 1648.

— *De utriusque Ecclesiae Occidentalis atque Orientalis perpetua in dogmate de Purgatorio consensione*, Rome, 1655.

AMANTOS, K. I., *Οἱ 'Αργένται τῆς Χίου*, in *Χιακὰ Χρονικά*, vol. iv, Athens, 1919, pp. 83–119.

— *'Η Μονὴ τῶν Μουνδῶν ἐν Χίῳ*, Athens, 1931.

ANDREADIS, J. M., *'Ιστορία τῆς ἐν Χίῳ 'Ορθοδόξου 'Εκκλησίας*, Athens, 1940.

ANDROUTSOS, C., *Δογματικὴ τῆς 'Ορθοδόξου 'Ανατολικῆς 'Εκκλησίας*, Athens, 1907.

ARCUDIUS, P., *De Concordia Ecclesiae Occidentalis et Orientalis in septem Sacramentorum administratione*, Paris, 1626.

— *Utrum detur Purgatorium et an illud sit per ignem*, Rome, 1632.

ARGENTI, P. P., *'Ιστορία τοῦ Χιακοῦ οἴκου 'Αργέντη*, Athens, 1922.

— *The Occupation of Chios by the Venetians (1694)*, London, 1935.

— *Bibliography of Chios*, Oxford, 1940.

— *Chios A.D. 1089–A.D. 1912*, Oxford, 1941.

— *Chius Vincta or the occupation of Chios by the Turks (1566) and their administration of the island (1566–1912)*, Cambridge, 1941.

— *Diplomatic Archive of Chios 1577–1841*, 2 vols., Cambridge, 1954.

— and KYRIAKIDIS, S. P., *'Η Χίος παρὰ τοῖς γεωγράφοις καὶ περιηγηταῖς*, 3 vols., Athens, 1946.

ATCHLEY, E. G. C. F., *On the Epiclesis of the Eucharistic Liturgy and in the Consecration of the Font*, Alcuin Club Collections No. XXXI, London, 1935.

ATHANASIUS OF PAROS, *'Επιτομὴ εἴτε συλλογὴ τῶν θείων τῆς πίστεως δογμάτων*, Leipzig, 1806.

BARENTON, HILAIRE DE, *La France catholique en orient*, Paris, 1902.

BENT, J. T., *Early Voyages and Travels in the Levant. I. The Diary of Master Thomas Dallam, 1599–1600. II. Extracts from the Diaries of Dr. John Covel, 1670–1679* (Hakluyt Society, vol. 87), London, 1893.

BESSON, J., *La Syrie sainte*, Paris, 1660.

Βιβλίον καλούμενον 'Ραντισμοῦ Στηλήτευσις ἐν ᾧ περιέχεται κεφαλαίων ἀριθμὸς ὀγδοήκοντα ἑνός, ὧν ἕκαστον ταῖς ἀκτῖσι τῆς γραφῆς ὡς ἱστὸν ἀράχνης, φαίνεται διαλύον ῥαντισμάτων τὸ σκότος, Constantinople, 1756.

BIRKBECK, W. J., *Russia and the English Church*, London, 1895.

BLACKMORE, R. W., *The Doctrine of the Russian Church*, London, 1845.

BULGAKOV, S., *The Orthodox Church*, London, 1935.

BULGARIS, N., *The Holy Catechism*, edited by W. E. Daniel and R. Raikes Bromage, London, 1893.

CANTEMIR, DEMETRIUS, Prince of Moldavia, *The History of the Growth and Decay of the Othman Empire*, translated by N. Tindal, London, 1734.

CARAYON, A., *Relations inédites des missions de la Compagnie de Jésus à Constantinople et dans le Levant au XVIIe siècle*, Paris, 1864.

CHASSIOTIS, G., *L'instruction publique chez les Grecs depuis la prise de Constantinople par les Turcs jusqu'à nos jours*, Paris, 1881.

COVEL, J., *Some Account of the Present Greek Church, with Reflections on their Present Doctrine and Discipline; Particularly in the Eucharist, and the Rest of their Seven Pretended Sacraments*, Cambridge, 1722.

CRUSIUS, M., *Germanograecia*, Basel, 1585.

DAPONTE, K., *Καθρέπτης γυναικῶν*, 2 vols., Leipzig, 1766.

— *Ἱστορικὸς Κατάλογος*, in K. N. Sathas, *Μεσαιωνικὴ Βιβλιοθήκη*, vol. iii, Venice, 1872, pp. 71–200.

DAPPER, O., *Description exacte des isles de l'Archipel, et de quelques autres adjacentes*, Amsterdam, 1703.

DAWKINS, R. M., *The Monks of Athos*, London, 1936.

DEKIGALLAS, J., *Σχεδίασμα κατόπτρου τῆς Νεοελληνικῆς Φιλολογίας*, Hermopolis, 1846.

DELIKANIS, K., *Τὰ ἐν τοῖς κώδιξι τοῦ Πατριαρχικοῦ Ἀρχειοφυλακείου σῳζόμενα ἐπίσημα ἐκκλησιαστικὰ ἔγγραφα τὰ ἀφορῶντα εἰς τὰς σχέσεις τοῦ Οἰκουμενικοῦ Πατριαρχειόυ πρὸς τὰς ἐκκλησίας Ἀλεξανδρείας, Ἀντιοχείας, Ἱεροσολύμων καὶ Κύπρου*, Constantinople, 1904.

DEMETRAKOPOULOS, A. K., *Προσθῆκαι καὶ διορθώσεις εἰς τὴν Νεοελληνικὴν Φιλολογίαν Κωνσταντίνου Σάθα*, Leipzig, 1871.

— *Ὀρθόδοξος Ἑλλάς*, Leipzig, 1872.

DE VRIES, W., 'Das Problem der "communicatio in sacris cum dissidentibus" im Nahen Osten zur Zeit der Union (17. und 18. Jahrhundert)', in *Ostkirchliche Studien*, vol. vi, Würzburg, 1957, pp. 81–106.

— 'Eine Denkschrift zur Frage der "communicatio in sacris cum dissidentibus" aus dem Jahre 1721', in *Ostkirchliche Studien*, vol. vii, Würzburg, 1958, pp. 253–66.

DOSITHEOS, Patriarch of Jerusalem, *Ἐγχειρίδιον ἐλέγχον τὴν Καλβινικὴν φρενοβλάβειαν*, Bucharest, 1690.

— *Τόμος Καταλλαγῆς*, Jassy, 1694.

— *Τόμος Ἀγάπης*, Jassy, 1698.

— *Τόμος Χαρᾶς*, Rimnic, 1705.

— *Ἱστορία περὶ τῶν ἐν Ἱεροσολύμοις πατριαρχευσάντων*, Bucharest, 1715.

EVANGELIDIS, T., *Ἡ Παιδεία ἐπὶ Τουρκοκρατίας*, 2 vols., Athens, 1936.

EVERY, G., *The Byzantine Patriarchate 451–1204*, 2nd edition, London, 1962.

FINLAY, G., *A History of Greece*, vol. v, Oxford, 1877.

FORTESCUE, A. K., *The Orthodox Eastern Church*, London, 1916.

GAVIN, F., *Some Aspects of Contemporary Greek Orthodox Thought*, Milwaukee, 1923.

GEDEON, M. J., *'Ετεροδιδασκαλίαι ἐν τῇ 'Εκκλησίᾳ Κωνσταντινουπόλεως μετὰ τὴν ἅλωσιν*, in *'Εκκλησιαστικὴ 'Αλήθεια*, vol. iii, Constantinople, 1883, pp. 774–80.

— *Πατριαρχικοὶ Πίνακες*, Constantinople, 1885–90.

GEORGIADIS, B., *'Ανέκδοτος ἐπιστολὴ τοῦ πρώην Κωνσταντινουπόλεως Καλλινίκου τοῦ Γ'*, in *'Εκκλησιαστικὴ 'Αλήθεια*, vol. iii, Constantinople, 1883, pp. 601–604, 617–20, 633–4.

GEORGIRENES, J., *A Description of the Present State of Samos, Nicaria, Patmos, and Mount Athos*, London, 1678.

GILL, J., *The Council of Florence*, Cambridge, 1959.

GRAF, A., *Jeórjiosz Zavírasz Budapesti könyvtárának katalógusa*, Magyar-Görög Tanulmányok, No. 2, Budapest, 1935.

GRAF, G., *Geschichte der christlichen arabischen Literatur*, vol. iii, Studi e Testi 146, Rome, 1949.

GRIGORIOU, P., *Σχέσεις καθολικῶν καὶ ὀρθοδόξων*, Athens, 1958.

GRITSOPOULOS, T. A., *'Ο Πατριάρχης Κωνσταντινουπόλεως Κύριλλος ὁ Καράκαλλος*, in *'Επετηρὶς 'Εταιρείας Βυζαντινῶν Σπουδῶν*, vol. xxix, Athens, 1959, pp. 367–89.

HADJIANTONIOU, G. A., *Protestant Patriarch. The Life of Cyril Lucaris (1572–1638), Patriarch of Constantinople*, London, 1961.

HAJJAR, J., *Les chrétiens uniates du Proche-Orient*, Paris, 1962.

HAJNÓCZY, I., *A Kecskeméti Görögség Története*, Magyar-Görög Tanulmányok, No. 8, Budapest, 1939.

HELLADIUS, A., *Status Praesens Ecclesiae Graecae*, no place (? Altdorf), 1714.

HILL, A., *A Full and Just Account of the Present State of the Ottoman Empire in all its Branches*, London, 1709.

HOFMANN, G., *Athos e Roma, Orientalia Christiana*, vol. v, No. 19, Rome, 1925.

— *Rom und Athosklöster, Orientalia Christiana*, vol. viii, No. 28, Rome, 1926.

— *Sinai und Rom, Orientalia Christiana*, vol. ix, No. 37, Rome, 1927.

— *Patmos und Rom, Orientalia Christiana*, vol. xi, No. 41, Rome, 1928.

— *Griechische Patriarchen und Römische Päpste. Untersuchungen und Texte, Orientalia Christiana*, vol. xiii, No. 47; vol. xv, No. 52; vol. xix, No. 63; vol. xx, No. 64; vol. xxv, No. 76; vol. xxx, No. 84; vol. xxxvi, No. 97. Rome, 1928–34.

— 'Griechische Klöster und Rom', in *Orientalia Christiana*, vol. xx, No. 66, Rome, 1930, pp. 5–15.
— 'Byzantinische Bischöfe und Rom', in *Orientalia Christiana*, vol. xxii, No. 70, Rome, 1931, pp. 12–34.
— 'Byzantina', in *Orientalia Christiana*, vol. xxvi, No. 78, Rome, 1932, pp. 74–85.
— 'Patriarchen von Konstantinopel', in *Orientalia Christiana*, vol. xxxii, No. 89, Rome, 1933, pp. 5–39.
— *Vescovadi cattolici della Grecia. I. Chios, Orientalia Christiana*, vol. xxxiv, No. 92, Rome, 1934.
— *V. c. d. G. II. Tinos, Orientalia Christiana Analecta* 107, Rome, 1936.
— *V. c. d. G. III. Syros, Orientalia Christiana Analecta* 112, Rome, 1937.
— *V. c. d. G. IV. Naxos, Orientalia Christiana Analecta* 115, Rome, 1938.
— *V. c. d. G. V. Thera, Orientalia Christiana Analecta* 130, Rome, 1941.
— *Il Vicariato Apostolico di Constantinopoli, 1453–1830, Orientalia Christiana Analecta* 103, Rome, 1935.
— 'Apostolato dei Gesuiti nell' oriente greco (1583–1773)', in *Orientalia Christiana Periodica*, vol. i, Rome, 1935, pp. 139–63.
— 'La Chiesa cattolica in Grecia (1600–1830)', in *Orientalia Christiana Periodica*, vol. ii, Rome, 1936, pp. 164–90, 395–436.
— 'Lettere pontificie edite ed inedite intorno ai monasteri del Monte Sinai', in *Orientalia Christiana Periodica*, vol. xvii, Rome, 1951, pp. 283–303.
— 'Der Metropolit von Chios, Parthenios, (später Patriarch von Konstantinopel) an Papst Urban VIII', in *Ostkirchliche Studien*, vol. i, Würzburg, 1952, pp. 297–300.
— 'Neue Quellen zur inneren Kirchengeschichte des griechischen Ostens im dritten Jahrzent des XVII. Jahrhunderts', in *Revue des Études Byzantines*, vol. xi, Paris, 1953, pp. 165–74.
— *Rom und der Athos. Briefwechsel zwischen dem Missionar auf dem Athos Nikolaus Rossi und der Kongregation De Propaganda Fide, Orientalia Christiana Analecta* 142, Rome, 1954.

HYPSILANTIS, A. K., *Τὰ μετὰ τὴν ἅλωσιν*, Constantinople, 1870.

JOHN IV OXITA, *De Azymis*, edited by B. Leib in *Orientalia Christiana*, vol. ii, No. 9, Rome, 1924.

JUGIE, M., *Theologia Dogmatica Christianorum Orientalium ab Ecclesia Catholica Dissidentium*, 5 vols., Paris, 1926–35.

KARALEVSKIJ, C., (né Charon), 'Antioche', *Dictionnaire d'histoire et de géographie ecclésiastiques*, vol. iii, Paris, 1924, cols. 563–703.

KARMIRIS, J. N., *'Ετερόδοξοι ἐπιδράσεις ἐπὶ τὰς ὁμολογίας τοῦ ιζ' αἰῶνος*, Jerusalem, 1949.

— *Τὰ Δογματικὰ καὶ Συμβολικὰ Μνημεῖα τῆς 'Ορθοδόξου Καθολικῆς 'Εκκλησίας*, 2 vols., Athens: vol. i, 2nd edition, 1960; vol. ii, 1st edition, 1953.

— *Σύνοψις τῆς δογματικῆς διδασκαλίας τῆς 'Ορθοδόξου Καθολικῆς 'Εκκλησίας*, Athens, 1957.

KARNAPAS, K., *'Ιάκωβος ὁ Πάτμιος ὡς διδάσκαλος ἐν τῷ 'Αντιοχικῷ καὶ 'Ιεροσολυμιτικῷ θρόνῳ κατὰ τὸν ιη' αἰῶνα*, Jerusalem, 1906.

KIDD, B. J., *The Churches of Eastern Christendom*, London, 1927.

KOTSONIS, J., *'Η κανονικὴ ἄποψις περὶ τῆς ἐπικοινωνίας μετὰ τῶν ἑτεροδόξων* (*Intercommunio*), Athens, 1957.

— *Προβλήματα τῆς 'Εκκλησιαστικῆς Οἰκονομίας*, Athens, 1957.

LAMBROS, P., *'Ιστορικὴ πραγματεία περὶ τῆς ἀρχῆς καὶ προόδου τῆς τυπογραφίας ἐν 'Ελλάδι*, in *Χρυσαλλίς*, vol. iv, Athens, 1866, pp. 169–72.

LEGRAND, E., *Bibliographie hellénique . . . au dix-septième siècle*, 5 vols., Paris, 1894–1903.

— *Bibliographie hellénique . . . au dix-huitième siècle*, 2 vols., Paris, 1918–28.

LE GUILLOU, M.-J., *Mission et Unité. Les exigences de la communion* (*Unam Sanctam*, 33, 34), 2 vols., Paris, 1960.

— 'Aux sources des mouvements spirituels de l'Église orthodoxe de Grèce: I. La renaissance spirituelle du XVIIIe siècle', in *Istina*, Paris, 1960, No. 1, pp. 95–128.

LEIB, B., *Deux inédits byzantins sur les azymes, au début du XIIe siècle*, *Orientalia Christiana*, vol. ii, No. 9, Rome, 1924.

LE QUIEN, M., *Oriens Christianus*, 3 vols., Paris, 1740.

LUCAS, P., *Voyage du Sieur Paul Lucas, fait par ordre du Roy dans la Grèce, l'Asie Mineure, la Macedoine et l'Afrique*, 2 vols., Paris, 1712.

MAKRAIOS, S., *'Υπομνήματα 'Εκκλησιαστικῆς 'Ιστορίας*, in K. N. Sathas, *Μεσαιωνικὴ Βιβλιοθήκη*, vol. iii, Venice, 1872, pp. 201–419.

MALVY, A., and VILLER, M., *La Confession Orthodoxe de Pierre Moghila*, *Orientalia Christiana*, vol. x, No. 39, Rome, 1927.

MAXIMOS THE PELOPONNESIAN, *'Εγχειρίδιον κατὰ τοῦ σχίσματος τῶν παπιστῶν*, Bucharest, 1690.

MAZARAKIS, G. G., *Συμβολὴ εἰς τὴν ἱστορίαν τῆς ἐν Αἰγύπτῳ 'Ορθοδόξου 'Εκκλησίας*, Alexandria, 1932.

MERCATI, A., 'Complementi a notizie sull'unione di orientali con Roma', in *Orientalia Christiana Periodica*, vol. xv, Rome, 1949, pp. 291–312.

— 'Nuovi documenti pontifici sui monasteri del Sinai e del monte Athos', in *Orientalia Christiana Periodica*, vol. xviii, Rome, 1952, pp. 89–112.

MEYENDORFF, J., 'Projets de concile oecuménique en 1367: un dialogue inédit entre Jean Cantacuzène et le légat Paul', in *Dumbarton Oaks Papers*, vol. xiv, Washington (D.C.), 1960, pp. 147–77.

MILLER, W., *Essays on the Latin Orient*, Cambridge, 1921.

MINIATI, E., *Πέτρα Σκανδάλου*, Athens, 1863.

MUSSET, H., *Histoire du Christianisme spécialement en orient*, 3 vols., Harissa (Lebanon) and Jerusalem, 1948–9.

NEKTARIOS, Patriarch of Jerusalem, *Πρὸς τὰς προσκομισθείσας θέσεις παρὰ τῶν ἐν Ἱεροσολύμοις φρατόρων διὰ Πέτρου τοῦ αὐτῶν Μαΐστορος περὶ τῆς ἀρχῆς τοῦ πάπα Ἀντίῤῥησις*, Jassy, 1682.

NICODEMUS of the Holy Mountain, Saint, *Πηδάλιον . . . ἤτοι ἅπαντες οἱ ἱεροὶ, καὶ θεῖοι κανόνες*, Leipzig, 1800.

OIKONOMOS, K., *Τὰ σῳζόμενα ἐκκλησιαστικὰ συγγράμματα*, vol. i, Athens, 1862.

PALMER, W., *Dissertations on subjects relating to the 'Orthodox' or 'Eastern-Catholic' Communion*, London, 1853.

PALMIERI, A. P., 'La rebaptisation des Latins chez les Grecs', in *Revue de l'orient chrétien*, vol. vii, Paris, 1902, pp. 618–46, and vol. viii, 1903, pp. 111–32.

— 'Un document inédit sur la rebaptisation des Latins chez les Grecs', in *Revue Bénédictine*, vol. xxiii, Maredsous, 1906, pp. 215–31.

PAPADOPOULLOS, T. H., *The History of the Greek Church and People under Turkish Domination*, Brussels, 1952.

PAPADOPOULOS, C. A., *Περὶ τοῦ βαπτίσματος τῶν ἑτεροδόξων*, in *Ἐκκλησιαστικὸς Φάρος*, vol. xiv, Alexandria, 1915, pp. 469–83.

— *Ἀνέκδοτος ἀλληλογραφία τοῦ Πατριάρχου Ἀλεξανδρείας Ματθαίου Ψάλτου*, in *Ἐκκλησιαστικὸς Φάρος*, vol. xvii, Alexandria, 1918, p. 401–35.

— *Ἱστορία τῆς Ἐκκλησίας Ἀλεξανδρείας, 62–1934*, Alexandria, 1935.

— *Ἱστορία τῆς Ἐκκλησίας Ἀντιοχείας*, Alexandria, 1951.

PAPADOPOULOS-VRETOS, A., *Νεοελληνικὴ Φιλολογία*, Athens, 1854–7.

Parius, Athanasius: see *Athanasius of Paros*.

PASCHALIS, D. P., *Ματθαῖος ὁ Ἄνδριος, πάπας καὶ πατριάρχης Ἀλεξανδρείας*, Athens, 1901.

PETIT, L., 'L'entrée des catholiques dans l'Église orthodoxe', in *Échos d'Orient*, vol. ii, Paris, 1899, pp. 129–38.

PIGAS, Meletios, *Διάλογος Ὀρθόδοξος Χριστιανός*, Vilna, 1596.

PITTON DE TOURNEFORT, J., *Relation d'un Voyage du Levant, fait par ordre du Roy*, 2 vols., Paris, 1717.

POCOCKE, R., *A Description of the East*, 2 vols., London, 1743–5.

RABBATH, A., *Documents inédits pour servir à l'histoire du Christianisme en orient*, 2 vols., Paris and Beirut, 1905–21.

RICHARD, F., *Relation de ce qui s'est passé de plus remarquable à Sant-Erini isle de l'Archipel, depuis l'établissement des Pères de la Compagnie de Jésus en icelle*, Paris, 1657.

RILEY, A., *Athos or the Mountain of the Monks*, London, 1887.

— *Birkbeck and the Russian Church*, London, 1917.

ROBERTSON, J. N. W. B., *The Acts and Decrees of the Synod of Jerusalem sometimes called the Council of Bethlehem*, London, 1899.

RYCAUT, P., *The Present State of the Greek and Armenian Churches, Anno Christi 1678*, London, 1679.

SAROU, A. K., *Βίος Ἁγίου Ἀνδρέου Ἀργέντη τοῦ Χίου*, Athens, 1935.

— *Βίος Εὐστρατίου Ἀργέντη τοῦ Χίου Θεολόγου*, Athens, 1938.

— *Περὶ μεικτῶν ναῶν ὀρθοδόξων καὶ καθολικῶν ἐν Χίῳ*, in *Ἐπετηρὶς Ἑταιρείας Βυζαντινῶν Σπουδῶν*, vol. xix, Athens, 1949, pp. 194–208.

SATHAS, K. N., *Νεοελληνικὴ Φιλολογία*, Athens, 1868.

SAVRAMIS, E., *Ἡ πρώτη καθαίρεσις τοῦ Οἰκουμενικοῦ Πατριάρχου Κυρίλλου Ε' τοῦ Καρακάλου*, in *Ἐπετηρὶς Ἑταιρείας Βυζαντινῶν Σπουδῶν*, vol. x, Athens, 1933, pp. 161–86.

SEVERUS, GABRIEL, *Ἔκθεσις κατὰ τῶν ἀμαθῶς λεγόντων καὶ παρανόμως διδασκόντων, ὅτι ἡμεῖς οἱ τῆς Ἀνατολικῆς Ἐκκλησίας γνήσιοι καὶ ὀρθόδοξοι παῖδες ἐσμὲν σχισματικοὶ παρὰ τῆς ἁγίας καὶ καθόλου Ἐκκλησίας*, no place, no date (? London, circa 1625).

SHERRARD, P., *The Greek East and the Latin West*, London, 1959.

SIMON, R., *The Critical History of the Religions and Customs of the Eastern Nations*, translated by A. Lovell, London, 1685.

SMITH, T., *An Account of the Greek Church*, London, 1680.

STEPHANIDIS, B. K., *Ἐκκλησιαστικὴ Ἱστορία*, Athens, 1948.

THEOTOKAS, M. G., *Νομολογία τοῦ Οἰκουμενικοῦ Πατριαρχείου*, Constantinople, 1897.

TOTT, F. DE, *Mémoires du Baron de Tott sur les Turcs et les Tartares*, 2 vols., Paris, 1785.

Tournefort, Pitton de: see *Pitton de Tournefort.*

USPENSKI, K. A. (Archimandrite Porphyry), *The Patriarchate of Alexandria* (in Russian), vol. i, Saint Petersburg, 1898.

VENDOTIS, G., *Προσθήκη τῆς Ἐκκλησιαστικῆς Ἱστορίας Μελετίου*, Vienna, 1795.

VLASOPOULOS, S., *Ἡ ὑπεράσπισις τῆς Γραικικῆς Ἐκκλησίας*, translated from the Italian by C. Philetas, Athens, 1848.

VLASTOS, A. M., *Χιακά*, 2 vols., Hermopolis, 1840.

WENGER, A., 'La réconciliation des hérétiques dans l'Église russe. Le Trebnik de Pierre Moghila', in *Revue des Études Byzantines*, vol. xii, Paris, 1954, pp. 144–75.

Wheler, G., *A Journey into Greece . . . in company of Dr. Spon of Lyons*, London, 1682.

Williams, G., *The Orthodox Church of the East in the Eighteenth Century, being the correspondence between the Eastern Patriarchs and the Nonjuring Bishops*, London, 1868. (A new edition of this correspondence is at present being prepared by W. Jardine Grisbrooke, and will be published shortly.)

— *A Collection of Documents: relating chiefly to the visit of Alexander Archbishop of Syros and Tenos to England in 1870*, Occasional Paper of the Eastern Church Association No. 14, London, 1872.

Woolley, R. M., *The Bread of the Eucharist*, Alcuin Club Tracts No. 10, London, 1913.

Zaviras, G., *Νέα Ἑλλὰς ἢ Ἑλληνικὸν Θέατρον*, Athens, 1872.

Zolotas, G. I., *Ἱστορία τῆς Χίου*, 3 vols., Athens, 1921–8.

INDEX

www.ingramcontent.com/pod-product-compliance
Lightning Source LLC
LaVergne TN
LVHW050630100826
845148LV00011B/1807

* 9 7 8 1 6 2 5 6 4 0 8 2 6 *